Peddling Poison

Peddling Poison

The Tobacco Industry and Kids

Clete Snell

Criminal Justice, Delinquency, and Corrections

Marilyn D. McShane and Frank Williams, Series Editors

Westport, Connecticut
London

Library of Congress Cataloging-in-Publication Data

Snell, Clete.
 Peddling poison : the tobacco industry and kids / Clete Snell.
  p. cm.—(Criminal justice, delinquency, and corrections, ISSN 1535–0371)
 Includes bibliographical references and index.
 ISBN 0–275–98239–4 (alk. paper)
 1. Teenagers—Tobacco use—United States—Prevention. 2. Tobacco habit—United
States—Prevention. 3. Advertising—Tobacco—United States. 4. Products liability—
Tobacco—United States. 5. Tobacco industry—Law and legislation—United States.
I. Title. II. Series.
HV5745.S54 2005
362.29'6'08350973—dc22   2004028033

British Library Cataloguing in Publication Data is available.

Library of Congress Catalog Card Number: 2004028033
ISBN: 0–275–98239–4
ISSN: 1535–0371

First published in 2005

Praeger Publishers, 88 Post Road West, Westport, CT 06881
An imprint of Greenwood Publishing Group, Inc.
www.praeger.com

Printed in the United States of America

The paper used in this book complies with the
Permanent Paper Standard issued by the National
Information Standards Organization (Z39.48–1984).

10 9 8 7 6 5 4 3 2 1

To my mother, Faye Snell, for her love and support

Contents

Foreword

The complex relationships of smokers, the government, and the tobacco industry have long been studied by sociologists, political scientists, and public administrators. However, the information we now have available in works such as this clarify the issues with powerful evidence and statistics that make our continued apathy regarding this medical crisis unconscionable. Based on the material presented here, the reader is left to question whether juvenile smoking may—and perhaps should—replace other drug and alcohol abuse issues as a top priority for health and human service intervention.

As a researcher for a Texas task force, Clete Snell has studied the regulation of tobacco among children from every conceivable angle. He gives us a comprehensive picture of the way the industry still employs its masterful one-upsmanship on the public, all the time aided and abetted by politicians and voting blocs. Not only have conservative, business-minded administrations left the children dangling in a smoke-friendly environment but they have, in Grinch-like fashion, run off with the tobacco settlement money intended for use in addressing the escalating health problems related to smoking. It is a frightening scenario. The politicians nod their heads throughout the testimony of tobacco company executives who say they have no idea whether smoking is dangerous. These same politicians proudly support criminal laws to prosecute parents—in particular pregnant women—for exposing their children to a myriad of substances, many of which are less dangerous than tobacco. This danger is not hypothetical: one expert demonstrated how more people die from tobacco each and every week than were killed in the World Trade Center attacks. Snell explains that each week hundreds of children will smoke their first cigarette, setting themselves up for eventual reckoning with cancer, emphysema, strokes, and other health problems.

As Snell demonstrates, the political and business worlds can no longer make their claims of innocence, and users can no longer deny the long-term effects of smoking. In terms of public health, smoking is a drug epidemic with long-term health care costs. This is a book that should be read by all parents, those who currently smoke, those in the health professions, and those tasked with regulating smoking.

Marilyn D. McShane
Frank Williams
Series Editors

Acknowledgments

This book would not be possible without the contributions of several people. Marilyn McShane first suggested I write a book about tobacco policy over a cup of coffee at an American Society of Criminology conference, and by the time the coffee was gone an outline was completed. Her helpful suggestions contributed tremendously to the final product. I would also like to thank Suzanne Staszak-Silva and the staff at Greenwood Publishing for their helpful suggestions and—most of all—patience. My knowledge of issues concerning tobacco policy and youth was developed from my close working relationship with the Texas Department of Health's Bureau of Chronic Disease and Tobacco Control. It has been a tremendous honor to work with their staff and my other colleagues in the Texas Tobacco Prevention Initiative toward the goal of lowering youth tobacco use. My former colleagues in the College of Juvenile Justice & Psychology at Prairie View A&M University provided a friendly and collegial environment and listened patiently to my rants about the tobacco industry. In particular, I would like to thank Tana McCoy, Anthony Carona, JoAnn Burbridge-Jones, and Myrna Cintron. Finally, I would like to thank my girls, Katie and Emma, for their patience while their dad typed away on the computer.

Introduction

The field of criminal justice has a long history of examining adolescent drug use as a social problem. Because of the social acceptance of cigarette smoking, tobacco is rarely considered a dangerous drug. In the opinion of many, tobacco is not considered a drug at all. However, not only does tobacco kill more people per year than all illegal drugs combined, it kills more people per year than alcohol, AIDS, car accidents, murders, suicides, and illegal drugs *combined*. The social acceptance of tobacco use in this country obscures the fact that it is the single greatest preventable cause of death in the United States. Additionally, almost 90% of those who use tobacco products started the habit before adulthood. Despite all we know about the dangers of smoking, this assembly line of addiction continues largely unabated. Approximately 750,000 kids become new, regular smokers each year. These children consume approximately 900 million packs of cigarettes each year; almost one-third will ultimately die from smoking.

Criminal justice as a discipline also has a history of examining issues of social justice and corporate misbehavior. The United States tobacco industry's decades of deception are likely the greatest example of corporate wrongdoing in the nation's history. In fact, the United States Justice Department is currently pursuing criminal charges against several cigarette companies. Tobacco industry documents reveal the following facts: (1) tobacco manufacturers were aware of the health hazards due to smoking from at least the 1960s and deliberately hid this knowledge from the public; (2) big tobacco manipulated their products to make cigarettes more addictive; and (3) the industry purposely marketed their products to children. Children have been the greatest source of replacement smokers for the thousands that quit or die each year. The full story of the industry's deception is yet to be revealed as thousands of pages of industry documents have yet to be examined.

Finally, criminal justice as a discipline has a strong interest in developing substance abuse and delinquency prevention programs that work. The track record concerning the success of substance abuse and delinquency prevention programs has not been that impressive. Youth tobacco prevention programs may be a useful model. Despite being greatly outspent by the tobacco industry, the public health community has developed and implemented innovative tobacco control programs that have resulted in significant reductions in youth tobacco use. Many experts in the areas of substance abuse have an eye on these model programs with the hope of adapting their approach to other types of illicit drugs. In fact, the comprehensive programs approach developed by the Centers for Disease Control and Prevention may be a model for many different types of delinquency prevention programs.

This book charts the recent history of the tobacco wars between the tobacco industry and public health advocates. While cigarette smoking has decreased steadily among adults in recent decades, cigarette use among adolescents actually increased throughout most of the 1990s. Currently, about 13% of middle school and 28% of high school students use some type of tobacco products. Youth begin smoking in five progressive stages ranging from experimentation to addiction. Psychosocial and personal factors affect the decision to start smoking and to persist in the behavior, among them the availability of cigarettes, the social acceptance of smoking, peer and parenting influences, perceptions of the social environment, self-esteem, and self-image.

Much of the explanation for tobacco's social acceptance is due to the pervasiveness of tobacco industry marketing and advertising. Despite total bans of tobacco advertising on television and radio, only the auto industry spends more than "big tobacco" on advertising and marketing. Tobacco industry documents reveal that much of this advertising has targeted youth. Tobacco advertisements often give the impression that the user is sophisticated, confident, and beautiful—messages that are appealing to kids. It also gives the impression that tobacco use is widespread and socially accepted. Despite promises to only market their products to adult consumers, a great deal of tobacco advertising continues to reach children through convenience stores, magazines, and even through popular films.

The Food and Drug Administration (FDA), under Dr. David Kessler, responded to a petition to assert jurisdiction over cigarettes as a drug. This simple request led to a massive investigation of the tobacco industry. If Kessler could prove that the tobacco industry purposely manipulated their products to have some intended effect on smokers, his agency had a legal responsibility to regulate tobacco products. The investigation and disclosures from tobacco industry insiders revealed that the industry purposely manipulated the nicotine content of cigarettes to make them more addictive.

FDA regulation over tobacco products remains elusive, but much of the information from this investigation led to the first successful lawsuits against the tobacco industry. The Master Settlement Agreement between forty-one states' attorney generals and the tobacco industry resulted in a $246 billion payoff to offset the healthcare costs of smoking. The states' attorney generals, state legislators, and state governors agreed to use these funds to offset healthcare costs, and to develop tobacco control programs. Despite the promises, less than 5% of the settlement is being used to prevent youth tobacco use.

In 1999, the Centers for Disease Control and Prevention published a manual titled *Best Practices for Comprehensive Tobacco Control Programs*, which outlined comprehensive tobacco control programs. The best practices address nine different components of comprehensive tobacco control programs that include; community programs to reduce tobacco use, chronic disease programs to reduce the burden of tobacco-related diseases, school programs, enforcement, statewide programs, counter-marketing, cessation programs, surveillance and evaluation, and administration and management. The comprehensive tobacco control program approach has been replicated nationwide and has enjoyed enormous success in reducing youth tobacco use.

In addition to state-sponsored tobacco control programs, a number of youth tobacco prevention organizations have developed innovative and aggressive approaches in the cause of tobacco control. One of the greatest challenges in reducing youth tobacco use is changing the popular mindset that smoking is normative, popular, and cool, especially among young people. These programs have developed innovative approaches using classroom presentations, sponsored contests, and the Internet that effectively deliver the opposite message.

I conclude this book by discussing the future of tobacco control. After tremendous declines in tobacco use during the 1970s, African American tobacco use is currently on the rise. Developing tobacco control programs in African American communities is especially problematic because the industry has provided economic support over a long period of time. The issue of tobacco control has become a global concern as deaths from tobacco use are projected to become the leading cause of death in the world. The Framework Convention on Tobacco Control organized by the World Health Organization recently ratified a global tobacco control treaty that has real promise to reduce tobacco use among developing nations. Cigarettes are increasingly being sold over the Internet without proper age verification controls. The result is that it may be easier than ever for kids to buy cigarettes. Meanwhile, the tobacco industry led by Philip Morris, has changed its tone and position concerning the health hazards related to smoking. This change of position is a calculated strategy to improve the industry's sagging image and its odds of survival. The future of youth tobacco prevention efforts in the United States rests with a Congress that has failed to develop comprehensive tobacco control legislation. The future also depends on changing the view shared by many young people that tobacco use is socially acceptable and a matter of choice. Once addiction sets in, the choice is gone.

I

Youth Tobacco Use: The Health Effects, Trends in Smoking Rates, and Reasons Why Kids Use Tobacco

INTRODUCTION

Smoking kills an estimated 434,000 Americans every year. The vast majority of these smokers began smoking in their teen and preteen years. Very few people begin tobacco use as adults. In fact, by the age of eighteen, approximately one in three people in America use tobacco products. Moreover, the earlier adolescents initiate tobacco use, the heavier their tobacco use becomes in adulthood and the longer potential time they have to be users. Long-term chronic health problems such as cancer, emphysema, and heart disease are related to the duration and amount of tobacco use. The focus of public health officials for the last couple of decades has been to reduce deaths from tobacco by attempting to prevent young people from taking up the habit.

THE HEALTH EFFECTS OF TOBACCO USE AMONG YOUTH

Tobacco use—especially cigarette smoking—is considered the chief preventable cause of premature death in America. Several reports by the Surgeon General's Office has documented a causal link between cigarette smoking and lung cancer and other fatal cancers, arteriosclerosis and coronary heart disease, chronic obstructive pulmonary disease, and a wide array of other serious health problems.[1] More recently, research has found that passive or environmental tobacco smoke can lead to serious health problems—such as lung cancer—in otherwise healthy nonsmokers. In fact, every three weeks in the United States, secondhand smoke kills about the same number of nonsmokers as were killed in the September 11th terrorist attacks on the World Trade Center.[2]

Many young people have the false impression that the health effects of smoking and other tobacco use are problems they will have to combat much later in life. Many youth who just start smoking also believe that they can quit at anytime. The truth is that smoking has immediate and serious effects on the health of children. Cigarette smoking in adolescence appears to retard the rate of lung growth and the maximum lung function that can be achieved. Young smokers are less likely to be physically fit than young nonsmokers, and more likely to experience shortness of breath, coughing spells, wheezing, and other physical health problems.

Heart disease is the leading cause of death in the United States. Atherosclerosis is a precursor to heart disease and may begin in childhood or young adulthood as a consequence of smoking. Smoking by children and adolescents is related to an increased risk of early atherosclerotic lesions that are a risk factor for heart disease.

Smokeless tobacco (frequently termed snuff or chew) is related to health problems that range from halitosis to severe health problems such as several different forms of oral cancer (cancers of mouth, tongue, and esophagus). Reports by the Surgeon General have documented that smokeless tobacco use is as addictive for young people as it is for adults. Furthermore, smokeless tobacco users are more likely than nonusers to become cigarette smokers.

Drug use among youth has been a public policy concern for decades, but rarely has cigarette smoking been considered to be among serious drug problems. Nicotine dependence from cigarette smoking is the most common form of drug addiction in the nation. Moreover, to emphasize the seriousness of nicotine addiction, it causes more death and disease than all other addictions combined.[3] The two medical disorders associated with nicotine addiction identified by the American Psychological Association are nicotine addiction and nicotine withdrawal. Symptoms of nicotine withdrawal includes "craving for nicotine; irritability, frustration, or anger; anxiety, difficulty concentrating; restlessness; decreased heart rate; and increased appetite or weight gain."[4]

Physical dependence on any type of substance refers to the condition in which withdrawal symptoms are present. Physical dependence makes it much more difficult to achieve and maintain abstinence from a drug and makes it more likely that the user will relapse. Surveys conducted by the National Institute on Drug Abuse (NIDA) have found that severe withdrawal symptoms and the inability to maintain abstinence from use of a drug are more commonly associated with heroin and cigarette smoking than any other forms of addictive drugs, including cocaine and marijuana.

Each year about 20 million Americans attempt to quit smoking, but only about 3% have long-term success.[5] In fact, even among addicted cigarette smokers who have lost a lung due to cancer or have had major heart surgery, only about 50% kick the habit for more than a few weeks.[6]

This startling fact is something I witnessed firsthand while visiting my wife who at the time, worked for MD Anderson Cancer Hospital in Houston. Quite frequently cancer patients, who were obviously receiving chemotherapy evidenced by hair loss, weight loss, and pale skin, could be found outside the hospital connected to IV's and smoking cigarettes.

Nicotine's addictive potential is realized very soon after regular use. Data from the 1985 National Household Survey on Drug Abuse (NHSDA) found that 84% of 12- through 17-year-olds who smoked one pack of cigarettes or more per day felt that they needed or were dependent on cigarettes. The NHSDA research found that young people develop tolerance and dependence for nicotine, increase the amount they smoke over time, and are unable to abstain from cigarettes. This suggests that the addictive processes in adolescents are similar or the same as that for adults.[7]

OVERALL TRENDS IN CIGARETTE USE IN THE PAST CENTURY

It is important to develop an understanding of the magnitude of the problem of tobacco use in the United States and how that has changed over recent years. The National Health Interview Survey (NHIS) has been conducted by the Centers for Disease Control (CDC) since 1965. It uses very large probability samples and interviews are conducted within the home. NHIS respondents are considered current smokers if they have ever smoked at least 100 cigarettes and that they continue to smoke. Former smokers are those who have smoked at least 100 cigarettes and are not current smokers. Those classified as having never smoked have either smoked no cigarettes or less than 100 in their lifetimes. The NHIS also asks questions concerning other types of tobacco use such as cigar, pipe, and chewing tobacco.[8]

Total annual consumption of cigarettes in the United States was 2.5 billion cigarettes in 1900 according to records from the U.S. Department of Agriculture. Consumption increased steadily and dramatically over the years until reaching a peak of 640 billion cigarettes in 1981. The largest increases occurred in the 1910s, 1920s, and 1940s. For instance, total cigarette consumption was 8.6 billion in 1910 and increased to 44.6 billion in 1920. In 1940, consumption had more than tripled to 181.9 billion cigarettes. Since the peak consumption of cigarettes in 1981, cigarette use has steadily declined to approximately 480 billion cigarettes in 2003.[9]

Because overall cigarette consumption does not take into account the overall population changes over the last century, it is more useful to examine cigarette consumption per capita. The trends are similar to that of overall consumption. Per capita use of cigarettes was 54 in 1900 (54 cigarettes consumed per person), 665 in 1920, 1,976 in 1940, and reached a peak of 4,345 in 1963.[10]

The NHIS first asked questions about cigarette smoking in 1965. At that time an estimated 42% of American adults were current smokers, including 52% of men and 34% of women. By 1991, cigarette smoking prevalence had decreased to 26% overall, 28% for men and 24% for women. Throughout this period of time (1965–1991), blacks were more likely to smoke than whites, and Hispanics were less likely to smoke than non-Hispanics. Prevalence by age was highest among persons aged 25–44 years. During the period studied, smoking decreased dramatically for all sociodemographic groups. From 1965 to 1991, the prevalence of cigarette smoking decreased 46% among men and 31% among women. The decrease in cigarette use was about equal between blacks and whites, and decreased more dramatically among Hispanics. Cigarette smoking prevalence also declined most rapidly among younger adults and among people with more education.[11]

There has also been a large increase in the number of smokers who were able to quit smoking. This is generally referred to as *cessation* in the language of epidemiologists. The number of people who were regular smokers but quit nearly doubled between 1965 and 1991. By 1990, more than half of U.S. men and more than half of American white adults who had ever smoked cigarettes had quit. The prevalence of quitting was higher for men than women, for whites than blacks, and for non-Hispanics than Hispanics. The likelihood of quitting the habit increased with both age and education.[12]

TRENDS IN YOUTH TOBACCO USE

There have been a limited number of research projects that have followed adolescent tobacco use over a long period of time. The Monitoring the Future Project is one that has followed teen smoking since 1976. In one publication, daily cigarette smoking among high school seniors was tracked from 1976 to 1993. Daily cigarette smoking was defined as smoking at least one cigarette per day during the past thirty days. The overall prevalence of daily smoking was approximately 35% lower in 1984 than in 1976. However, from 1976 to 1993 there was a 2% increase in daily smoking. In contrast, smoking prevalence among adults in 1991 was about 20% lower than in 1983. Similarly, daily smoking among white high school seniors increased 14% between 1984 and 1993, while it decreased 20% among white adults. Male high school seniors increased their daily tobacco use by 21% between 1984 and 1993, while it decreased 20% among adult males. Among female high school seniors, on the other hand, the prevalence of daily smoking was 11% lower in 1993 than in 1984. Among adult women between 1983 and 1991, the decrease in current smoking was even more striking (20% reduction).[13]

The greatest reduction in daily smoking among high school seniors was among blacks. Their self-reported prevalence was 51% lower in 1993 than in 1984. But, in keeping with the overall trends among youth during that time period, the reduction in daily smoking among black high school students was less pronounced (19%).[14]

The National Youth Risk Behavior Survey (YRBS) is another source of information regarding cigarette smoking among high school students. The YRBS measures the prevalence of health risk behaviors among high school students through representative biennial national, state, and local surveys. The samples from this study are representative of students in grades 9–12 in all fifty states and the District of Columbia. A recent publication using this data tracked cigarette consumption between 1991 and 2001. Three types of tobacco behavior were assessed: (1) lifetime smoking, defined as having ever smoked cigarettes; (2) current smoking, defined as smoking at least one day in the last 30 days; and (3) current frequent smoking, defined as smoking on at least twenty of the last thirty days. The report concludes that cigarette smoking rates increased steadily from 1991 to 1997, and since that time they have been declining significantly.[15]

The prevalence of lifetime smoking remained stable throughout the 1990s, but declined significantly from 70.4% in 1999 to 63.9% in 2001. The prevalence of current smoking increased from 27.5% in 1991 to 36.4% in 1997, and then declined significantly to 28.5% in 2001. Current frequent smoking increased from 12.7% in 1991 to 16.7% in 1997 and 16.8% in 1999, and then declined significantly to 13.8% in 2001.[16]

Among female students, the prevalence of current smoking increased steadily from 27.3% in 1991, peaked at 34.9% in 1999, and declined significantly to 27.7% by 2001. Similar trends occurred among white female, black male, Hispanic, Hispanic female, Hispanic male, ninth, and eleventh grade students. In all these cases, smoking prevalence peaked by 1999 and then declined significantly by 2001.

The trend was similar for all males; the prevalence of current smoking increased steadily from 27.6% in 1991, peaked at 37.7% in 1997, and declined significantly to 29.2% in 2001. A similar pattern occurred among white, white male, black, tenth, and twelfth grade students.

CURRENT YOUTH TOBACCO USE

According to the National Youth Tobacco Survey (NYTS) in 2002, about 13.3% of middle school students (grades 6–8) reported current use of any tobacco products. Cigarettes (10.1%) were the most popular tobacco choice among middle school youth, followed by cigars (6%), smokeless tobacco (3.7%), pipes (3.5%), bidis (2.4%), and kreteks (2%). Middle school boys were more likely than girls to use all types of tobacco products except for cigarettes. Middle school boys and girls were about equally likely to smoke cigarettes.[17]

High school students used tobacco products at a rate of about 28.4% in 2002. As with middle school youth, high school students were most likely to smoke cigarettes (22.9%), followed by cigars (11.6%), smokeless tobacco (6.1%), pipes (3.2%), kreteks (2.7%), and bidis (2.6%). Males were significantly more likely to use any tobacco products than females students (32.9% for males compared to 23.9% for females). However, male high school students were only slightly more likely to smoke cigarettes than females (24.6% for males compared to 21.2% for females).[18]

To summarize trends in youth tobacco use, smoking among adolescents declined sharply in the 1970s, but the decline slowed significantly in the 1980s, increased throughout most of the 1990s, then decreased in the late 1990s and continues to drop at the present time. Female adolescent smoking actually exceeded that among males by the mid- to late 1970s, however both sexes are about equally likely to smoke at the present time. Boys are much more likely to experiment with other types of tobacco products than girls. Nationally, white adolescents are more likely to use all forms of tobacco products than are blacks and Hispanics. The decline in the prevalence of cigarette smoking among black adolescents has been dramatic and has occurred over a period of about fifty years.

Why have youth smoking rates dropped in recent years? Experts at the Centers for Disease Control believe that the following factors may have been influential: (1) a 70% increase in the retail price of cigarettes from December 1997 to May 2001; (2) an increase in the number and effectiveness of school-based efforts to prevent tobacco use; and (3) an increase in the exposure of youth to national and state mass-media smoking prevention campaigns. Despite the progress, especially among high school students, over one-quarter (28.5%) of high school youth are current smokers and almost 14% are frequent smokers with probable nicotine dependence.[19]

WHY KIDS START SMOKING

The earliest research concerning how to prevent youth from starting to smoke was the result of the landmark 1964 Surgeon General's report on smoking and health.[20] Early research was not theory-based and did not focus on the question of what motivates young people to smoke. This research viewed cigarette smoking as a health behavior, rather than a social behavior with social causes, functions, and reinforcements. By the mid-1970s, support for theory-based research was provided by the National Clearinghouse for Smoking and Health, the National Institutes of Health (NIH), NIDA, and private health organizations such as the American Lung Association, the American Cancer Society, and the American Heart Association.

The application of psychosocial theories to the area of youth smoking was a major breakthrough in attempts to understand why youth begin to experiment with smoking and what sustains their tobacco use. The early works of Leventhal, Bandura, and McAlister, Perry, and Maccoby were pioneering, but limited in the sense that they tended to rely on simple correlations such as testing for a relationship between parental smoking and children's smoking behavior.[21] The problem with research that examines simple correlations is that it is impossible to come to any conclusions about the actual causes of youth smoking. Subsequent research became much more sophisticated, theory-driven, and longitudinal in nature. Longitudinal research tracks the same cohort of youth over a period of time (usually several years) and can provide much more useful information as to why kids initiate tobacco use and why they continue to use tobacco products. Conrad, Flay, and Hill reviewed twenty-seven studies concerning why kids start smoking that had been published since 1980.[22] The fairly large number of rather sophisticated studies allows us to begin to draw some conclusions as the why kids smoke.

Developmental Stages of Smoking

Flay developed a useful model of the five primary stages of smoking initiation among children and adolescents.[23] In the first stage or preparatory stage, general attitudes and beliefs about the value of smoking are formed. Even if an adolescent does not begin to smoke, they come to see smoking as having a useful purpose: to appear mature, cope with stress, fit in with a new peer group, or display independence from the influence of authority figures such as parents.[24] Certain psychosocial risk factors discussed in the next section, such as tobacco advertising and adult or sibling role models who smoke, may provide an influence at this stage.

The second stage is termed "the trying stage" where an adolescent actually experiments for the first time with cigarette smoking, usually smoking two or three times. The psychosocial risk factors involved in this stage include peer reinforcement or encouragement to try smoking, the perception that smoking is normative or socially acceptable behavior, and the availability of cigarettes.

The third stage is the experimental stage where adolescents engage in repeated but irregular smoking. Some of the psychosocial risk factors involved in this stage include social situations such as parties where smoking is often prevalent and important peers such as a best friend who supports smoking, low self-efficacy or the inability to refuse offers to smoke, and the availability of cigarettes. These influences may impact a youth enough to smoke in particular social situations or around certain people, but not become a regular smoker.

The fourth stage is termed "regular use" when adolescents smoke on a regular basis, at least weekly, and increasingly across a variety of situations and personal interactions. The psychosocial influences at this stage include socializing with peers that smoke and reinforce smoking, the perception that smoking has personal utility such as reducing stress or weight loss, and the availability of cigarettes.

The final stage is nicotine dependence and addiction. As discussed earlier, this involves a physiological need for nicotine. This need includes a tolerance for nicotine, withdrawal symptoms if the person attempts to quit, and a high likelihood of relapse if the person quits.

While there is much variation among adolescents in the length of time between an initial attempt at smoking and regular use, on average it takes only two to three years. In fact, McNeill found that of those youth who experimented with cigarettes, about half were smoking on a daily basis within a year.[25] Thus, prevention efforts have focused on delaying or preventing the first attempts at smoking, as well as preventing the progression to regular use of cigarettes. Because an adolescent may become a regular smoker in a fairly short period of time (two to three years), a high percentage of adolescents at least try cigarettes, and because adolescents who become regular smokers generally progress to addiction as adults, it is critical to target prevention efforts at middle school, junior high school, and high school youth.[26]

Psychological and Social Risk Factors

In the Surgeon General's report *Preventing Tobacco Use Among Young People*, various psychological and sociological (psychosocial) risk factors were identified—through a thorough examination of research—as greatly increasing the chances that adolescents will begin using tobacco products. These risk factors were grouped into the following categories: sociodemographic, environmental, behavioral, and personal. These risk factors are believed to be the first link in the causal chain that leads to tobacco-related health problems. Thus, prevention efforts should take these factors into account.

Sociodemographic Factors

Sociodemographic factors such as socioeconomic status or gender do not generally directly impact decisions to start smoking, but rather indirectly impact decisions to start smoking by impacting behavioral and personal factors. Tobacco use may vary according to socioeconomic status, family structure, age, gender, and ethnicity.

Low socioeconomic status (SES) has been found to predict smoking initiation in several longitudinal studies.[27] One German study found that seventh- and eighth-grade students from a school in a low-income area had higher rates of tobacco use and were more likely to start smoking over a six-month period than youth from a higher-income area. Low-in-

come students also had greater expectations of certain positive consequences of smoking, more friends who smoked, and lower scores on a
self-image scale. A possible explanation is that lower-income students
may start cigarette smoking to cope with the stress that comes with a lack
of financial and material resources or with living in a one-parent household. They may find that tobacco use is a quick and easy coping strategy
for stress or loneliness.[28] Youth from low-income families may also have
more peers or other role models who smoke and less supervision to discourage experimentation than youth from higher-income families.[29] While
low socioeconomic status is related to initiating cigarette smoking, it is
not a strong predictor of experimenting with smokeless tobacco.

The life stage of adolescence has become a consistent and strong predictor of initiating both cigarette and smokeless tobacco use.[30] In particular, the transition between elementary school and high school seems to
be a high-risk period for the adolescent's initiation of tobacco use. In fact,
the rate of the onset of smoking and the prevalence of smoking may actually level off during the high school years.[31] There are three major types
of developmental challenges that youth face during adolescence. First,
youth become physically and sexually mature and begin to establish relationships with the opposite sex. Second, adolescence is a time of responding to cultural pressures to begin making the transition to adult
social roles and responsibilities. Third, youth during this developmental
period begin to establish a coherent sense of self and a set of values to
guide future behavior. Many youth confront these challenges through experimentation and risk-taking behavior.[32] Tobacco use is one of many
risky behaviors that many youth believe may make them more attractive
to certain peers and may contribute to a positive self-image in many social settings.[33]

Currently, the rate of smoking among boys and girls is roughly equal
in the United States. However, that has not always been the case. Males
were much more likely to smoke and use other tobacco products until
the mid-1970s and mid-1980s. During that time, tobacco use among
young men dropped from about 45% to 33% but remained constant at
about 34% among young women.[34] Two studies suggest that changing
gender roles, or more women are in traditionally male positions of power
and authority, may explain why young women have been more resist-
ant to the general trend of lower smoking rates. One review of research
on the influence of gender on smoking behavior found that peers and
parental models equally influenced both girls and boys. The study did
find that girls who smoked were more socially skilled (e.g., at ease with
their peers, strangers, and adults) than nonsmoking girls, and more socially skilled than boys who smoked.[35] Girls are also more likely to be
concerned with body weight and to believe that smoking may help control weight gain.[36]

Environmental Factors

Environmental factors that may influence the decision to initiate smoking include the availability of cigarettes in the community, the social acceptability of smoking, the influences of peer and parental smoking, and the perceptions youth hold of their environment.

Adolescent smoking behavior has been found to be effected by the acceptability and availability of cigarette use within society or the community. The acceptability of smoking and the availability of tobacco products is affected by the pervasive advertising and promotional activities of the tobacco industry (this is discussed in more detail in Chapter 2). Multiple role models, including family members, friends, and even television and film actors, also affect the social acceptance of tobacco. Finally, community norms, policies, and ordinances impact the acceptability of smoking by either sending clear signals that tobacco use by youth is tolerated through allowing sales or access to underage buyers, or by enforcing strong ordinances that work to keep tobacco out of the hands of kids.

In a study conducted by the National Adolescent Student Health Survey, 79% of eighth graders and 92% of tenth graders considered it to be "very easy" or "fairly easy" to obtain cigarettes.[37] Similarly, the 1991 Monitoring the Future Project found that 73% of eighth graders and 88% of tenth graders reported that it would be "fairly easy" or "very easy" to get cigarettes. Another study conducted by the Centers for Disease Control found that among a national sample, of the 2.6 million underage smokers, 1.5 million purchase their own cigarettes.[38] Among those who buy their own cigarettes, 84% purchase them from small convenience stores, 50% from large stores such as grocery stores, and 14% obtain them from self-serve vending machines. There have been a number of studies observing cigarette buying behaviors of teens that tend to confirm these reports. The general availability of cigarettes is important because a number of studies have found that the more available cigarettes are in a community, the earlier the onset of smoking among youth.[39]

My own experience in first trying cigarettes was, in most respects, not unlike other adolescents. I was in a car with three of my peers. We were all juniors in high school. We had just left a party and all three of us had been drinking beer. Someone suggested that we drive up to the local ski resort (I lived in Montana at the time). On the way up, another friend passed around cigarettes. I remember smoking two cigarettes and experiencing a terrible burning sensation in my throat. One of my friends asked if I had ever tried Copenhagen, a brand of smokeless tobacco; I lied and said "of course." I had tried other forms of smokeless tobacco which were very popular in Montana. He offered his can and I took as small a pinch as I could. When I awkwardly placed the tobacco between my lip and bottom teeth, he laughed, acknowledging that I was not a very experienced "dipper." Within five minutes I felt a distinct light-headedness and a burning sensation in my stomach (I was swallowing the tobacco juices). We eventually made it to the ski resort after climbing to approximately 6,000 feet in elevation. The combination of beer, cigarettes, smokeless tobacco, and high elevation made me as nauseous and dizzy as I have ever been in my life. We pulled up to the parking lot just in time for me to open the car door and vomit in a snowdrift for several minutes. I remember the humiliation of my friends' laughter and the curious look of strangers walking through the parking lot. My first experience with tobacco use had been decidedly negative and I remember thinking, "Why in the world would anyone decide to do this?" Most adolescents' first experience using tobacco is not positive in terms of physical sensations. It is the social cues in initial tobacco use that reinforces subsequent use; positive reinforcement from peers and the general feeling of social acceptance and fitting in.

The impact of role models such as parents, siblings, and peers on decisions to start smoking have been carefully examined in research. Role models not only provide the necessary attitudes for the social acceptance of tobacco use, they also provide common social settings, such as parties, in which cigarettes are tried for the first time.[40] These role models and social settings provide the context in which youth come to view smoking as either a positive or negative experience.

The evidence concerning the influence of parents' smoking behavior on their children's cigarette use has been mixed. On the one hand, a number of studies have found a strong and consistent relationship between parental and adolescent smoking.[41] By contrast, parental smoking was a weak predictor of children's smoking in other studies.[42] Conrad, Flay, and Hill examined the findings of twenty-seven prospective studies concerning the onset of smoking among youth.[43] Fifteen of these studies examined parental influences and less than half (seven) found that parental smoking was a strong predictor of their children's smoking behavior. Chassin and his coauthors believe that parental smoking may influence the decision to try cigarettes, but is far less important in the transition to regular smoking behavior.[44]

Parents are not the only family members who may influence decisions to use tobacco products. I started using smokeless or chew tobacco (for only a short time) after seeing my older brothers use it (and before the beer-tobacco-altitude induced vomit incident). Unlike parents, there is considerable support for the influence of the smoking behavior of older siblings on the smoking behavior of younger siblings. One ten-year longitudinal study of over 6,000 adolescents found that sibling smoking was one of only four factors that predicted risk of regular smoking and also predicted whether or not respondents would still be smoking after ten years.[45] A study by Hunter and colleagues found race and gender differences in the effect of sibling smoking.[46] Sibling smoking was a strong influence for white males, a sister's smoking was an influence for white females, and a brother's smoking influenced both black males and females.

The influence of one's peers (persons of about the same age who feel a social identification with one another) on smoking behavior has been a topic of considerable research. The findings suggest that peers may be the single most important factor in determining when and how youth first try cigarettes. As I described in my own experience, smoking is frequently a behavior designed to achieve social acceptance from peers, as well as an effort to experiment with an otherwise adult activity within a familiar and friendly social setting.[47]

Studies of varying sophistication from all over the world have found a strong relationship between smoking initiation and the influence of peers' or friends' smoking.[48] In the stage of first experimentation with tobacco most youth are in the company of their best friends. Hahn and associates found that 60% of the 11- through 17-year-olds in their study admitted to first smoking with close friends, and 72% reported smoking most recently with close friends.[49] Among a group of 12- through 14-year-olds, those whose best friend smoked were four times more likely to smoke than those whose best friend did not smoke. The influence of best friends' smoking influenced both experimentation with smoking and smoking prevalence. In a review of sixteen well-designed longitudinal studies there was a positive association between peer smoking and the decision to start smoking in all but one study, and peers appear to influence other stages of tobacco use as well.[50] In other words, youth with friends who smoke are much more likely to smoke themselves. The fact that this association was found in 88% of well-designed studies suggests a clear link between friends' smoking behavior and cigarette use. This link appears to be influenced by other personal factors, such as one's self confidence, and it's greatest influence is on the earliest stages of smoking. Finally, the strength of the bond or attachment to a peer that smokes appears to also have a strong impact on smoking behavior.

Perceptions of the Social Environment

The perceptions or beliefs that youth have about their social environment can influence their behavior, regardless of whether those perceptions are true or not. For example, middle school kids may believe that "lots of kids" their age smoke and thus may be more likely to begin smoking to fit in. The reality is that only a small percentage of children that age are regular smokers. Perceptions that have been examined for their influence on youth smoking include smoking-related norms, social support, expectations, reactions by peers and parents, and barriers that youth believe to be in place within their environment.

Norms can be thought of as what a person within a particular group believes he or she ought to do or what is believed to be acceptable behavior for a given age group, gender, or other type of social group. Gerber and Newman asked adolescents how many of their classmates were smokers.[51] Youth who increased their smoking over the course of year were much more likely to believe that a high number of their classmates were smokers than kids who had decreased their smoking in the same period. Similarly, Leventhal and colleagues found that all kids in their study greatly overestimated the number of adults and kids who smoke.[52] Adolescents in their research believed that 66% of their peers and 90% of adults were smokers. They overestimated the prevalence of smoking in both groups by a factor of three. One large study of approximately 3,300 junior high students in California found that adolescents who made rather high estimates of regular smoking prevalence were more likely to try smoking, to become smokers, or to increase the amount they smoked over the course of the study.[53]

Social support includes the perceived approval or disapproval of adolescent cigarette smoking by parents, siblings, peers, and other important people in a youth's life such as teachers or employers. One important source of social support is peer pressure. Peer pressure is not always negative. Peers may actually discourage smoking and this has been used successfully in many prevention programs.[54] In the community where I grew up, alcohol use was strongly encouraged, cigarette use was accepted but not strongly encouraged, and other types of drug use such as marijuana smoking were strongly discouraged by my peers.

Despite the lack of strong encouragement to smoke by my own peers, there is tremendous peer pressure to smoke. Hahn and colleagues found that the urging of one or more acquaintances, especially peers or close friends, prompted over half of the adolescents in their study to try a cigarette for the first time.[55] Another study found that girls who believed that their friends were more supportive than critical about their smoking were more likely than those who saw their friends as less supportive to become regular smokers one year later.[56] Similarly, many adolescents in another study claimed "my friends like me because I smoke." In the same study, nonsmokers were more likely to report, "my parents don't want me to smoke."[57]

Social support can also include the general support or approval of others who are important in the adolescent's life. This type of support seems to play an important role in the beginning stages of smoking. One study found that adolescents who claimed that their parents were generally supportive of them were less likely to start smoking than youth who believed their parents were not supportive. In contrast though, the same adolescents who believed that their friends were supportive of them were *more* likely to start smoking. Similarly, male adolescents who believed they had limited involvement in family decisions were more likely to become regular smokers than male adolescents from families where high involvement in family decisions was reported.[58] Finally, adolescents who believed that parents, siblings, friends, and teachers would not care if they smoked were at much greater risk of taking up smoking than those who believed these role models would care.[59]

Behavioral Factors

There are several behavioral factors such as academic achievement, risk taking and other problem behaviors, health enhancing behaviors, and smoking-related skills that have been examined for their influence on the risk of smoking among adolescents. These behavioral patterns may provide opportunities to look at smoking as something that has a purpose; it is useful or appropriate in certain situations.

Poor academic achievement measured in a variety of ways (grades, truancy rates, and future professional or educational aspirations) has repeatedly been found to be related to the onset of smoking. For example, Borland and Rudolph looked at the relationship between scholastic performance, parental smoking, and socioeconomic status among 1,814 high school students in Pennsylvania.[60] They found that among those variables, scholastic performance was the strongest predictor of smoking. In other words, those with the highest grades were much less likely to smoke than adolescents with lower grades. This result has been found in a study of urban black male adolescents in Harlem, New York, as well as among Hispanic and Asian adolescents in southern California.[61] Similarly, kids who disliked school and feared school failure were more likely to start smoking in early adolescence than those who liked school and expected to be successful in school.[62] Conrad and colleagues found that of the twenty-seven longitudinal studies they examined concerning the onset of smoking, 80% found a positive relationship between low academic achievement and the onset of smoking.[63] Finally, in a study by Newcomb and colleagues, what they termed "academic lifestyle orientation" (measured by grades, educational aspirations, personal and professional plans, and expectations) was the principal influence on teenage smoking behavior, teenage emotional well-being, social relationships with smokers, and adult smoking behavior.[64] Clearly, academic achievement plays an important role in adolescent smoking behavior.

Cigarette use among adolescents has been examined in association with other types of problem behaviors. For example, cigarette smoking has been linked to further illegal drug use. This suggests that smoking may be an entry-level or gateway drug in a sequence of increasingly serious drug use. This line of research is not claiming that smoking causes illegal drug use, but rather that those who use illegal drugs have most likely smoked cigarettes prior to becoming involved in illegal drugs. Studies by Fleming and colleagues and Newcomb and Bentler point to the crucial role of cigarette smoking in the progression to marijuana and harder drug use.[65] These researchers have found that the increased use of cigarettes was associated with the increased use of illegal drugs. For example, one study found that among a group of adolescents tracked for eight years, those who were using illegal drugs at adulthood were roughly twice as likely to have smoked than those who had not smoked.[66]

Risk-taking behavior has been defined as having an inclination toward excitement, and taking chances and is generally considered an indicator of overall deviance and rebelliousness. Risk taking has been found to be related to trying a cigarette for the first time in several studies.[67] However, among the twenty-seven well-designed studies reviewed by Conrad and colleagues, only five found a strong relationship between rebelliousness, risk taking, and proneness to deviance to the onset of smoking.[68]

Health-enhancing behavior, such as participation in sports, has been suggested as one means of decreasing the likelihood of deviant behavior. Swan and colleagues found that girls who were involved in at least one organized sport were less likely to smoke.[69] However, involvement in sports did not appear to impact boys' rate of smoking in this study. Similarly, McCaul and colleagues did not find a relationship between boys' smoking and participation in extracurricular activities such as sports.[70]

Other behavioral factors that have been examined are those related to the more immediate social situations surrounding smoking. For example, one study found that 42% of smoking experimenters had asked for their first cigarette.[71] Another study found that difficulty in refusing an offer to smoke was a strong predictor of smoking.[72] Furthermore, this difficulty in refusing an offered cigarette seems to be strongly influenced by the offering friend's attitudes and behaviors (e.g., being persistent or critical if refused), particularly for high-risk adolescents.[73] In the review of the onset of smoking conducted by Conrad and associates, three studies found that refusal or resistance skills against smoking were associated with lower rates of the onset of smoking.[74]

Personal Factors

Personal factors, those characteristics inherent within a person, include thought processes, personal values, personality, and overall emotional well-being. Personal risk factors are the filters through which sociodemographic and environmental factors pass as they influence behavior. Personal risk factors also help to explain why youth who are exposed to similar social environments may behave differently. Several personal factors have been examined for their relation to cigarette smoking including: knowledge of the health consequences of smoking, the utility of smoking for youth, self-esteem, self-image, self-efficacy, personality, and general emotional well-being.

Many, if not most, youth tobacco prevention programs have a strong emphasis on teaching kids about the negative long-term health consequences of smoking. They talk about death rates among smokers from cancer, heart disease, and emphysema. However, knowledge of the long-term health consequences of smoking has not been shown to be related to adolescent smoking behavior.[75] Virtually all adolescents—smokers and non-smokers—are aware of the long-term health effects of smoking, but most youth have a very short-term outlook on life and tend to feel invulnerable. Many also believe, falsely, that they can quit smoking at any time. Belief that smoking has short-term consequences appears to have a much stronger influence on kids.[76] One study found that knowing the health consequences of smoking had a minimal impact on adolescent smoking. However, adolescents in the beginning stages of smoking appear to begin actively denying the health consequences of their cigarette use.

In the search for the reasons why youth start smoking, many have begun to examine tobacco use from the perspective of the adolescent. Many adolescents who begin to smoke perceive several functional purposes of smoking. For instance, adolescent smokers are more like to view smoking as a way to act mature or more adult, have fun, cope with personal problems, stress, and boredom, or rebel against authority.[77] Castro and colleagues found that adolescents in their study smoked cigarettes to help cope with stressful and disruptive family events.[78] In one important study by Hahn and colleagues, regular smokers were asked why they first tried cigarettes and why they had most recently smoked.[79] The vast majority (60%) reported first trying cigarettes out of curiosity. Much smaller percentages of youth reported trying cigarettes to fit in (13%) or because of feeling pressured (10%). In the case of most recent use, these adolescents were most likely to claim that they smoked for pleasure (27%), as compared to feeling dependent (20%), out of curiosity (17%), and fitting in with a social group (10%). Similarly, Chassin and colleagues suggest that positive attitudes toward smoking, such as the idea that smoking is fun or pleasurable, are a better predictor of regular tobacco use than they are for initial experimentation.[80]

Adolescence is a period of identity formation and a time where a sense of self develops from interactions with parents, school, and peers. Self-esteem, or the qualitative self-evaluation emerges from this process. Several studies have found a link between self-esteem and the onset of smoking. For instance Young and Werch found that young nonsmokers and those with no intention to start smoking had higher levels of self-esteem relative to family, school, and peers than frequent users, and those who intended to smoke in the future.[81] Conrad, Flay, and Hill concluded in their review that self-esteem received fairly consistent support and that it was much better than what they had expected from their examination of earlier, less rigorous studies.[82]

It has been suggested that many adolescents may compensate for low self-esteem by attempting to improve their external image. They may want to appear to others as if they are mature or look "cool." One large study found that youth in all racial and ethnic groups viewed smoking as a way to improve their self-image.[83] Chassin and colleagues found that among adolescents in their study, smoking role models were viewed as tough, sociable, and sexually attractive.[84] Thus, youth who assume that smoking creates these positive attributes may also believe that it is a powerful mechanism for self-enhancement. Smoking becomes a vehicle that they perceive will create a positive social image and improve the way others view them—particularly peers.

An adolescent's efficacy (or confidence) in performing certain behaviors has been found to significantly counter the influences of peers who smoke. Devries, Kok, and Dijkstra found that self-efficacy in resisting offers to smoke was the strongest factor in predicting adolescent smoking over a one-year period in the Netherlands.[85] Thus, self-efficacy or personal confidence appears to act as a strong internal buffer in protecting many adolescents from the tremendous social pressure to smoke.[86]

Several studies have found a relationship between cigarette smoking and symptoms of depression among adolescents. For instance, Covey and Tam found a relationship between depressed mood and smoking, and further, that depression scores correlated with the number of cigarettes smoked.[87] Smoking may act as a short-term self-medicating response to depression by increasing alertness, feelings of euphoria and calm, but these effects would dissipate in the long run as tolerance to nicotine increases.[88]

CONCLUSION

Tobacco use is the most common cause of premature death in the United States, killing over 400,000 Americans each year. Despite being linked to chronic health problems such as cancer, emphysema, and heart disease, many young people suffer under the illusion that they can quit smoking at any time and that any negative health effects will occur much later in life. The truth is that the nicotine within tobacco products is highly addictive; teens who smoke regularly become dependent on cigarettes and find it as difficult to quit as adults. Also, cigarette smoking has immediate health effects ranging from decreased physical fitness to arteriosclerosis, an early precursor to heart disease. Smokeless tobacco products have even more immediate health effects. They may lead to oral or stomach cancers within a few years of use.

Cigarette use increased steadily and dramatically in the 1900s, reaching their peak in the 1960s when 42% of adults were smokers. Cigarette use has steadily declined after the first Surgeon General's Report on the health effects on smoking was released in 1964. While cigarette smoking decreased steadily among adults in the 1970s, 1980s, and 1990s, cigarette use declined less rapidly among youth, and actually increased throughout most of the 1990s. Currently, about 13% of middle school and 28% of high school students use some type of tobacco products.

Youth start smoking in progressive stages. In the first stage, general positive attitudes about smoking are formed. Stage 2 is when a youth actually experiments with tobacco for the first time. Stage 3 involves repeated but irregular tobacco use. In stage 4, regular tobacco use leads to addiction and dependence in stage 5. Throughout each of these stages, a number of psychosocial and personal factors are involved in the decision to start smoking and to persist as a smoker including; the availability of cigarettes, the social acceptance of smoking, peer and parenting influences, perceptions of the social environment, self-esteem, and self-image. One of the reasons that many youth come to believe in the social acceptance of smoking has to do with the pervasiveness of pro-tobacco messages. The tobacco industry spends more than $10 billion a year to convince consumers that smoking will enhance one's personal image, their social acceptance, and to make it look as though tobacco use is normative and valued in American culture. Despite the tobacco industry's claims, these messages continue to impress youth.

2

Marketing Tobacco Products to Youth

INTRODUCTION

All types of American businesses use marketing tools and strategies to advertise their products and attempt to influence customers. The goal is to attempt to attract new customers and thereby increase the market share of a given product. Among American manufacturers, only the automobile industry markets its products more heavily than the tobacco industry.[1] Despite the negative media attention the tobacco industry has received in recent years (or perhaps because of it), as well as new restrictions in advertising, the tobacco industry has increased its advertising expenditures to record highs of over $10 billion. The cigarette is the only legally available product in the United States that when "used as directed" will kill the user and injure others.[2] Tobacco companies have lobbied successfully to keep this information, along with the ingredients of tobacco products, from the public. Tobacco products are the only consumable retail products not required by the U.S. Food and Drug Administration to list ingredients on its packaging. These ingredients include over forty distinctive cancer-causing agents as well as nicotine—the chemical that makes cigarettes and other forms of tobacco as addictive as heroin or cocaine.

The question of just how much influence tobacco advertising and promotion has on tobacco consumption has been a subject of debate and research for many years.[3] Much of the debate has focused upon whether or not consumers are aware of the adverse health effects of smoking and can make informed choices; whether or not tobacco companies inappropriately target certain consumer groups in their advertising and promotional activities (such as youth or minorities); and whether or not children and adolescents are exposed to and affected by tobacco advertising and promotion. Another area of debate concerns whether or not tobacco advertising and promotion stimulates demand and if so, what should the role of the government be in regulating tobacco marketing and protecting consumers.

The tobacco industry has argued continuously that their primary purpose in advertising is to maintain brand loyalty and capture a greater market share of current smokers by convincing customers to change brands. A review of the research on tobacco marketing and promotion, as well as internal industry documents uncovered in court cases suggest otherwise. First of all, there is a strong correlation between the level of tobacco advertising and overall tobacco use. That is, as the tobacco industry increases their spending on advertisement and promotions, the amount of tobacco products purchased by consumers also increases.[4] Second, several recent judicial opinions, with the help of tobacco industry insiders and tobacco industry memos, have called in to question whether the enormous investment in advertising only serves brand loyalty. There is strong evidence that a significant portion of the advertising investment is being targeted toward specific market segments such as adolescents, as well as cultural and ethnic minorities.[5]

One basic business principal is that for any business to be successful, its product must not only retain its current consumers but also gain new consumers over time. Gaining new consumers for the tobacco industry is particularly difficult in modern times. If the tobacco industry is to maintain current levels of tobacco consumption or even slow the ongoing decline of smoking, the industry must aggressively seek replacement smokers for the estimated 3,500 Americans who quit smoking each day and for the additional 1,200 tobacco customers who die each day due to smoking-related illnesses.[6]

Of course, these facts are known to the tobacco industry and strongly suggest where new consumers must come from. Epidemiologists claim that almost all first use of tobacco occurs before high school graduation.[7] While the tobacco industry makes rigorous assertions that they do not advertise to youth, it is clear that tobacco advertising and promotion messages are making their way to kids. Several surveys have found that most adolescents can recall certain tobacco advertisements, logos, or brand insignia. The greater the recall of tobacco advertising and promotions, the greater the intent to smoke, initiation of smoking, and level of consumption of cigarettes.[8]

The American Medical Association and a broad coalition of public health organizations have called for much stricter regulation of cigarette advertisements or even a complete ban.[9] These groups claim that tobacco marketing overwhelms smoking prevention campaigns. For example, in 2002, approximately $10 million was spent by the Texas Department of Health on tobacco prevention efforts, including an aggressive media campaign. This figure is dwarfed by the $260 million spent on advertisement and promotions by the tobacco industry in the state of Texas alone in the same year. These antitobacco groups also argue that tobacco marketing increases the number of young people who begin smoking each year. The tobacco industry counters these arguments by stating that they do not target particular groups of people or segments of the population. They also assert that most of the American population is aware of the health risks associated with smoking and can make informed decisions for themselves. Finally, the tobacco industry claims that it has a constitutional right under the First Amendment to promote its products.[10] These arguments and counterarguments have been at the heart of a thirty-year debate concerning the regulation of tobacco advertising and promotions.

THE HISTORY OF ATTEMPTS TO REGULATE TOBACCO ADS

On January 11, 1964, the Surgeon General's Advisory Committee released its landmark report documenting the overwhelming scientific evidence concerning the health hazards of smoking. One week later, the Federal Trade Commission (FTC) filed a notice stating its tentative views of how the requirements of the Federal Trade Commission Act would apply to cigarette advertising and labeling of cigarettes in light of the Surgeon General's Report. The Federal Trade Commission Act states that "unfair or deceptive acts or practices are declared unlawful" and thus, the commission has the power to take action against them. The FTC claimed that tobacco advertisements at the time could be unlawfully misrepresenting or concealing the health hazards of smoking in two ways.

First, the FTC believed that many tobacco advertisements falsely stated or gave the false impression that cigarette smoking promotes health or physical well-being or is not a health hazard, or that smoking the advertised brand was less of a health hazard than smoking other brands.[11] The second concern was that much cigarette advertising portrayed smoking as pleasurable, desirable, compatible with physical fitness, or indispensable to personal development or social success without informing the consumer of the hazards involved in smoking. The FTC believed that consumers had to be made aware of the tremendous health dangers associated with cigarette smoking and this knowledge would likely influence the decision to smoke. On June 22, 1964, the FTC required warning labels on cigarette packaging and in advertisements for cigarettes that cigarette smoking is dangerous to human health. The exact wording of health warnings on tobacco products and advertisements was determined by Congress, in the Federal Cigarette Labeling and Advertising Act of 1965, before the FTC had a chance to act. After heavy lobbying efforts by the tobacco industry, Congress decided that the label should be in small print on one side of the panels of each cigarette package and should read, "Cigarette Smoking May be Hazardous to Your Health."[12]

In 1969, Congress passed the Public Health Cigarette Smoking Act. This act prohibited cigarette advertising on radio and television broadcasting.[13] The act also required that cigarette packaging include the stronger warning label, "Warning: The Surgeon General Has Determined That Cigarette Smoking Is Dangerous to Your Health."[14] The prohibition on broadcast advertising was unsuccessfully challenged in court—not by the tobacco industry, but by a group of broadcasters.[15] Despite the victory, the result of the broadcast ban was not only the elimination of tobacco advertising, but also the cost-free counteradvertising that had been in place since 1969. The Fairness Doctrine states that whenever material covering "a controversial issue of public importance" is aired, the broadcaster has an obligation to present, to some degree, both sides of the issue. The Fairness Doctrine was being used to broadcast public service announcements on radio and television concerning the health effects of smoking. After implementation of the broadcast ban, these public service announcements largely disappeared. It is an historical irony that it appears that the counteradvertising was so effective that the tobacco industry actually favored a broadcast ban on tobacco advertising. To bolster this claim, cigarette smoking had declined since the Surgeon General's report, but had leveled off and increased after cigarette advertising was removed from radio and television in 1971.

Advertising to Adolescents and Young Adults

In May of 1981, the FTC issued a report concerning cigarette advertising.[16] The official version of the report stated that the overriding message of cigarette advertising was that smoking is a positive, desirable experience. The dominant themes of these ads were that "smoking was associated with youthful vigor, good health, good looks and personal, social and professional acceptance and success, and that it is compatible with a wide range of athletic and healthful activities."[17] The FTC went on to state that the advertisements included the legally required general warning, but otherwise made no mention of the adverse health consequences of smoking.

The unofficial and nonpublic version of the report reveals much more about the true motives of the tobacco industry. Ted Bates and Company, Inc., hired a marketing and research firm who conducted focus groups to develop a marketable image for Viceroy cigarettes. Results of the research revealed that many smokers viewed the habit as a dirty and dangerous one engaged in only by "very stupid people."[18] A report developed by the marketing firm concluded, "Smokers have to face the fact that they are illogical, irrational, and stupid. People find it hard to go throughout life with such negative presentation and evaluation of self."[19] The marketing report went on to state that because there "are not any real, absolute, positive qualities or attributes in a cigarette" the most effective advertising is designed to "reduce objections."[20] Advertisements, the report said, must project an image of cigarettes as beneficial, such as improving the self-image of smokers, gaining social acceptance, or serving as a stimulant or tranquilizer. The analysis recommended that advertisers should start from the "assumption that cigarette smoking is dangerous to your health" and then try to circumvent the problem rather than fight a losing battle.[21]

One particular interesting passage from the report concerns how to persuade the young person to smoke:

> For the young smoker, the cigarette is not yet an integral part of life, of day-to-day life, in spite of the fact that [young smokers] try to project the image of a regular, run-of-the-mill smoker. For them, a cigarette, and the whole smoking process, is part of the illicit pleasure category. . . . In the young smoker's mind a cigarette falls into the same category with wine, beer, shaving, wearing a bra (or purposely not wearing one), declaration of independence and striving for self-identity. For the young starter, a cigarette is associated with introduction to sex life, with courtship, with smoking "pot" and keeping late study hours.[22]

The strategy this marketing firm recommended for attracting young people to start smoking was to present cigarettes as one of a number of initiations into adulthood and show cigarettes as one part of the illicit pleasures of drinking alcohol, smoking marijuana, or having sex.[23] Brown & Williamson Tobacco Corporation claims that it never implemented these ideas.

Whether Brown & Williamson implemented these specific marketing ideas is not clear, but it is clear that the tobacco industry had been very aware of it's need to target young smokers in order to increase or maintain their profit levels. Internal documents provided by industry insiders and from court cases reveal a pattern of deception by big tobacco and the need to promote their products to youth. The following are some tobacco industry internal memos demonstrating the necessity of marketing to youth:

> To Ensure Increased and Longer-term Growth for the Camel Filter, the Brand Must Increase Its Share Penetration Among the 14–24 Age Group Which Have a New Set of More Liberal Values and Which Represent Tomorrow's Cigarette Business.[24]

> The success of Marlboro Red during its most rapid growth period was because it became the brand of choice among teenagers who then stuck with it as they grew older.[25]

The same FTC *Staff Report on the Cigarette Advertising Investigation* also concluded that the warning labels on cigarette packages and advertisements had little impact on the level of knowledge about and attitudes toward smoking held by the general public. The FTC recommended new warning labels that specifically referred to addiction, miscarriage, and death. They also suggested that packages of cigarettes should reveal the brand's yields of tar, nicotine, and carbon monoxide. Finally, the FTC suggested that warning labels should be circled in red with arrows to important terms. After heavy lobbying by the tobacco industry, Congress did not implement these suggestions, but required the warning labels that we have now through the Comprehensive Smoking Education Act of 1984.[26] These labels are as follows:

SURGEON GENERAL'S WARNING: Smoking Causes Lung Cancer, Heart Disease, Emphysema, and May Complicate Pregnancy.

SURGEON GENERAL'S WARNING: Quitting Smoking Now Greatly Reduces Serious Risks to Your Health.

SURGEON GENERAL'S WARNING: Smoking by Pregnant Women May Result in Fetal Injury, Premature Birth, and Low Birth Weight.

SURGEON GENERAL'S WARNING: Cigarette Smoke Contains Carbon Monoxide.

Smokeless tobacco products had not been required to carry warning labels until the late 1980s despite considerable evidence that smokeless tobacco caused oral cancer, nicotine addiction, and other health problems. Massachusetts decided to enact legislation to require warning labels, and twenty-five other states decided to follow suit. However, the federal government enacted the Smokeless Tobacco Health Education Act of 1986.[27] The act required three rotating warning labels. This time they carried the circle-and-arrow format that the FTC had recommended earlier. The three warning labels read as follows:

WARNING: This product may cause mouth cancer.

WARNING: This product may cause gum disease and tooth loss.

WARNING: This product is not a safe alternative to cigarettes.

Tobacco Advertising: A First Amendment Right?

Despite the successes of campaign to require warning labels on tobacco products and removing tobacco advertising from television and radio, regulating tobacco advertising has proven to be difficult because the tobacco industry has a First Amendment right to advertise and market a legal product. However, these protections are not absolute. In 1976, the Supreme Court ruled that commercial speech found in product advertisements is not afforded the same level of protections as other types of speech and may be regulated if there is a valid public interest.[28] The government may regulate commercial speech for the following public interests: avoiding deceptive and misleading claims, preventing unlawful activities such as promoting the sale of alcohol to minors, and protecting public health.

The Supreme Court uses a four-pronged test in deciding whether regulations of commercial speech violate the First Amendment. The first part of the test asks the question: Is the advertising unlawful or misleading? The United States Supreme Court's definition of "inherently misleading" refers to advertisements that promote fraud, are overreaching, or create consumer confusion.[29] While it would seem to make sense that tobacco advertisements would easily fit into this category, courts have ruled that imagery alone is not misleading. For example, courts have ruled that advertisements for alcoholic beverages that project images of drinkers as successful and fun-loving yet do not warn of the dangers of alcohol abuse are not legally misleading.[30]

A cigarette advertisement would be ruled misleading if it included unsubstantiated health claims. Advertisements could not claim that cigarette smoking poses little or no risk to health or does not affect breathing. The Federal Trade Commission successfully challenged an R. J. Reynolds Tobacco Company advertisement that stated smoking is not as hazardous to health as the public has been led to believe.[31]

Furthermore, with recent revelations and documents proving that the tobacco industry purposely marketed their products to minors, the courts may conclude that this represents illegal advertising. Courts do not protect speech that leads to an illegal activity such as the sale of cigarettes to minors. The tobacco company Liggett Group Inc. has admitted that the entire tobacco industry has conspired to market cigarettes to youth.[32] Thus, regulation of some tobacco advertising is likely to pass the first prong of the test.

The second part of the test concerns whether or not the government's interest is substantial. Appellate courts have consistently ruled that the government has a substantial interest in limiting tobacco advertisements due the overwhelming evidence associating smoking with lung cancer, heart disease, and other diseases.[33] However, the Federal Cigarette Labeling and Advertising Act does not allow state and local governments to regulate cigarette advertising based on smoking and health. The tobacco industry successfully lobbied Congress to exclude this type of regulation. Thus, cities such as New York and Baltimore are regulating tobacco advertising on the basis of preventing minors from being involved in the illegal purchase of tobacco.

The third prong of the test requires that the government regulation of commercial speech must benefit the public interest. There is extensive social science research regarding the effect of tobacco advertising on the purchasing habits of teen smokers and on the effect of some of the images projected in tobacco advertising. After R. J. Reynolds introduced the Joe Camel advertising campaign in the late 1980s, the market share of Camel cigarettes among teenagers increased at least twenty-fold. In the same time period, there had been an overall decline in teen smoking. Once this campaign was introduced, that decline was reversed.[34] An association between a rise in young girls' smoking habits and the tobacco industry's decision to market their products to adolescent girls has also been documented.[35] The Supreme Court has not given a clear indication as to what level of evidence is needed to regulate tobacco advertising to serve the public interest. The Court has been demanding scientific and statistical evidence in similar cases. However, it is quite likely that tobacco advertising restrictions would likely stand up to this test due to the increasing volume of evidence to suggest that tobacco marketing is still reaching adolescents and has had the impact of increasing youth tobacco use.

The fourth and final prong of the test is whether the regulation of advertising is a reasonable fit; in other words the regulation must be "the least restrictive" possible. The restriction cannot be overly sweeping and broad. Restrictions on tobacco advertising likely meet this test by restricting advertisements that target areas where children gather, such as schools and playgrounds. The tobacco industry still has alternative venues for advertising their products to adult consumers such as through the mail, promotions, sporting events, magazines, and at the points of purchase of tobacco products. In fact, antitobacco advocates argue that magazine and points of purchase advertisements reach a significant number of kids.

After the Master Settlement: Tobacco Advertisements Are Still Reaching Youth

The Master Settlement Agreement (MSA) between the states' Attorneys General and the tobacco industry requires the elimination of certain types of outdoor tobacco advertisements, including those found on billboards, in arenas, stadiums, shopping malls, video arcades and advertisements on private or public transportation waiting areas. The MSA also forbids the tobacco industry from "directly or indirectly targeting youth in their promotional activities, or engaging in activities with the primary purpose of initiating, maintaining, or increasing youth smoking."[36] The Master Settlement Agreement with the states will be discussed in more detail in Chapter 4.

Philip Morris took out an advertisement in March of 2000 stating: "Perhaps the most visible change is the removal of tobacco advertising from billboards in the United States. The goal of this provision is to limit the exposure of kids to tobacco advertising, a step defined by the public health community as a way to help reduce the incidence of youth smoking."[37] Several recent studies and reports seem to counter those assertions. First of all, while the overall sale of cigarettes fell by 15.6 billion cigarettes from 2000 to 2001, the tobacco industry increased their advertising and promotional expenditures by $1.6 billion to a record high of $11.22 billion.[38] The $11.22 billion figure represents an increase of 17% from the $9.59 billion spent in 2000, and an increase of 66% from the $6.73 billion spent in 1998.[39] Thus, the tobacco industry has increased its expenditures on advertising and marketing by 66% since the Master Settlement Agreement of 1998.

Also, two recent studies have shown that both cigarette and smokeless tobacco marketing to teens through magazine advertising increased after the Master Settlement Agreement took effect in November 1998. The Food and Drug Administration restricts tobacco advertising for any magazine or publication where 15% or more of their readers are under age 18.[40] Despite this restriction, cigarette advertising expenditures in magazines with more than 15% youth readership increased by $30 million after the MSA.[41] The tobacco industry spent almost $120 million on advertising in nineteen magazines with more than 15% youth readers in the first nine months of 1999. This represents over one-third of their total magazine expenditures for that period.[42]

Much of the increased advertising in youth magazines came from the brands that most youth prefer. Marlboro is the most popular brand of cigarettes with youth. Marlboro spent $26.1 million in the first nine months of 1999 on advertising in magazine with more than 15% youth readers. That is the highest expenditure of any brand, and was an increase of $5.2 million since 1998. During the first nine months of 1999, the most popular cigarette brands (Marlboro, Camel, Kool, Winston, and Newport) spent a combined $71.1 million on advertising in magazines with youth readerships of more than 15%. Kool increased their magazine expenditures by almost 76% since the Master Settlement Agreement.[43]

The United States Smokeless Tobacco Company (USST) settled with 44 states' Attorneys General regarding tobacco-related heath costs. The settlement required exactly the same provisions as the Master Settlement Agreement concerning cigarettes discussed above: the elimination of outdoor tobacco advertisements and advertising in magazines with youth readerships greater than 15%. One study conducted by the Massachusetts Department of Public Health found that overall smokeless tobacco magazine advertising expenditures increased from $9.4 million to $24 million from 1997 to 2001. This represents a 150% increase. More importantly, youth magazine advertising increased from $4.7 million in 1997 to $11.1 million in 2001 for all companies. However, the United States Smokeless

Tobacco Company was the only smokeless tobacco maker to sign the settlement agreement. Their spending increased 161% from $3.6 million in 1997 to $9.4 million in 2001.[44]

It's also been argued that these advertisements are directed at youth. One series of ads for United States Smokeless Tobacco's Rooster brand features headlines such as "Cock-A-Doodle-Freakin'-Do," "Birds of a Feather Party Together" and "Where's the Chicks?" A recent Skoal campaign features a picture of a jet skier and the headline "A Splash Bolder." These advertisements have appeared in *Rolling Stone* and *Sports Illustrated*, which have a large youth readership.[45]

The Massachusetts Department of Public Health studies discussed here were released in the wake of multimillion dollar public relations campaigns by the tobacco industry in which they attempted to portray themselves as a reformed and changed industry marketing responsibly, only to adults. A Brown & Williamson executive has stated publicly that the company does not place advertisements in magazines with more than 15% youth readership. Similarly, Philip Morris' web site states, "Cigarette brand advertising does not appear in publications directed primarily to those under 21 years of age." Finally, R. J. Reynolds' web site states, "We do not want children to smoke, nor do we market this adult product to minors."[46]

Point-of-Purchase Advertising and Promotions

While tobacco advertising in magazines has increased since the Master Settlement Agreement, the areas with the greatest increases in expenditures and where the greatest percentage of tobacco industry advertising occurs are promotional allowances and retail value-added expenditures. Promotional allowances are payments to retailers and any other persons in order to facilitate the sale of cigarettes, excluding expenditures in connection with newspapers, magazines, outdoor, audiovisual, transit, and direct mail. Examples of promotional allowances include payments to retailers for displaying and merchandising brands and volume discounts given to wholesalers. Promotions made up almost 40% of tobacco marketing expenditures in 2000.[47] Retail value-added expenditures are the costs associated with offers such as "buy one, get one free" and "buy three, get a free T-shirt," where the bonus item is distributed at retail when the cigarettes are purchased. The cigarettes and bonus item are often packaged together as a single unit. Retail value added costs made up almost 43% of tobacco marketing expenditures in 2000.[48]

The tobacco industry spends more than $3.8 billion on vendor allowances and retail value-added promotions and advertisements at sales outlets or "points of purchase" throughout the United States.[49] Point-of-purchase advertising and promotions are meant to target and attract shoppers at the places where they purchase specific products or brands.

Point-of-purchase tobacco advertising consists of cigarette and spit tobacco advertisements and functional items (such as counter mats, change cups, clocks, grocery baskets, and cigarette and smokeless tobacco dispensers). These items are found both inside and outside the property of convenience stores, drug stores, gas stations, and other retail sales outlets. Tobacco product advertising at retail outlets has increased significantly since the ban on tobacco billboard advertising went into effect in 1999.[50] Wakefield and colleagues found that 80% of retail outlets had interior advertising, 70% had tobacco functional items, and 60% had exterior tobacco advertising. Similarly, a 1991 study of retail stores in Buffalo, New York, found that 87% of stores had promotional items advertising tobacco products, and two-thirds had tobacco posters.[51]

As mentioned earlier, tobacco industry promotions are distinct from advertising in the sense that incentives are provided to the consumer or the retailer. Incentives to retailers include coupons, multipack discounts (buy two, get one free), free gifts with tobacco product purchases, and other types of discounts and merchandise. Incentives to retailers generally include payments to display the company's brands, advertisements, and related materials prominently or in specific store locations. Thus, industry officials pay retailers for "good" shelving space, termed slotting allowances. This usually includes counter space or highly visible racks. It also includes spaces next to candy products, display cases that are self-serve (tobacco products can be accessed without the aid of a clerk), and walls and counters below four feet (the eye-level of young children). A study in Santa Clara County, California, found that 62% of stores had received slotting/display allowances from the tobacco industry. This is higher than allowances for other popular convenience store products such as candy, snack foods, and soft drinks. Obviously these incentives provide a strong motivation for retailers to display, promote, and advertise tobacco products. The primary reason for discussing tobacco industry advertising in retail stores is that three out of four teenagers shop at convenience stores at least once a week. According to the trade association, Point of Purchasing Advertising International, point-of-purchase advertising and promotions target consumers at the place where they actually purchase the product, they are meant to attract the attention of the shopper, and they remind consumers of previous seen selling messages.[52]

Point-of-purchase advertising and promotions seem to especially impact kids. A 1999 study found that teens are more likely than adults to be influenced by promotional pieces in convenience stores (73% to 47%). This study also found that 51% of teenagers admit they are influenced by in-store displays, 47% are influenced by exterior banners or window signs, and 44% are influenced by in-store promotional signs.[53]

A recent study compared photographs of stores with no tobacco advertising and stores with tobacco advertising and found that students perceived easier access to tobacco products at the stores with tobacco advertising.[54] Biener and Siegel (1999) conducted a study of seventh graders and found that more than 99% reported seeing tobacco advertising and promotions and 70% indicated a level of receptivity to tobacco marketing materials.[55]

Another study found that adolescents who owned a tobacco promotional item and named a cigarette brand whose advertising attracted their attention were twice as likely to become established smokers than those who did neither.[56] Despite the claims by the tobacco industry that promotional items are meant for smokers over age 21, one study found that 30% of all kids in the sample (ages 12 to 17) owned at least one promotional item, such as T-shirts, backpacks, and CD players.[57] These promotional items appear to have a tremendous impact on teens. One study found a strong association between youth awareness of, and involvement with, tobacco promotions and being at risk for tobacco use.[58]

According to a 1994 U.S. Surgeon General's report, the use of value-added or coupon promotions makes cigarettes appear more affordable, especially to those with less financial resources, including kids. Coupons also affect new users by encouraging them to smoke more, moving them from the trial stage to being a regular smoker.[59] Self-service displays or displays that allow access to tobacco products without a clerk's assistance make it easier for kids to purchase cigarettes or even steal them, and research suggests that approximately 5% of young smokers steal cigarettes.[60] Finally, a study of seventh graders found that youth who have experimented with smoking are more likely than other respondents to report seeing tobacco advertising in stores.[61]

Restrictions on Advertising and Marketing of Tobacco

After its investigation of the tobacco industry, the Food and Drug Administration (FDA) assumed regulatory control over tobacco products (this is the subject of Chapter 3). The FDA used this power to immediately pass a series of marketing and advertising restrictions on cigarettes and smokeless tobacco products. The FDA also used their regulatory power to limit underage access to cigarettes. The tobacco industry challenged the authority of the FDA to regulate tobacco all the way to the United States Supreme Court. In a five-to-four decision, the Supreme Court decided that only Congress could give the FDA authority to regulate tobacco.

However, in the interim, many states passed their own restrictions on youth access to tobacco and the advertising and marketing of tobacco products to youth. While selling tobacco products to anyone under age

18 is illegal in all states and Washington, D.C., there is tremendous variation in how these laws are enforced. For example, only thirty-two states designate any type of enforcement authority to enforce minors' access to tobacco laws. Texas designates local law enforcement agencies to enforce tobacco retailer laws, but has no specific funding set aside for this purpose; this is the norm throughout the nation. The penalties for selling tobacco to minors are generally small fines. About half the states (twenty-four) allow for either tobacco licenses to be suspended or revoked for selling tobacco to minors, but this generally occurs after multiple violations and is quite rare. An important method for restricting youth access to tobacco is banning tobacco vending machines in places open to youth; forty-one states and Washington, D.C. have enacted such a ban.[62]

The Food and Drug Administration initially banned outdoor tobacco advertisements within 1,000 feet of schools and public playgrounds. They also banned selling or giving away products such as caps, T-shirts, and gym bags that bear tobacco product brand names or logos. However, the tobacco industry successfully challenged these regulations. Currently, only four states ban outdoor tobacco advertisements near places kids go to school or play.[63]

TOBACCO RETAILERS IN TEXAS

In 2000, on the request of the Texas Department of Health, I had a small group of graduate students at Prairie View A&M University count the frequency and types of tobacco advertising and promotions in a random sample of retail stores legally accessible to youth and licensed to sell tobacco products. The students also checked whether the stores were in compliance with several Texas tobacco retailer laws. They found 1,301 legal violations in 409 stores. The most common legal violation was failure to post the state license to sell tobacco. The next most common violation was failure to post the Texas Comptroller's Warning Sign (24% of stores). This 10-by-18 inch sign in black and red print states the following:

> Buying or selling tobacco products? WARNING, Purchasing or attempting to purchase tobacco products by a minor under age 18 years of age is prohibited by law. Sale or provision of tobacco products to a minor under 18 years of age is prohibited by law. Upon conviction, a Class C misdemeanor, including a fine of up to $500, may be imposed.

The irony of the license and warning signs are that they are mailed to the retailer together when a tobacco license is purchased. There is no good reason for failing to post either the license or the warning sign.[64]

The graduate students found a total of 6,908 tobacco advertisements inside and outside the 409 stores. They also found that coupons for free tobacco products were the most common promotional efforts within the stores. Marlboro was the most advertised tobacco product and had the most promotional items, followed more distantly by Camel and Newport. These products combine for only about 35% of the overall cigarette market share. However, 86% of minors who smoke currently purchase or use one of these three brands.[65] Other findings of interest include: 39 stores had tobacco ads next to candy; 23 stores had outdoor tobacco ads next to churches and schools; 136 stores had tobacco ads below four feet; and the frequency of tobacco ads were much higher in African American neighborhoods, neighborhoods with a high percentage of kids, and high poverty neighborhoods. We have continued this survey in subsequent years and the frequency of tobacco advertisements and legal violations have declined substantially, perhaps due to the establishment in 1999 of an aggressive tobacco control program in the Houston area.

CANDY CIGARETTES

Public health advocates consider candy cigarettes as another way in which tobacco products are promoted to children. In many cases, candy cigarette packaging closely mirrors the packaging of real cigarettes. The United States candy cigarettes industry has been around since at least 1915.[66] By 1939, tobacco manufacturers had authorized the use of cigarette pack designs on packs for candy cigarettes. One candy cigarette maker boasted, "we put out the candy cigarette pack by the millions" and touted "the tremendous advertising factor" to "coming up cigarette smokers."[67]

Currently there are two large manufacturers of candy cigarettes in the United States—New England Confectionery and World Candies. New England Confectionery produces candy cigarettes resembling several Brown & Williamson brands. World Candies produces candy cigarettes mimicking the brand names of Marlboro, Winston, Salem, More, and Advantage.[68] World Candies also produces bubble gum cigarettes. This gum comes in white paper with a brown paper end to closely resemble a real cigarette. These were one of my personal favorites as a child because you could blow one end and powdered sugar would escape from the other side like smoke. By 1998, candy cigarette packaging could no longer duplicate the names of particular cigarette brands. However, candy cigarette packaging continued to resemble cigarette packaging. The presidents of both World Candies and New England Confectionery continue to deny that their companies made products that could be considered candy cigarettes.

A recent study in the British Medical Journal examined documents from the tobacco industry as well as other sources concerning candy cigarettes.[69] The results indicate a long-term relationship between both industries. One document from the National Automatic Merchandising Association Special Committee on Cigarette Vending, dated just before the release of the 1964 Surgeon General's report, warned tobacco manufacturers that it found candy cigarettes in packs "so real looking it's startling" and stated its concern that this would add "another argument to bolster the claim that the tobacco companies are trying to lure youngsters into the smoking habit."[70] After that, the tobacco industry began to distance itself from candy cigarettes. However, the tobacco industry continued to allow trademark infringements. In fact, as, late as 1991, a South American candy company wrote to Philip Morris, reluctantly agreeing to the company's request that they discontinue using its brand names for chocolate cigarettes. The candy company protested by stating, "over all these years, candy cigarettes have been sold to thousands of children and the brands 'daddy smoked' have been receiving propaganda completely free of charge."[71]

The tobacco industry has made only minimal attempts to stop cigarette candy makers from selling their products in packaging resembling cigarette brands. In fact Klein and St. Clair found only one lawsuit filed by R. J. Reynolds against World Candies. This lawsuit was filed in the wake of an article published in the New England Journal of Medicine concerning candy cigarettes. The lawsuit was apparently settled before it was filed, and no payment was required despite the alleged thirty years of trademark infringement. Similarly, in 1990 Philip Morris announced a "crackdown" on children's merchandise containing their trademarks, including candy products. However, there is no evidence that lawsuits were ever filed either before or after the crackdown. In contrast, Philip Morris has vigorously enforced their trademark against rival tobacco companies.[72]

In 1990, World Candies funded a study conducted by Dr. Howard Kassinove, a psychologist from Hofstra University in reaction to a proposed ban on candy cigarettes by the U.S. Congress. The cost of the study was shared with New England Confectionary. The study concluded that it seemed unlikely that candy cigarettes were a major contributor to adolescent smoking after only 5.3% of smokers considered candy cigarettes to have contributed to their later smoking. However, after showing candy cigarette packages to thirty-one young children, they found that boxes which were similar in size to real cigarettes, were cellophane wrapped, and had a tax seal on the end were most likely to be identified as "candy cigarettes," even when the word cigarette did not appear on packaging. They also concluded that there was "little doubt that some of the children were pretending to be smoking as they held candy cigarettes in their hands, and some of the children will likely begin to smoke when they get older." Dr. Kassinove recommended that candy cigarette manufacturers "package their material in ways that are appealing to children but are not suggestive of cigarettes." World Candies and New England confectionery removed the word "cigarette" from their products but otherwise made no changes in their packaging designs.[73]

More troubling is the admission from Dr. Kassinove that he had changed his original report at the insistence of World Candies. In the revised report, references to the health hazards of smoking and to the proposed ban on candy cigarettes, and a listing of countries that had banned candy tobacco products were all eliminated. The study also dropped the reference to the 5.3% of adults who considered candy cigarettes as a contributor to their smoking. Finally, all descriptions of youth mimicking adult smokers and the researchers' concerns about design features resembling tobacco cigarettes were deleted.[74]

SMOKING IN FILMS

If you have ever watched old movies from the 1940s and 1950s, you may have noticed that smoking was prominent in a lot of those films. In fact, if you watch Turner Classic movies you may notice how frequently smoking takes place. The actors in those films tended to be upper class and sophisticated people who portrayed smoking as seductive and mysterious. They were also paid to smoke in those films by the tobacco industry. In fact, the industry had contracts with the major studios to include their products in movies. But that was in the 1940s and 1950s, right? It might surprise you to know that Sylvester Stallone took $500,000 from Brown & Williamson to smoke their brand in three of his films. Similarly, in *Superman II*, Lois Lane, who is a nonsmoker in the comic book series, chain-smoked Marlboros in the movie. The Marlboro brand name appeared some forty times in the film. A clause in the contract between Warner Brothers and Philip Morris states that the producers will edit the film to avoid any negative portrayal of Marlboros. Philip Morris paid a mere $40,000 to the producers for this sort of advertising. More recently, the producers of the James Bond film *License to Kill* took a $350,000 payment to have James Bond smoke Larks in the movie. Since that time and after much criticism, Pierce Brosnan has decided that in his portrayal of James Bond, the agent no longer smokes any brand. In the children's films *Who Framed Roger Rabbit?* and *The Muppet Movie*, Philip Morris also paid to have their products appear on screen.[75]

In one recent case, U.S. Tobacco actually helped finance a film starring country singer George Strait called *Pure Country*, and displayed its products prominently in it. There have been more recent reports of cigar companies paying to promote cigars in films such as *Independence Day*.[76]

In the 1990s, there was actually a noticeable upsurge in the amount of smoking in movies and television. Characters in 1990s movies were much more likely to smoke than a person in real life.[77] John Travolta smoked in nearly every film he made in the 1990s. Julia Roberts smoked in several of hers as well. After declining over three decades, smoking in movies has returned to levels comparable to those observed in the 1960s before the issuance of the first Surgeon General's report on smoking and health in 1964. Stockwell and Glantz believe that the presentation of smoking in films remains pro-tobacco with only 14% of tobacco screen-time presenting adverse social or health effects from tobacco use. The researchers found that in movies from the 1960s, tobacco was used about once for every five minutes of film time. In films from the 1970s and 1980s, tobacco was used about once every ten to fifteen minutes, but in movies from the 1990s, tobacco was used an average of every three to five minutes. Thus, not only is tobacco use in films increasing, despite the tobacco industry's claims that they no longer pay to place their products in films, these images tend to reinforce messages that smoking today is a widespread and socially desirable activity. The researchers believe that the portrayal of tobacco use, whether in a positive or negative context, leads to changes in attitudes that predispose children to smoking. In an era in which the tobacco industry is finding traditional advertising media increasingly restricted, the appearance of tobacco in motion pictures is an important mechanism to promote and reinforce its use, particularly among young people.[78]

CONCLUSION

The tobacco industry loses over 4,500 customers each day because they either quit or die. To gain new customers, the tobacco industry uses aggressive and sophisticated marketing and advertising practices. Despite total bans of tobacco advertising on radio and television, the industry spends more money on advertising than any other American manufacturer except the auto industry, and those expenditures have increased dramatically in recent years. Replacement smokers tend to come from youth because almost all first time tobacco use occurs before high school graduation. Tobacco companies are well aware of this, and industry documents reveal a long history of direct marketing to kids. Despite current claims that the tobacco industry only markets their products to adult consumers, a large amount of tobacco advertising continues to reach kids. Kids see tobacco advertisements through magazines, promotions, retail stores, and even through candy cigarettes and movies.

Advertising agencies use extremely sophisticated methods to display a product in such a way that it leaves an impression on the unconscious mind. In the case of tobacco, advertisements often give the impression that the user is sophisticated, confident, and beautiful. It also gives the impression that tobacco use is widespread and socially accepted. Until recent years, we were not fully aware that the tobacco industry purposely marketed their products to kids. We were also not aware of many other deadly secrets that the industry managed to maintain for several decades. The FDA investigation of the 1990s changed all of that, and forever changed the way we look at big tobacco.

3

The FDA Investigation of Big Tobacco

INTRODUCTION

David Kessler became the commissioner of the Food and Drug Administration in October 1990 during the first Bush administration. He was a lawyer and a doctor, taught food and drug law courses, and had worked in Washington for Senator Orrin Hatch. His experiences made him a natural choice to head an agency that was underfunded, understaffed, and had much of its authority stripped during the Reagan administration. Dr. Kessler's primary goal when taking his new position was to make the agency a strong regulator—to vigorously enforce the nation's food and drug laws. He had no intention of taking on the tobacco industry, but take it on he did, and that is the legacy of his tenure at the FDA. He led a massive investigation of the tobacco industry, and with the help of industry insiders revealed how the American public was deceived by big tobacco companies for decades. The decision to investigate the tobacco industry and the ultimate decision to regulate tobacco were acts of tremendous political courage. The tobacco industry has had enormous influence over many politicians and tremendous resources at their disposal. For Kessler, once he had preliminary evidence that the industry intentionally manipulated tobacco products, he had no choice but to investigate. Much of the information for this chapter comes from David Kessler's book *A Question of Intent: A Great American Battle with a Deadly Industry*.[1]

CAN THE FDA REGULATE TOBACCO?

The decision to regulate tobacco products or any product is not a policy choice, but a legal decision. The FDA has a responsibility to ensure that the food we consume and the pharmaceutical drugs we use are safe.

Before any food or drug is marketed to consumers, it undergoes rigid testing by the FDA. So, why is that cigarettes are not included as a product or drug under FDA jurisdiction? The legal definition of a drug is an "article (other than food) *intended* to affect the structure or any function of the body." In other words, a substance not only had to affect the structure or function of the body, but the manufacturer had to intend that it do so. In 1977, the public interest group Action on Smoking and Health (ASH) filed a petition asking the FDA to assert jurisdiction over cigarettes as a drug. The commissioner, Don Kennedy, denied the petition. ASH filed suit, and in *Ash v. Harris*, the Court of Appeals upheld the FDA's decision not to regulate cigarettes as drugs because there was no evidence that the industry intended the effects that tobacco products have on the body.[2]

David Kessler was asked to revisit this question after several citizen petitions had been filed asking the FDA to regulate tobacco. Scott Ballin, the Chairman of the Coalition on Smoking and Health, sponsored these petitions. The Coalition on Smoking and Health united the American Heart Association, the American Lung Association, and the American Cancer Society. Meanwhile, Mike Synar, a Democratic senator from Oklahoma, had introduced legislation that would place tobacco regulation under the FDA. The legislation had no chance of passing, but Synar also met with Kessler and suggested that he needed to do something about tobacco. Kessler was also receiving pressure from within his own agency to do something about tobacco. As one FDA attorney stated, "this is the most important thing we can do, and if we take it up I'm willing to spend the rest of my career on it."[3]

Despite the passionate pleas, Kessler was reluctant to investigate tobacco, noting that it would burn up administration resources and provoke reprisals in the form of budget cuts from the White House or Congress. He also had other priorities such as developing permanent food labels and speeding up the process of approving potentially life-saving drugs. Kessler also recognized that once cigarettes were classified as drugs, they would likely have to be banned altogether. Banning tobacco would not only bring on the wrath of the tobacco industry and political leaders from tobacco states such as Virginia, North Carolina, and Kentucky, but also quite likely the 50 million Americans who would simultaneously go through withdrawal. Finally, he believed that Congress sets the agenda for the FDA and would likely have to give the FDA the power to regulate tobacco.

With the tacit approval of Dr. Kessler, a small group of people within the FDA began discussing ideas on regulation and amassing information on nicotine, addiction, tobacco control, and the tobacco-related efforts of other agencies within the federal government. They met with Jack Henningfield who headed the clinical pharmacology branch of the National

Institute on Drug Abuse (NIDA). Henningfield was a major contributor to the 1988 Surgeon General's report that declared nicotine in drugs as addictive and had over 200 publications to his credit. Henningfield found that both in animals and humans, when given the opportunity, both will self-administer nicotine to themselves. This is a defining characteristic of addiction. Henningfield had to end his research on the addictive nature of nicotine after Carlton Turner, the Reagan Drug Czar threatened to cut NIDA's budget should it continue. Kessler suggests that this was the result of the Tobacco Institute (the lobbying arm of the tobacco industry) pressuring congressional allies to stop NIDA from studying the addictive properties of tobacco.

Despite the work of the tobacco group within the FDA, Kessler was not convinced the FDA had the jurisdiction to regulate tobacco. What changed his mind was a suggestion by David Adams, an FDA attorney who was an expert in drug advertising and labeling. He told Kessler that he felt there was a way to regulate cigarettes if Kessler wanted to. The FDA tobacco group had learned that nicotine was a variable or ingredient in tobacco, not an absolute component. He went on to say that he believed that cigarette manufacturers can take nicotine out, but they choose not to. That gets at the question of the industry's intent. The FDA had been thinking about regulating tobacco; Adams suggested regulating nicotine as a drug. From that point, Kessler decided to focus on the issue of tobacco regulation. If the tobacco industry intended that their products contain nicotine to satisfy an addiction, he was going to have to find evidence to prove it.

The FDA tobacco group received information from a former R. J. Reynolds manager about the process of making cigarettes. The industry insider code named "Deep Cough" claimed that the industry manipulated tobacco products and specifically nicotine levels in cigarettes. That was enough information for Dr. Kessler to write a letter responding to the petitions by the Coalition on Smoking and Health. The letter stated, "the petitions were not sufficiently far-reaching" (they were limited to industry claims about low-tar cigarettes). "The focus should be on the presence of nicotine in cigarettes in amounts associated with addiction." The letter went on to say, "Although it has been well-known for many years that some people smoke for the drug effects of nicotine. . . . Cigarettes vendors have in the past been given the benefit of the doubt as to whether they intend cigarettes to be used for this purpose, because some people smoke for no reason other than the drug effect." The letter continues by stating that the FDA has reason to believe that there is new evidence that "suggests that cigarette vendors intend the obvious—that many people buy cigarettes to satisfy nicotine addiction. Should the agency make this finding based on an appropriate record or be able to prove these facts in court, it would have a legal basis on which to regulate these products under the drug provisions of the ACT" (the Food and Drug Cosmetic Act). The letter concluded, "The proper forum for this discussion, and for the resolution of these issues, is not the FDA, but the Congress."[4]

The reaction to the letter was swift and dramatic. The FDA alerted John Schwartz at the *Washington Post* about the letter. His reaction was, "Holy shit" and later stated, "I knew immediately that the world had changed." Jack Henningfield, the expert on addiction from NIDA said he was "stunned, awed, and amazed" when he learned of the release. Rip Forbes, an aide to Congressman Waxman said to himself, "This is going to make a great hearing." The tobacco industry was caught completely off guard and they quickly scrambled to find out how their intelligence networks had failed so miserably. However, the official reaction from the Tobacco Institute was, "We are surprised that this FDA letter is getting the attention it is. The bottom line of this letter is that FDA won't act without further action from Congress. Nothing has happened."[5]

Congressmen Henry Waxman and Mike Synar were both supporters of antitobacco initiatives for years and had unsuccessfully attempted to pass legislation to regulate tobacco products. Their reaction was to call for congressional hearings and stated that Dr. Kessler would need to come to Capitol Hill to "make his case." The only problem was that Kessler's evidence came from a handful of documents, one informant, and the insights of other experts. He did not have "a case" to assert jurisdiction over tobacco at the time. He pulled together a team charged with the mission of learning everything possible about the industry's knowledge of nicotine and to determine whether the tobacco industry was manipulating and controlling nicotine levels. They had a few weeks to learn what the tobacco industry had skillfully hidden for decades.

THE INITIAL INVESTIGATION

Deep Cough

Before the letter from the FDA to the Coalition on Smoking and Health had been sent, the FDA began a series of conversations with a former R. J. Reynolds employee codenamed "Deep Cough." All tobacco industry employees are required to sign confidentiality agreements stating that they will not divulge company secrets. These agreements are legally binding even after an employee leaves the company. Despite fears of legal retribution, Deep Cough was willing to talk to the FDA about R. J. Reynolds' manufacturing process. He was also being pressed for an interview with ABC's *Day One* program, which was developing a story about the tobacco industry.

Deep Cough stated that "vats of nicotine" were used in reconstituted tobacco. Later the FDA learned that as far back as the 1950s, the tobacco industry developed a process for using stems, scraps, and other leftovers from tobacco plants. A solvent is added to the mix and the nicotine contained in the scraps dissolves in the solvent. The concentrated nicotine is than sprayed back onto paper sheets in a process called "reconstituting tobacco." This process is done in virtually all American cigarettes. Deep Cough hinted that R. J. Reynolds had conducted nicotine research on humans. He described one research project concerning the development of a Super Ultra–Low Tar Cigarette. The development of low-tar cigarettes reflected the belief by the industry that people associate cancer with tar and not other ingredients such as nicotine. Volunteer employees who smoked a certain number of cigarettes were asked to donate urine, saliva, and blood samples.

Deep Cough stated that they were told by tobacco lawyers never to use the word nicotine, because it could open them up to regulation by the FDA. Thus they used terms like "satisfaction" or "impact." In another project where the tobacco product had little "impact," there were directions to adjust the amount of nicotine or the PH, the alkalinity, to increase "impact."

Later on *Day One*, Deep Cough stated, "They put nicotine in the form of tobacco extract into a product to keep the consumer happy." The reporter for *Day One*, John Martin, asked how much they added. Deep Cough stated that it "depended on what level the process called for," but it could be at "one percent, five percent, ten percent. . . ."[6] However, Deep Cough offered no evidence of this. The tobacco industry vehemently denied the allegations and eventually sued *Day One* concerning the broadcast.

Vedpal Singh Malik

Vedpal Singh Malik was a senior scientist with Philip Morris. He was among eight former Philip Morris employees suing the tobacco giant after being fired. Malik was working on two projects that involved genetic engineering. One project had the goal of creating a nicotine-free plant; the other project involved the development of a tobacco plant with fewer carcinogens. He felt that he was making real progress when suddenly he was told that his projects were being shut down and that he was out of a job.

Malik told investigators from the Office of Criminal Investigation about an experimental, nicotine-free cigarette called "Next." He stated that the nicotine extracted from Next was added to Marlboro. When pressed by Dr. Kessler, Malik stated that once the nicotine was extracted, "They absorbed the nicotine on the stems."[7] These stems were than used in the development of Marlboro cigarettes. Malik quoted a senior manager as saying that "a cigarette without nicotine is like sex without an orgasm."[8] Malik also put FDA investigators in touch with other potential informants including a chemist they codenamed "Philip" and a behavioral scientist they codenamed "Cigarette."

Philip

Philip had been the director of applied research at Philip Morris for five years. He had tremendous knowledge of both the research and the production processes. He made few friends at Philip Morris because he advocated regulation of tobacco so that the issues of health and safety could be out in the open.

Philip provided detailed information about how cigarettes were made. He discussed the technology that existed to make tobacco nicotine-free, and stated that the industry had its own sources of nicotine—including nicotine collected from the nicotine removal process described by Malik. He also described a complex computer model that allowed tobacco companies to control the porosity of the paper and the design of the filter-to-burn rate in order to determine exactly how much nicotine a given brand of cigarettes would deliver.

Philip also discussed the elaborate chemistry involved in the process of making cigarettes and discussed the particles that contain nicotine and other chemicals found in tobacco smoke. If the chemicals are too small, than the smoker does not retain the particles. If the particles are too large, they become lodged in the back of the throat. He stated, "If you get the particles the right size, they get all the way down in your lungs."[9]

Later, Philip discussed the development of filtered cigarettes in the 1950s in the face of evidence that smoking was linked to certain cancers. Filtered cigarettes did reduce tar levels, but they also reduced the level of nicotine. Philip claimed that this resulted in a less "satisfying" cigarette to the addicted smoker. Thus, the industry started to experiment with new approaches such as using tobacco plants that were richer in certain volatile compounds.

Cigarette (Victor DeNoble)

Cigarette was the code name for a Philip Morris informant and behavioral psychologist who was charged with studying the impact of nicotine on the central nervous system and developing a safe cigarette through nicotine substitutes. The idea was to create a nicotine analog that would inflict less damage on humans than nicotine itself. The goal was to create a molecule that could either be engineered into tobacco or sprayed onto a tobacco plant. Cigarette believed that his lab had succeeded in developing the nicotine analog. In response, Philip Morris fired Cigarette, destroyed his work, and closed the lab. A Philip Morris attorney realized that research conducted on the effect of nicotine on the central nervous system could lead to evidence that nicotine was addictive, a result that opened the company to legal liability.

Cigarette described conducting experiments to discover what made nicotine "reinforcing." Early in his research he attempted to determine what laboratory rats would do to obtain nicotine and how quickly they would do it. The rats were given the choice of two levers. One administered a dose of nicotine, the other a placebo. Cigarette found that the rats chose the nicotine after a few attempts. Over several days the rats conditioned themselves to self-administer almost ninety doses of nicotine in a twenty-four-hour period. This research was significant because Philip Morris was sponsoring research on the self-administration of nicotine—a hallmark property of an addictive drug—while publicly denying knowledge that nicotine was addictive.

Cigarette went on to discuss his efforts to produce a safe cigarette. The ultimate goal was to discover a molecule that would have the same biological effects as nicotine on the brain without damaging the heart. Cigarette and a colleague believed they had discovered the nicotine-like compound. It was called 2-methyl nicotine.[10]

FDA investigators found Cigarette's research colleague and nicknamed him "Cigarette Jr." Cigarette Jr. confirmed the information that Cigarette had provided. He felt misled by Philip Morris and that years of research to develop a safe cigarette had been wasted. Cigarette Jr. also stated that he and Cigarette had submitted a paper for the journal *Psychopharmacology*, but Philip Morris made them withdraw it. The company told the scientists that the "data you're generating are inconsistent with our position in lawsuits, and why should you be allowed to risk a billion dollar enterprise for lever-pushing rats?"[11] The authors decided to launch a silent protest. An abstract of the paper had been accepted and published at the American Psychological Association annual meeting. Authors of papers accepted as abstracts stand in front of posters describing their research. Cigarette stood in front of a blank poster board and explained to anyone willing to listen that he was not allowed to present his data. Shortly afterward, Philip Morris ordered the scientists to kill all of their animals and suspend further research. Shortly thereafter they were fired. Neither of the scientists retained a copy of the paper. The journal editor also did not have a copy but he had distributed it to other scientists. Kessler happened to ask his addiction specialist, Jack Henningfield, if he was aware of the research that Cigarette had conducted. As it turned out, Henningfield was not only aware of the research, but was one of the scientists that reviewed the original manuscript, and he had kept a copy.

Kessler's Own Research, the FDA Labs, and a Visit to Philip Morris

While gaining more and more information from industry insiders, Dr. Kessler and his team were doing their own research. Dr. Kessler brought home boxes of any information he could find about the tobacco industry, tobacco, nicotine, and the modern cigarette. He learned that tar is not part of the tobacco plant but is the result of combustion when a cigarette is burned. Nicotine, on the other hand, is a natural component of tobacco leaves. When extracted from a plant, nicotine is an oily, liquid poison. One-tenth of a teaspoon of free nicotine can be fatal to humans if absorbed through the skin. Kessler also discovered that nicotine levels in tobacco plants not only vary from breed to breed, but also from one plant to the next. Even within the same plant, the leaf, stem, and ribs produce different concentrations of nicotine. Despite this, every cigarette brand's nicotine level is extremely uniform. Kessler sent a young FDA employee to the North Carolina State University library, which had one of the largest collections of tobacco industry documents. She found an industry ad in the *Tobacco Encyclopedia* with the headline "MORE OR LESS NICOTINE." In smaller print the ad read: "Nicotine levels are becoming a growing concern for the designers of modern cigarettes, particularly those with lower tar deliveries. The Kimberly-Clark tobacco reconstitution process used by LTR Industries permits adjustments of nicotine to your exact requirements. We can help you control your tobacco."[12]

Despite the 1988 Surgeon General's report declaring nicotine addictive as well as near consensus among the scientific community, the tobacco industry argued that because there was a lack of an intoxicating effect from smoking, nicotine was not addictive. In order to refute those claims Dr. Kessler needed to develop a solid understanding of addiction. It has not been until recent times that science has come to understand the biological basis of addiction.

Randy Wykoff, an FDA specialist on cancer gave Dr. Kessler some simple statistical facts that placed the topic of addiction into proper context. There are approximately 49 million smokers in the United States. Three-fourths of these smokers say they are addicted to cigarettes, and two-thirds state that they want to quit. About seventeen million smokers attempt to quit every year and over 90% fail. In fact, after surgery for lung cancer, nearly 50% of those who survive resume smoking. Even when the larynx of a smoker is removed, 40% begin smoking again.

Dr. Kessler asked Jack Henningfield how much nicotine must a cigarette deliver in order to addict the smoker? Henningfield suggested that smokers trying to quit generally smoked twelve or thirteen cigarettes a day. However, a small number of smokers termed "chippers" smoke about five cigarettes a day without becoming addicted. Thus, he estimated that ten to fifteen milligrams a day or about ten to fifteen cigarettes would make a smoker addicted. Henningfield went on to coauthor a paper on the topic that was published in the *New England Journal of Medicine* concluding that regulations be developed mandating cigarettes with nicotine contents below that threshold level.[13]

Meanwhile, William Campbell, the CEO of Philip Morris responded to Dr. Kessler's letter to the coalition with a letter of his own printed in the *New York Times*. In the letter, Campbell stated that nicotine occurs naturally in tobacco and that nothing in the processing of tobacco or the manufacture of cigarettes increases the nicotine in their products above what is naturally found in tobacco. He went on to claim that consumer preferences had led them to develop lower tar cigarettes that also had lower nicotine levels. He stated that the reconstitution process had been going on for over 150 years to efficiently use all parts of the tobacco plant and resulted in cigarettes with lower levels of nicotine than what is found in unprocessed tobacco. Finally, he stated that cigarettes were legal products and more than 50 million Americans "choose" to smoke.[14]

Kessler saw the letter as an opportunity. He sent a letter to Campbell requesting a meeting with members of Philip Morris's research, scientific, technical, and production staffs in order to obtain a better understanding of their processes. To Kessler's surprise, Campbell granted the request. A tobacco company was inviting the FDA inside their complex just a few days before Kessler's testimony on Capitol Hill.

FDA investigators peppered members of Philip Morris's research team asking if they took steps to determine the correct amount of nicotine in a cigarette, and did they ever add nicotine? Philip Morris representatives stated no emphatically. Rather, they claimed that there was a 15-to-1 ratio of tar to nicotine, and as tar was decreased in a cigarette, so was the nicotine. According to Philip Morris, the processing of cigarettes was designed for tar, and nicotine levels change only as tar levels change. Later in the interview, the representative of Philip Morris backed off his statement about the ratio of tar to nicotine. At the request of the FDA, Philip Morris representatives provided two pages of formulas for Merit cigarettes. After examining the formulas, Mitch Zeller, the Deputy Commissioner of the FDA realized that different types of tobacco had been mixed together to make Merit; each had a different level of nicotine. Mitch briefed Dr. Kessler on the visit stating, "Look, David, they don't have to spike. They don't have to add nicotine. They can do it through blending."[15]

During this time, Kessler had FDA labs in St. Louis examine twenty brands of cigarettes for their nicotine levels. Among the Merit family of cigarettes, the "ultra–low tar" cigarette had the highest percentage of nicotine (2.0%). The Regular Merit (full-flavor) cigarette had only 1.46% nicotine. Additionally, the Federal Trade Commission collected data on tar and nicotine levels of cigarettes from 1982 to 1991. Kessler had a FDA statistician examine the data closely. He returned with computer print-outs of graphs showing that nicotine levels had increased about 10 to 15% in those years, while tar levels had decreased. This flatly contradicted industry claims that they did not set levels of nicotine for particular brands of cigarettes.

THE WAXMAN HEARINGS

Less than a week before Congressman Waxman's hearing concerning tobacco regulation, Dr. Kessler received a letter from Republican Congressman Thomas Bliley Jr. Bliley was the ranking minority member of Waxman's subcommittee and represented Richmond, Virginia. The letter asked the FDA to provide a long list of information and documents prior to the hearing. It asked for all evidence in the FDA's possession that suggested that the industry intended their products contain nicotine to satisfy an addiction. He wanted written summaries of conversations and copies of documents pertaining to nicotine addiction, including the names, addresses, and titles of informants. Finally, he asked for "all other information or evidence brought to the FDA's attention." The letter asked for the information the day it arrived at the FDA. Bliley wanted to know what the FDA knew and how they knew it. Kessler suspected that Bliley was being influenced by the tobacco industry. Later Kessler got his hands on an internal Philip Morris document dating to the same period that listed "letter to Kessler from Bliley" as one of its agenda items.[16] Kessler sent Bliley a list of published references but did not reveal his confidential sources.

The first Waxman hearing took place on March 25, 1994. Congressional hearings are less informative to congressmen than they are opportunities to present an issue to the press and to the American public. Henry Waxman stated that the morning's testimony would be about "drug addiction, which claims the lives of four hundred thirty thousand Americans a year. The drug is nicotine." Waxman discussed the letter to the Coalition and explained that Dr. Kessler had been invited to the hearing "to elaborate on the possible application of the Federal Food, Drug, and Cosmetic Act to tobacco products." Waxman made it clear that he was unhappy that the CEOs of the major tobacco companies declined the subcommittee's invitation to the hearing. The tobacco industry was instead represented by the Tobacco Institute's Charles Whitley, a former congressman. Waxman mentioned that Mike Miles, the CEO of Philip Morris, had time to hold a press conference concerning their lawsuit against ABC News over the *Day One* story, but couldn't find the time to discuss this issue with Congress. Waxman commended Mike Synar on his efforts to raise the issue of tobacco regulation by the FDA and his efforts on tobacco control in general. Waxman then turned to Bliley for his opening statement.

Bliley read from a prepared script: "I know that the tobacco industry is not very popular in some quarters, but that does not excuse federal officials from their duty to proceed cautiously and responsibly before leveling serious accusations. Commissioner Kessler has not done so in this instance. I view this hearing as an opportunity for Dr. Kessler to explain his precipitous and reckless conduct and to set the record straight."[17]

Congressman Durbin of Illinois spoke next and argued for greater regulation of tobacco. James Clyburn of South Carolina argued that there was nothing new to warrant an FDA investigation of the issue. He also accused Dr. Kessler of "scaremongering" at the expense of his constituents. Later Kessler learned that the tobacco industry had developed a list of sympathetic people willing to testify on its behalf. Clyburn was among them and the industry intended to "write one-two pagers" for them.

Martin Lancaster of North Carolina suggested that the FDA was having difficulty meeting its current responsibilities and should not take on the additional burden of tobacco. He stated, "FDA's recent actions on this issue of nicotine in cigarettes suggests to me that the Agency, in its eagerness to come after the tobacco industry with both barrels blazing, has in fact run off with its pistols half-cocked and its barrels loaded with blanks."[18] The following month, Lancaster was rewarded when top Philip Morris executives were asked to make $200–$250 contributions to his reelection campaign. The executives were told to state in their letters that they were Philip Morris executives.

Finally, Dr. Kessler was allowed to speak. He began by saying, "The cigarette industry has attempted to frame the debate on smoking as the right of each American to choose. The question we must ask is whether smokers really have that choice. Consider these facts. Two thirds of adults who smoke say they wish they could quit. Seventeen million try to quit each year but for every one who quits, at least nine try and fail. Three out of four adult smokers say they are addicted. Mr. Chairman, the issue I will address today is simple: Whose choice is actually driving the demand for cigarettes in this country? Is it a choice by consumers to continue smoking? Or is it a choice by cigarette companies to maintain addictive levels of nicotine in their cigarettes?"[19]

Dr. Kessler than presented his evidence. He described nicotine as "highly addictive" and explained how it affected the brain. He discussed the significance of animal self-administration studies, and listed the major medical organizations that had declared nicotine addictive. Kessler discussed the evidence his team had discovered concerning the control of nicotine levels. He was careful to state that not all of the evidence is in, but "a picture is beginning to emerge." He went on to state, "The public may think of cigarettes as no more than blended tobacco rolled in paper. But they are more than that. Some of today's cigarettes may in fact qualify as high-technology nicotine delivery systems that deliver nicotine in quantities sufficient to create and sustain addiction in the vast majority of individuals who smoke regularly. . . . The research undertaken by the cigarette industry is more and more resembling drug development."[20]

Dr. Kessler went on to discuss actual nicotine levels in cigarettes. He presented the data concerning Merit cigarettes, emphasizing that the brand advertised as having the lowest levels of tar had the highest concentration of nicotine. He also presented the FTC data that demonstrated that nicotine levels had increased over a ten-year period while tar levels had decreased.

Dr. Kessler ended his testimony by discussing the possible consequences of FDA regulation: "Clearly, the possibility of FDA exerting jurisdiction over cigarettes raises many broader social issues for Congress to contemplate. It could lead to the possible removal of nicotine in cigarettes to levels that are not addictive, or restricting access to them, unless the industry could show that nicotine-containing cigarettes are safe and effective." Kessler acknowledged that the removal of nicotine could cause millions of Americans to go through withdrawal and create an enormous black market. He stated, "On these issues we seek guidance from Congress."[21]

Henry Waxman began his questions by stating, "Dr. Kessler, you have laid out a really astounding picture, not only of the tobacco companies manipulating the levels of nicotine, but by doing that, manipulating the American people who take up cigarette smoking." He asked a series of basic health questions in order to get the information on the record. Then he asked, "Dr. Kessler, on the critical issue of the industry's intent, have you found any studies by the tobacco industry that would support the proposition that nicotine is retained in tobacco for addictive purposes?"[22]

Kessler responded by stating that self-administration is a classic characteristic of an addictive substance and that self-administration studies had shown that nicotine is addictive. Kessler then dropped a bombshell, "We recently learned that a team of industry researchers had carried out such studies in the 1980s and reached similar conclusions."[23] He was referring to the information gathered from the informants Cigarette and Cigarette Jr.

Waxman responded, "Are you saying, in other words, that the tobacco industry sponsored studies of animals that would indicate that nicotine was addictive to these animals? . . . What happened to these studies?"[24]

Kessler answered, "We have been told that both manuscripts were withdrawn by the researchers before publication. We have a copy of a letter from an editor of the journal to the researcher."[25]

Waxman summed up, "In other words the tobacco industry sponsored studies on their own where they found out that nicotine was addictive and before the public could know about it, they acted to suppress those studies?"[26] Waxman asked Dr. Kessler to identify the company but Kessler refused, not wanting to single out any specific tobacco company.

Kessler then engaged in a number of exchanges with Congressman Bliley who brought up issues such as denatured alcohol and the spiking of nicotine. These were topics not addressed by Kessler's testimony, which only made sense later when Kessler learned that Bliley was given a "list of questions for use in examining Kessler" by the tobacco industry.

Mike Synar spoke last and was only slightly overdramatic when saying, "I don't think I would be exaggerating to suggest that we have just witnessed some of the most historic testimony in the history of Congress on any subject."[27] For the first time in American history evidence was presented before Congress and the American people that strongly suggested that the tobacco industry deliberately intended to addict people.

The tobacco industry had obviously underestimated the depth of the FDA investigation and immediately took steps to counter it. Documents discovered later by Kessler described a "ferocious defense" strategy and an Action Team to confront the FDA investigation. Shortly after Kessler's testimony, Murray Bring, general counsel to Philip Morris called the FDA investigation "by far the most threatening" of recent developments against the industry and described Kessler's activities as "ominous." Bring was thinking beyond regulation of tobacco when he said, "If he [Kessler] were to declare that nicotine in cigarettes is addictive, and must be regulated, that action could affect the way in which jurors approach the issues of addiction and choice."[28]

Steve Parish, an executive vice president at Philip Morris, had developed a four-pronged Tobacco Strategic Attack Plan. The first approach was the "frontal assault," direct actions taken in Philip Morris's own name including opening other plants to FDA investigators, briefing government officials, running aggressive ad campaigns, and working at the state level to preempt legislation. The second approach was termed "surgical strikes" or the company's individual lawsuits that they believed gave them media opportunities. They referred to the suit against ABC News as an example that had the effect of removing the word "spiked" from antitobacco vocabulary. Third, were allied attacks from friendly third parties who sided with the tobacco industry but did not have obvious connections to the industry. The final approach was termed "air cover" from the newly formed National Smokers Alliance, an organization developed by Philip Morris and described as "our NRA" by one Philip Morris representative.[29]

Henry Waxman called for another hearing. He wanted the CEOs of the major tobacco companies to respond to Dr. Kessler's charges. He invited each to appear rather than subpoena them. Congressman Bliley warned the executives that if they failed to appear, he would not provide cover for them. In the end, all seven CEOs agreed to appear. After two decades of hearings in Congress on tobacco control, this was the first opportunity to question tobacco executives directly. Jim Johnston from R. J. Reynolds was asked if smoking caused cancer. He stated that it may, but he did not know if it did. Andrew Tisch was asked the same question and stated that he did not believe that cigarette smoking caused cancer. Bill Campbell of Philip Morris stated in a deposition, "To my knowledge, it has not been proven that cigarette smoking causes cancer." He was asked if he would ever be convinced. He admitted, "Yes, I may be convinced," but added, "We don't know what causes cancer, in general, right now." But the most dramatic moment of the day came when Congressman Ron Wyden asked, "Let me ask you first, and I'd like you to just go down the row, whether each of you believes that nicotine is not addictive. Yes or no, do you believe nicotine is not addictive?" In quick sequence, the CEOs all gave the same answer: "I believe that nicotine is not addictive."[30]

While the hearing included a good deal of aggressive tactics and a harsh tone by several subcommittee members, the sight of seven tobacco company CEOs raising their hands and testifying under oath to tell the truth is what is most remembered. In fact, I show this picture to young people when making presentations concerning the tobacco industry's influence on youth. In almost every case at least one child in the crowd recognizes that the people in the picture are tobacco company executives. Much later a senior tobacco executive that Kessler called "Veritas" stated that the CEOs' testimony made them look like fools and that their scripts no longer made sense. Within a few years all seven executives were no longer in their tobacco company positions.

EVEN MORE EVIDENCE

Ammonia Technology

The FDA learned of yet another informant codenamed "Research." Research was a biochemist and a former vice president of research for Brown & Williamson. He was lured away from the pharmaceutical industry with a $300,000 a year salary and given the assignment to reduce the toxins in cigarettes. Research was fired when he argued that the tobacco additive coumarin was toxic and should be removed from all Brown & Williamson products. Research was reluctant to talk to the FDA and took great pains to conceal his conversations. After a conversation with Waxman's staff, Research claimed that he received a phone call with the message, "Leave tobacco alone or watch your kids."[31] Research told Kessler to watch his mail.

Shortly afterwards, a number of internal Brown & Williamson documents arrived at the FDA that dealt with ammonia technology. The documents identified a secret project utilizing ammonia to increase the potency of nicotine. The document stated, "Ammonia can liberate free nicotine from the blend which is associated with increases in impact and satisfaction."[32] Research would not admit to sending the documents but stated that he believed that ammonia was the ingredient that gave Marlboro its appeal. The chemists in the FDA labs later discovered that ammonia allowed one to "free base" nicotine. The process changed the charge on the nicotine molecule and increased the rate at which nicotine was absorbed in the bloodstream. Later, Dr. Kessler discovered industry documents that explicitly stated that ammonia increased nicotine delivery to the smoker.

The Story of Y-I

In addition to the information on ammonia, Research mentioned tobacco plants that had been genetically manipulated for high nicotine levels. Kessler was stunned by this information. Research explained that there were two ways of breeding for higher nicotine levels. Hybridization involves crossing different plants and selecting offspring with certain desired characteristics. The problem with this technique is that it's slow and the plants tend to revert back to their original form over time. The second technique was genetic engineering where a gene for the desired trait is actually inserted into a seed. Both techniques had been used to create a tobacco plant with as much as an 8% nicotine level. The average nicotine level in flu-cured tobacco was 2.5 to 3%.

A Washington tobacco lobbyist was overheard boasting that the FDA was looking in the wrong place. "It all begins in the fields."[33] When pressed about where these plants are grown, Research mentioned several domestic farms and hinted that it might have been grown in South America in much larger quantities. The name of the hybrid, genetically engineered plant was Y-I. When asked how the FDA could get their hands on the plant, Research stated that they had to do it before the manufacturing process, but that there was an inventory of about 6.2 million pounds in the United States. That large a quantity suggested to Kessler that these plants were not experimental, but widely used in the manufacturing of cigarettes.

Later, Research was identified as Jeffrey Wigand. Wigand told his story on CBS's *60 Minutes* to correspondent Mike Wallace and producer Lowell Bergman. Dr. Kessler was indignant that after the tremendous steps he took to protect Wigand's identity that he would decide to go to the press. The *60 Minutes* interview is a fascinating story in its own right that became the subject of the movie *The Insider*, starring Russell Crowe and Al Pacino.

Another informant from Brown & Williamson codenamed "Macon" confirmed the existence of a program, ten years in the making, to engineer a high-nicotine tobacco plant. Macon claimed that Brown & Williamson had successfully grown the plant in Brazil. Macon went on to say that Y-I had been added to Barclay cigarettes and while the cigarette certainly had "impact" and delivered "a buzz and a half,"[34] it also tasted terrible. To minimize the terrible taste, the company used it as expanded tobacco, which is cigarette filler pumped up with carbon dioxide. Macon stunned Kessler again when he added that Y-I was still in production at the time and could be found in Raleigh King, Raleigh King Lights, Viceroy 100s, Viceroy King, Viceroy Lights King, Richland King, and Richland Lights King. If these assertions were true and Kessler could prove it, he would have direct evidence of nicotine manipulation. However, with the investigation and hearings, Brown & Williamson was attempting to use their supply of Y-I plants as quickly as possible.

While the FDA tobacco team visited Brown & Williamson's facilities they specifically asked whether the company had conducted any genetic testing to raise or lower nicotine content. Shortly afterwards, Research told the team that company executives were "going crazy,"[35] and that during a Memorial Day weekend a meeting was held that included the company lawyers, research executives, and marketing executives. Kessler believed that the company must have realized just how much his team had learned.

Several informants identified James Chaplin, a former USDA scientist, as a key player in the development of Y-I. When interviewed, Chaplin stated that he became involved in the Y-I project at a late point; that the company had already produced a successful crossbred plant. He reluctantly admitted that the plant had been grown on a small farm outside Wilson, North Carolina and on a few farms in Brazil. While members of the FDA team traveled to the farm to collect samples of Y-I plants, Chaplin finally admitted that he was the person who succeeded in creating the high nicotine seeds. Dr. Kessler had investigators comb through U.S. Custom documents from port to port along the eastern seaboard. Finally, in Charleston, South Carolina an investigator found an invoice that read: "Your order: Project YI I 3/08/92." Dr. Kessler had proof "that Brown & Williamson had shipped almost half a million pounds of genetically manipulated high-nicotine tobacco into the United States."[36] Shortly afterwards, Drew McMurtrie, Brown & Williamson's director of product development, admitted that Y-I was developed because the company was interested in making a product that maintained nicotine levels while lowering tar. A company executive had actually admitted to manipulating nicotine levels in the offices of the FDA.

Saint

Saint was a chemical engineer formerly employed by Philip Morris to conduct research into how to develop a safe cigarette. With a background in thermodynamics, she was placed in charge of "supercritical extraction technology."[37] This is the same process used to remove caffeine from coffee. She told Kessler that she had been given a list of carcinogens in tobacco and asked to isolate and remove them using supercritical extraction. She stated that she had been able to do exactly that. She went on to say that management's attitude toward her work had begun to change and that other scientists' work had been destroyed, their labs were closed, and they were fired. Thus, she decided it was time to leave. An angry and stunned Kessler asked her to repeat what she was saying. She stated again that she had been able to remove most carcinogens from tobacco using supercritical extraction and that she had told company executives about this. A research scientist for Philip Morris was able to develop a much safer cigarette with the same technology used to make decaffeinated coffee.

The Tobacco Papers

While Dr. David Kessler and his team now had enough evidence to regulate nicotine as a drug, a singular event in May 1994 made that decision almost inevitable. Merrell Williams had been hired as a paralegal by a law firm representing Brown & Williamson. Williams was one of several paralegals assigned the task of reading and classifying company documents that were relevant to the company's efforts to defend itself against product liability suits. Williams understood the importance of the documents and began removing and copying the documents before returning them. In the end he had thousands of pages of these documents in his possession. Williams had been a lifelong smoker, and after a life-threatening triple bypass surgery, Williams decided to reveal the papers to an attorney in hopes of pursuing a personal injury lawsuit.[38]

When the FDA learned of the papers they attempted to obtain a copy, but Williams' attorney would not go for it. However, Philip Hilts of the *New York Times* managed to get a copy from a congressional staffer to whom they had been leaked. Hilts called Brown & Williamson to ask for a comment and was told that they were stolen documents and he could not print them. That was all he needed to verify that the documents were authentic. Excerpts were printed in the *Times* and were incredibly revealing. They presented decades of deception on the part of the industry. These papers along with others gathered later in trial discovery are commonly called the "tobacco papers" and can now be found on the Internet.[39]

Perhaps the most infamous line from the *New York Times* story came from Addison Yeaman, general counsel to Brown & Williamson: "We are, then, in the business of selling nicotine, an addictive drug."[40] Yeaman was attempting to get the company to assume responsibility to reveal the hazards of smoking so that it could openly pursue methods to remove the harmful chemicals in smoke.

Another document revealed that Brown & Williamson had debated whether to reveal information to the Surgeon General's office, which was preparing its report. "The executives chose to remain silent, to keep their research results secret, to stop work on a safer cigarette, and to pursue a legal and public relations strategy of admitting nothing."[41] Dr. Kessler felt that he may have crossed a professional line when he called Hilts to congratulate him. Meanwhile Kessler negotiated with Henry Waxman's office to get access to the documents. Kessler's staff was able to take extensive notes, but not to make copies.

Merrell Williams and his colleagues had developed labeling codes to categorize documents. "Confirmation of causation" was a label used for documents that confirmed the link between smoking and disease. The code "manipulation of research/data" was used for documents detailing the practice of recommending how research should be performed by research organizations. "Industry competition" was the code for documents that suggested Brown & Williamson might be able to obtain a competitive edge by designing cigarettes that allowed a smoker to "adjust his smoking habits to obtain greater delivery of nicotine." Advertising and marketing documents were also coded on the basis of their intended audiences including, "individuals attempting to quit," "persons who have not yet started smoking," and "smokers 18 years of age and younger."[42]

Another document written in 1965 titled "Report to the Executive Committee" by the head researcher at Brown & Williamson read in part, "Find ways of obtaining maximum nicotine for minimum tar," and offered possibilities such as "nicotine fortification of cigarette paper, addition of nicotine-containing powders to tobacco, and attention to blends."[43] To Kessler, these industry documents were significant because they were written proof that the effects of nicotine were intended.

Another set of documents were found under the care of an organization called Doctors Ought to Care. Many of these documents were written by William Dunn from Philip Morris. Dunn described "tentative plans to inject subjects with IV nicotine to examine effects of nicotine spike, level, and reinforcement characteristics of the substance."[44] Another research topic concerned ensuring "that total nicotine in the system remains at or near the nicotine need threshold."[45] "Hyperkinetic Child as Prospective Smoker" involved collecting data on elementary school children. Another proposal would give college students shock treatments to see whether they smoked more in times of stress.

Dunn was apparently in conflict with those at Philip Morris concerned about the legal implications of his work. He seemed to realize that the psychopharmacology of nicotine was very useful for product development, but also the area of greatest concern for legal liability. He states that this area of research is "where our attorneys least want us to be" and he asked a colleague "do we really want to tout cigarette smoke as a drug? It is, of course, but there are dangerous FDA implications to having such conceptualization go beyond these walls."[46]

Meanwhile, FDA sources described the contents of court documents under seal in a product liability case (*Haines v. Liggett Group*) that dealt extensively with nicotine. Notes from those sources read "Nicotine should be delivered at about 1.0–1.3 mg/cigarette, the minimum for confirmed smokers. The rate of absorption should be kept low by holding pH down, probably below 6."[47]

Ann Ritter was a trial lawyer in the case and found a gold mine of industry documents in a Charleston warehouse. In fact, these documents were the most revealing yet, and exactly what the tobacco team at the FDA was looking for. The team went through the documents, written by R. J. Reynolds executive Claude Teague, at Dr. Kessler's house and they read in part:

> Nicotine is known to be a habit-forming alkaloid, hence the confirmed user of tobacco products is primarily seeking the physiological "satisfaction" derived from nicotine—and perhaps other active compounds. Thus, a tobacco product is, in essence, a vehicle for delivery of nicotine, designed to deliver the nicotine in a generally acceptable and attractive form. Our industry is then based upon design, manufacture and sale of attractive dosage forms of nicotine, and our Company's position in our Industry is determined by our ability to produce dosage forms of nicotine which have more overall value, tangible or intangible, to the consumer than those of our competitors.
>
> If nicotine is the sine qua non of tobacco products and tobacco products are recognized as being attractive dosage forms of nicotine, then it is logical to design our products—and where possible, our advertising—around nicotine delivery rather than "tar" delivery or flavor. We may survey the market and conclude that current cigarette products delivering about 1.3 mg of nicotine appear to "satisfy" the typical smoker. This, somewhat crudely, establishes a target dosage level for design of new products.
>
> If nicotine is the sine qua non of smoking, and if we meekly accept the allegations of our critics and move toward reduction or elimination of nicotine from our products, then we shall eventually liquidate our business. In a sense, the tobacco industry may be thought of as being a specialized, highly ritualized and stylized segment of the pharmaceutical industry. Tobacco products uniquely contain and deliver nicotine, a potent drug with a variety of physiological effects.[48]

If there were any doubts before the arrival of these documents that nicotine was a drug, or that it was addictive, or that the tobacco industry was aware of this, those doubts were gone. Kessler knew with all of the overwhelming evidence that the FDA had to assume jurisdiction over tobacco. The question was, how to do it.

THE POLITICAL AND LEGAL BATTLE OVER REGULATION

If nicotine were classified a drug by the FDA, tobacco companies would be required to file an application that demonstrated cigarettes to be safe and effective. Because they would not be able to do that, the FDA would be required to ban cigarettes. This was something that the FDA desperately wanted to avoid for reasons already mentioned. One of the tobacco team members in the FDA suggested regulating cigarettes and smokeless tobacco as restricted devices. Under the Food, Drug, and Cosmetic Act, the agency could restrict the sale, use, and distribution of cigarettes without banning them if they were classified as medical devices. Nicotine would be considered the drug and the cigarettes and smokeless tobacco are drug delivery devices. According to this section of the statute the FDA could also regulate tobacco advertising.

In making a decision about how to regulate tobacco, Kessler decided to closely examine how the industry marketed their products. He came across two reports titled "Project 16" and a follow-up entitled "Project Plus/Minus." These reports detailed an overt attempt on the part of the industry to understand why children start to smoke and why they want to quit. Quotes from focus groups revealed that kids were experimenting with tobacco at ages eleven or twelve and soon found themselves in the grips of addiction. The regret of young teenagers who realized they were addicted and could not quit was what impacted Kessler. He came across a R. J. Reynolds memo instructing sales reps in Florida to identify stores "that are heavily frequented by young adult shoppers,"[49] especially those in close proximity to colleges and high schools, and to keep those stores properly stocked with tobacco products. A similar document was found in Oklahoma. One chain store marketing informant from R. J. Reynolds confirmed marketing efforts close to high schools and colleges. Another informant stated, "Whoever gets the people starting wins the game."[50] Dr. Kessler began to think of nicotine addiction as a pediatric disease and decided that regulation should have the goal of protecting children.

While Dr. Kessler could have acted unilaterally to regulate tobacco, he lived in a political world where the support of his boss, Secretary of the Department of Health and Human Services Donna Shalala, was vital, as was support from the White House. He made the case to the secretary by pointing out that most smokers begin when they're young, young people become addicted as adults, and youth smoking was increasing. He went on to say that three million young people were current smokers, about 516 million packs of cigarettes were illegally purchased by young people every year, and that 93% of young smokers who wanted to quit reported withdrawal symptoms. Kessler told the secretary that the goal of their regulation effort was to prevent future generations of children from becoming addicted to cigarettes. Knowing that public support was critical, Kessler reported that a recent Gallop Poll found that over three quarters of the population favored restrictions on cigarette advertising that appealed to youth. Significant majorities also favored bans on free product samples and billboards, as well as license suspensions for retailers who sold tobacco to underaged kids.

Kessler made the following proposals:

ending the use of cartoon characters and colorful graphics in magazines—only black and white and text-only ads would be allowed;

billboards would also only be allowed to use black and white text;

a ban on promotional techniques such as giveaways linked to proof-of-purchase coupons, and brand names on hats, T-shirts, and other nontobacco items;

sports and other events could be sponsored with only a corporate name and not a specific brand of tobacco;

access to cigarettes would be restricted by eliminating vending machines, free samples, mail-order sales, "kiddie packs" (small packs of cigarettes in quantities of 5 or 10 cigarettes), self-service displays (so that every purchase of cigarettes would involve a personal interaction);

a system to hold retailers accountable for illegal sales to minors; and

if the goal of reducing smoking by kids by 50% had not been reached within five years, other restrictions would be put in place.

Secretary Shalala only objected to the restrictions on sports sponsorship due to concerns of alienating the public. She stated that Kessler would have to work with department staff to get the final rule in shape. However, Kessler and his team had great difficulty in convincing Health and Human Resources department staff that the restrictions were pragmatic and reasonable. He eventually decided that he would have to go directly to the Clinton administration.

Convincing the Clinton administration of the necessity of regulation and the proposals that came with it also proved to be a challenge. In Kessler's only meeting with the president, Clinton told him that the House of Representatives was lost on two issues, gun control and tobacco. Kessler decided he needed the support of people who had the president's trust. Al Gore would prove to be a critical ally. He played a key role in reviewing executive branch regulations, he had a personal interest in the issue (he lost a sister to lung cancer), and he had a close personal relationship with the president. It did not take much convincing for Al Gore to take the issue to President Clinton.

Most of the president's staff was opposed to the idea, and the president himself had stated that if he approved the rule he would receive one day of media attention and lose five southern states (Virginia, North Carolina, Georgia, Kentucky, and Tennessee) in the 1994 election. Dick Morris, advisor to the president, commissioned a poll in those five southern states and found that 64% of voters favored government action to reduce teen smoking. Several top advisors suggested that the president negotiate with the industry instead.

However, Vice President Gore believed that it was time to confront tobacco as an issue and that it was the right thing to do, regardless of the political risks. Kessler stated that the president learned to trust Al Gore's judgment and often deferred to him when he took a strong position on an issue. The vice president kept up the pressure in meetings about the issue and during his weekly lunches with the president. After reading an article that summarized the Brown & Williamson documents and their knowledge of the effects of nicotine, Clinton held a meeting with Dr. Kessler. Kessler recalls the president saying, "I want to kill them. I just read all those documents, and I want to kill them."[51] In the end, the president was moved by the overwhelming evidence and gave his blessing on the proposed regulations.

Not long after the signing ceremony, the tobacco companies filed a lawsuit challenging the FDA's authority to regulate tobacco. They chose to file the suit in the U.S. District Court in Greensboro, North Carolina—the heart of tobacco country. The presiding judge came from a family who owned a tobacco farm, as an attorney he had represented a group of tobacco farmers, and as a judge had made several decisions in favor of tobacco interests. The legal questions were: (1) did Congress ever intend the FDA to have jurisdiction over tobacco products; (2) had the FDA appropriately classified tobacco products as drugs, as devices, or as a combination of drug delivery devices; and (3) did the specific proposed regulations fit within the agency's mandate? For all three questions, the North Carolina Court answered "yes." It did, however, strike the provisions concerning tobacco advertising to minors.[52]

The case was appealed to the Fourth Circuit Court, twice. After initial arguments, the presiding judge in the case died before a ruling was issued. After the case was reargued, the Appeals Court voted 2-to-1 against the FDA regulations and the case moved to the United States Supreme Court.

In oral arguments before the Supreme Court, Chief Justice Rehnquist stated that previous FDA commissioners had told Congress that the agency's governing statute did not cover tobacco. He demanded to know what had changed. Solicitor General Seth Waxman answered that the overwhelming evidence of the addictive properties of nicotine had only recently come to light. Rehnquist responded, "That certainly was not the first time that that scientific consensus evolved, was it?" Waxman reminded the justice that not long ago, seven CEOs testified under oath that they did not think cigarettes were addictive. Rehnquist responded, "Nobody believed them." Others on the bench were skeptical about what had changed as well. Dr. Kessler was in the audience and recalled that he wanted to shout that no previous commissioner had irrefutable evidence in the industry's own words. Kessler believed that the "everyone-knows-that" attitude was actually shaped by the evidence they had found. So much had come to light that to change popular thinking about tobacco and industry that even the perceptions of the justices had shifted. Four months later, in a 5-to-4 decision, the Supreme Court ruled in *FDA v. Brown & Williamson et al.* that the FDA did not have jurisdiction to regulate tobacco products.[53] In summarizing the majority position from the bench, Sandra Day O'Connor acknowledged smoking as one of the most serious health problems in the country and almost seemed to plead with Congress to allow the FDA the authority to regulate tobacco. Nonetheless, the majority held that the FDA did not have the legal authority to regulate tobacco on its own.

CONCLUSION

Much earlier in the investigation, Waldo Profitt, editor of the *Sarasota Herald-Tribune*, stated that the FDA letter to the Coalition on Smoking or Health was "one of the most fateful documents of the twentieth century." He predicted that it would ultimately "wipe out the tobacco industry as it now exists."[54] He went on the suggest that evidence that the industry manipulated nicotine levels would result in a rash of lawsuits seeking billions of dollars in punitive damages—and this time, the plaintiffs would win. Profitt was partially right, although the tobacco industry is still with us, plaintiffs in tobacco suits began winning after the release of the tobacco papers.

4

Tobacco Litigation and the Master Settlement

INTRODUCTION

While it may seem to the casual observer that tobacco lawsuits were a product of the 1990s, tobacco litigation in the United States has had a long and protracted history. The first wave of tobacco litigation actually started in the 1950s with the emergence of product liability case law. The second wave of tobacco litigation began in 1983 on the heels of the success of asbestos cases. Neither of these waves of litigation enjoyed any success. The third wave of litigation was inspired by the events discussed in the previous chapter. Specifically, the third wave started shortly after FDA Commissioner David Kessler sent his letter to the Coalition on Smoking and Health in 1994. That letter made national news, and with the *Day One* report broadcast by ABC three days later, new information was becoming available that made the tobacco industry vulnerable to lawsuits.

In fact, individual lawsuits, class action suits, and third-party suits filed by state attorneys general were successful in making the tobacco industry pay large settlements for the harm caused by tobacco products. The seemingly unending stream of lawsuits made the tobacco industry eager to develop a long-term and permanent settlement. The Master Settlement Agreement with the states was the end product of those negotiations.

TOBACCO LAWSUITS

The First Wave of Tobacco Litigation

The first wave of tobacco litigation began in 1954. These cases were inspired by new scientific and popular magazine reports that smoking caused lung cancer. Armed with this new evidence, plaintiffs' attorneys generally sued the tobacco industry using one of two theories. Under a theory of negligence, plaintiffs attempted to demonstrate that the tobacco industry knew enough about the potential harm of their products to require that they research the effects of tobacco, adopt warning labels, and stop advertising in a way that suggested that their products were safe. The problem with this approach was that plaintiffs' attorneys could not prove at the time that the industry knew or was aware of the potential harm of using tobacco products.[1]

The second theory that was more commonly used is that of implied warranty. In other words, even if the tobacco industry was unaware of the potential harm of their products, the marketing of a product not "reasonably fit for use" might support the recovery of damages by those who could show they were harmed by tobacco. One of the problems with this approach was that the industry was required to place warning labels on cigarette packaging and advertisements by 1966 (see Chapter 2).[2] Thus, smokers could not claim that they had not been warned about the health hazards surrounding smoking. Also, the tobacco industry was not making direct claims that their products had positive health effects—at least not explicitly.

The courts at the time were generally unreceptive to legal arguments made on the basis of negligence or express warranty. In *Lartique v. R. J. Reynolds Tobacco Co.*, the court decided that manufacturers are "insurers against foreseeable risks—but not unknowable risks."[3] Because plaintiffs in the 1950s through the 1980s could not demonstrate that the industry was aware of the health risks associated with smoking, their legal arguments made little progress in tobacco trials. The American Law Institute (ALI) validated this type of legal argument in 1973. The ALI consisted of a prestigious association of lawyers, judges, and legal scholars and their influence made strict liability tobacco cases even more challenging.

Much of the discussion concerning legal theory assumes that these early tobacco cases made it to trial. However, very few tobacco cases ever made it to that stage. The tobacco industry made a concerted effort to fight every claim with all the resources possible. They hired the most prestigious law firms and gave orders to spare no expenses in attacking product liability cases. As a consequence, industry lawyers delayed trials as much as possible, knowing that plaintiffs' attorneys could not afford the costs of protracted litigation. Most lawyers who brought suit against the industry worked in small private firms, and were only paid on contingency—in other words, if they won the case. Tobacco industry lawyers attacked the credibility of defendants by bringing up personal issues that only tangentially related to their health. While disavowing that tobacco products resulted in disease or injury to the plaintiff, they also made the claim that the plaintiff was warned and—in effect—should have known better.

The Centers for Disease Control (CDC) listed the possible benefits of private litigation against the tobacco industry in terms of reducing tobacco use. Among these benefits:

enlist the services of relentless advocates (attorneys) on the side of reducing tobacco use through the incentive of attorney fees;

force the industry to raise prices on tobacco products to offset losses from the settlement of lawsuits;

encourage the development of a safer cigarette (a noncarcinogenic nicotine delivery device);

discontinue dishonest practices that increase the risk of liability;

decrease the political power of the tobacco industry by making it difficult for politicians to maintain ties to the industry;

educate the public about the risks of tobacco use through the extensive media coverage generated by lawsuits; and

compensate injured parties and the healthcare system from the negative effects of tobacco use.[4]

The Second Wave of Tobacco Litigation

In the second wave of tobacco litigation came the development of new legal strategies by both plaintiffs' lawyers and the attorneys of the tobacco industry. In addition, industry attorneys continued their very successful strategy of delaying trials. Tobacco industry attorneys took countless depositions in these cases. Depositions are legal question-and-answer sessions with key witnesses in legal cases. Industry attorneys also filed countless motions. Motions are legal arguments generally concerning specific legal procedures that require a judge to make decisions. The main point is that both depositions and motions are time consuming in legal cases and work to delay trials. They also consume the time and financial resources of plaintiffs' attorneys. J. Michael Jordan was a highly successful attorney for R. J. Reynolds Tobacco Company in the 1980s. In an internal memo to his colleagues he stated, "The aggressive posture we have taken regarding depositions and discovery in general continues to make these cases extremely burdensome and expensive for plaintiffs' lawyers. . . . To paraphrase General Patton, the way we won these cases was not by spending all of [RJR's] money but by making that other son of a bitch spend all of his."[5]

To confront the tremendous disparity in resources that overwhelmed attorneys in the first wave of cases, attorneys for plaintiffs began to organize. The Tobacco Products Liability Project was a nonprofit advocacy group developed at Northeastern University in 1984. This group was established to encourage lawsuits against the tobacco industry and served as a clearinghouse of tobacco related information for attorneys, plaintiffs, medical experts, and the media. The organization held yearly conferences starting in 1984 to share information, new legal tactics, and to solve problems encountered within the first wave of litigation.

In addition to sharing resources, plaintiffs' attorneys attempted to develop new legal strategies. They shifted their focus from implied or express warranty to strict liability. This reflected an overall change as courts applied strict liability more frequently to other types of defective product cases.[6] The tobacco industry countered these tactics by arguing that defendants' were aware of the risks and had freedom of choice. While denying that any known risks existed in using tobacco products, industry lawyers simultaneously argued that smokers had freely chosen to smoke and had thereby assumed whatever risks there might be from smoking. Industry attorneys were quite successful in convincing juries that defendants had negligently contributed to their own harm.

Ironically, legislation designed to protect smokers was working to the benefit of the tobacco industry. The warning labels on cigarette packaging required by Federal Cigarette Labeling and Advertising Act greatly strengthened the tobacco industry's defense that plaintiffs had assumed their own health risk and were guilty of "contributory negligence." Instead of blaming the tobacco industry for producing a deadly product, jurors tended to blame the plaintiffs for their disease. When the argument was made that cigarettes were extremely addictive, the tobacco industry successfully pointed to the large number of people who quit smoking.[7]

As in the first wave of tobacco litigation, tobacco industry attorneys put the defendant on trial. They used aggressive pretrial discovery tactics to gain as much information as possible about the plaintiff and attempted to demonstrate that the plaintiff engaged in an overall risky lifestyle. The result in many cases was to negate any jury sympathy by placing the plaintiff's character on trial.

The most famous case of this era was *Cipollone v. Liggett Group Inc.*[8] Rose Cipollone filed suit in 1983, one year before her death. The case finally reached a jury five years later, which actually awarded the Cipollone estate $400,000. This verdict was overturned on appeal. In this case, over 100 motions were filed by the tobacco industry and most of the motions were argued before the judge. The District Court's decision was appealed to the Third Circuit Court of Appeals and finally the Supreme Court heard the case. The Supreme Court held that the Public Health Cigarette Smoking Act of 1969 preempted any claims based on the tobacco industry's failure to warn consumers in its advertising and promotions. Importantly, the Court did allow plaintiffs to use other legal strategies such as breach of express warranty, defective product design, and conspiracy to defraud.

After almost ten years of litigation the case was sent back to the trial court. However, plaintiff's attorneys found it difficult to prove that any of the above legal theories could connect the defendant with the death of Cipollone. Thus, five months after the Supreme Court ruling, the New Jersey federal district court approved a request of the Cipollone estate attorneys to withdraw from the case. Plaintiff's counsel spent $500,000 in out-of-pocket expenses and an additional $2 million in attorney and paralegal time.[9] Post-trial proceedings cost another $150,000 in out-of-pocket expenses and $900,000 in additional attorney and paralegal time. While the costs of losing this case were devastating to the plaintiffs, the victory did not come easily for the tobacco industry. *Time* magazine estimated that Liggett spent at least $75 million defending *Cipollone*.[10] In fact, *Cipollone* was the most costly case for the tobacco industry, which at the time was famous for not sparing any expenses in defending product liability cases. The Advocacy Institute, a public interest group dedicated to reducing tobacco use, had estimated that the tobacco industry was spending roughly $60 million per year defending the fifty or so cases pending against them in the mid-1980s.

The scorched earth legal tactics of the tobacco industry had made suing tobacco companies too costly a proposition for most attorneys. Additionally, the industry practice of never settling a case made it an all or nothing effort for attorneys working on contingency fees. It was a highly successful strategy by the tobacco industry. Of the 808 cases filed against the tobacco industry between 1954 and 1984, not one of the claims resulted in any plaintiff, or plaintiff's attorney, receiving a single dollar in financial compensation.

The Third Wave of Tobacco Litigation

While the *Cipollone* case ended badly for antitobacco advocates and the financially depleted attorneys for the plaintiffs, it proved to be an important forerunner for the next wave of tobacco litigation. First of all, the Supreme Court allowed a number of legal theories that would prove to be useful to future plaintiffs. Among these theories were the following:

1. cigarettes were defective products and unnecessarily dangerous, because preliminary evidence discovered by antitobacco activists and plaintiffs' attorneys strongly suggested that the tobacco industry knew how to produce cigarettes that were less likely to cause cancer;
2. cigarettes were defective products because they contained nontobacco carcinogenic substances;
3. a theory of civil conspiracy based on evidence that the tobacco industry had collaborated since the 1950s on strategies to market tobacco products while concealing knowledge about the harmful and addictive qualities to tobacco products in the face of growing scientific evidence of the dangers of tobacco products; and

4. a theory that the tobacco industry failed to deliver on their pledge to "objectively" investigate the possible dangers and take reasonable action on those findings.[11]

The *Cipollone* case revealed potential support for at least some of these theories. Documents discovered in the case provided evidence that the tobacco industry had fraudulently misrepresented the safety of their products and deliberately concealed knowledge about the harmful effects of cigarettes. (This occurred before the FDA investigation occurred.) Specifically, attorneys in the *Cipollone* case uncovered some of the evidence discussed in the previous chapter of the tobacco industry's conspiracy to defraud the American public by pretending to engage in or sponsor research to uncover whether or not there was a link between smoking and health problems. The industry made a promise to engage in this type of research in good faith, and obviously did not.

Additionally, a small number of the tobacco industry documents discussed in the previous chapter were revealed in the case *Haines v. Liggett Group, Inc.*[12] The judge in that case, H. Lee Sarokin, reviewed industry documents concerning the industry's use of the Council for Tobacco Research, and more specifically, its special projects division. The judge indicated that the documents uncovered evidence of research which suggested that smoking caused illness was directed to secret research projects, while findings of causes other than smoking for illnesses commonly thought to be associated with smoking were released to the public or published in journals. This led Judge Sarokin to remark that the tobacco industry was "the king of concealment and disinformation."[13] Importantly, Sarokin believed that the documents he reviewed were not protected by attorney-client privilege. His reasoning was that industry attorneys had been participating in an ongoing fraud, and that there is an exception to attorney-client privilege in that case. An appellate court agreed with Judge Sarokin that the documents could be used in this case and subsequent cases. However, the same appellate court dismissed Judge Sarokin for his "king of concealment" remark because he failed to appear impartial.[14]

The third wave of tobacco litigation was sparked by the FDA investigation and other revelations in the mid-1990s (see Chapter 3). These events were a public relations nightmare to the tobacco industry. The house of cards the industry had constructed began to collapse in spring of 1994. In the span of a few months the following events had occurred: the FDA's letter to the Coalition on Smoking or Health concerning evidence that nicotine was addictive had been published on the front page of major newspapers; ABC's *Day One* report, using industry informants, alleged that the industry manipulated nicotine levels in cigarettes; and internal Brown & Williamson documents were leaked to the press. By the

time that the seven chief executive officers for the tobacco industry testified under oath before the Waxman Congressional subcommittee that
they did not believe that nicotine was addictive, the public credibility of
the industry had plummeted. In the eyes of millions of Americans, the
tobacco industry appeared to be dishonest and disreputable. In the eyes
of plaintiffs' attorneys, the tobacco industry appeared much more vulnerable to lawsuits. By 1997, first hundreds, then thousands, and finally millions of tobacco industry documents began to surface due to the discovery
process in class action suits. These documents began to appear on the Internet web sites of the Commerce Committee of the U.S. House of Representatives, Minnesota Blue Cross and Blue Shield, and the Minnesota
District Court.[15] There is also a large online archive of industry documents.[16]

Plaintiffs' attorneys were now armed with a wealth of new information
to challenge traditional tobacco industry statements about tobacco and
health. The industry had consistently claimed that nicotine is not phar-
macologically active, that it is not addictive, and that anyone who smokes
makes a free choice to do so. The FDA investigation, statements of informants, and the tobacco industry's own documents made it clear none
of these statements were true. Even worse, the tobacco industry publicly
stated that there was no definitive proof that smoking causes cancer, yet
company documents showed by the 1960s that tobacco company researchers had proved in their own laboratories that cigarette tar causes
cancer in laboratory animals.

Now the tobacco industry had to contend with hundreds of new lawsuits instead of the 50 or so that they dealt with in the 1980s. For example,
R. J. Reynolds Tobacco Company reported that it had 68 cases to contend
with in July of 1995. The number of cases increased to 203 a year later,
and to 448 cases by August 1997.[17] In order to clear the large volume of
cases, courts set firm trial deadlines, consolidated cases, and allowed class
action suits. The scorched earth tactics of previous trials were no longer
permitted and the tobacco industry was no longer able to concentrate resources on defeating a few cases. The first clear victory for a plaintiff in
a lawsuit came in September 1995. A state court jury awarded $2 million,
including $700,000 in punitive damages, to a smoker that had developed
a type of cancer associated with asbestos exposure after smoking asbestos
filtered Kent cigarettes in the 1950s. Shortly afterwards, the industry had
begun to settle cases with individual litigants and concentrated resources
on class action suits.

Class Action Suits and Medicaid Reimbursement Cases

Class action suits allow a group of persons suffering from a common
injury to bring a single lawsuit together against an entity in an attempt

secure a remedy or award for the entire group. *Castano v. American To-bacco Co.* was filed on March 29, 1994 in a New Orleans federal court.[18] *Castano* represented a complete shift in tactics as a coalition of traditional plaintiffs' lawyers, mass disaster lawyers, and class action specialists from around the country joined forces in an attempt to overcome tobacco industry organizational resources. Each of a coalition of sixty-two law firms pledged $100,000 annually to fund this unparalleled class action suit, on behalf of millions of nicotine-dependent smokers. The plaintiffs requested damages for economic losses, emotional distress, and medical monitoring for future illness. In February 1995, Judge Okla Jones II granted class certification on a number of legal issues including fraud, negligence, and consumer protection issues. Before a trial began, Judge Jones allowed the defendants to appeal his certification decision to an appeals court. The Fifth Circuit appellate court vacated Judge Jones decision to certify the class action. They reasoned that the variations in the state laws of the fifty states, in which the injuries occurred, combined with trial management issues justified decertification of the case. They instructed Judge Jones to dismiss the class action. The coalition of lawyers decided to file statewide class action suits after this decision.

Two months after *Castano* was filed, another class action suit was filed in a Florida state court. *Engle v. R. J. Reynolds Tobacco Co.* sought billions in damages from all seven leading tobacco companies, the Council for Tobacco Research, and the Tobacco Institute, on behalf of smokers suffering from diseases like lung cancer and emphysema.[19] The suit claimed that the tobacco industry had deceived the public about the dangers of using tobacco products by denying that smoking is addictive and by suppressing research on the hazards of smoking.[20] Unlike the coalition of sixty-two law firms that filed the *Castano* suit, a single personal injury lawyer filed *Engle*. On October 31, 1994, *Engle* had the distinction of becoming the first tobacco-related class action suit to be granted class status.

While successes in individual suits and class actions undoubtedly had an enormous psychological impact on what was once considered an impenetrable industry, the real legal fallout occurred when the attorney general of Mississippi, Michael Moore, filed a lawsuit seeking reimbursement from the tobacco industry for the healthcare costs of ailments related to tobacco use.[21] The theory Moore used was that the state of Mississippi had been directly injured by the tobacco industry because Mississippi taxpayers had been forced to pay the state's Medicaid costs due to tobacco-related illnesses. The state planned to use statistical data to illustrate the percentage of Medicaid costs that can be attributed to tobacco use. If the suit was successful, the defendants would pay for Medicaid costs under a formula that calculates liability according to market share. The lawsuit was unique in that it did not seek compensation for individuals but instead sought compensation for the state as a healthcare provider. In this way, the tobacco industry could no longer defend itself on the basis of arguments about personal choice and that the smoker contributed to their own illness. As a result, on July 2, 1997, Mississippi settled its claims with the tobacco industry. The state would receive at least $3.3 billion over 25 years, with annual payments of at least $135 million. Importantly, the settlement had a provision granting Mississippi most favored nation status. This meant that Mississippi would get the benefit of any better agreement that another state might achieve in the future.[22] This proved extremely beneficial as the industry settled with three other states: Texas, Florida, and Minnesota.

In May 1998, the tobacco industry settled with the state of Minnesota and agreed to pay $6.1 billion over 25 years.[23] This had the effect of increasing the settlement amounts in the other three states. But, perhaps more importantly, the tobacco industry agreed to a number of public health concessions that would be reflected in the upcoming Master Settlement Agreement with the remaining states. Some of the unique concessions include: disbanding the Council for Tobacco Research, ending the practice of paying movie executives for placing tobacco products in films, the ten-year maintenance, at industry expense, of a depository of millions of tobacco documents located in Minneapolis, and reimbursement of fees to private attorneys who represented plaintiffs in the case ($440 million).

Florida filed suit in February 1995 seeking $4.4 billion from the tobacco industry. The Florida state legislature passed legislation for the specific purpose of amending a little used statute concerning Medicaid claims. This suit was the first to criticize the tobacco industry for targeting minors. Florida settled their case in 1997 for at least $11 billion over 25 years, with annual payments of at least $440 million continuing thereafter. The settlement called for an additional $200 million for a two-year initiative to reduce youth smoking, a ban on billboards and transit advertisements, and an agreement from the industry to lobby for a ban on cigarette vending machines.[24]

The final individual state to settle with the tobacco industry was Texas in January 1998. This case was unique in the sense that it was filed in federal rather than state court and it was the first to make claims under the federal RICO (Racketeer Influenced and Corrupt Organizations) Act. This act makes it unlawful to receive income derived directly or indirectly from a pattern of racketeering. The Texas suit was settled at a cost of $14.5 billion over 25 years, with annual payments of at least $580 million continuing thereafter, and public health provisions similar to those of Florida.[25]

THE MASTER SETTLEMENT AGREEMENT

On June 20, 1997, a group of forty-one state attorneys general proposed a tobacco settlement intended to resolve all pending lawsuits against the tobacco industry, including all suits by governmental entities as well as all remaining class action suits. The proposed settlement included provisions for FDA authority over tobacco, new warning labels, advertising restrictions, youth access provisions, rules to reduce public exposure to environmental tobacco smoke, and financial incentives to the tobacco industry to reduce sales to minors. The settlement assumed that Congress would enact the elements of the agreement into law.

The tobacco industry was eager for a settlement. With hundreds of individual lawsuits, multiple class action suits, and the attorneys general from each state to contend with, a final settlement that would preclude further legal action was intuitively appealing to the industry. On the other hand, there were a number of critics that understood that the settlement would likely become the overall national health policy tool for reducing tobacco use. Many, including former FDA Commissioner David Kessler, felt it would fail in this role. He believed that by limiting future lawsuits and by not granting the FDA broad authority to regulate tobacco, the settlement would likely benefit the tobacco industry in the end.

In September 1997, President Clinton outlined several principles that he felt must be present in any national tobacco legislation. These included the following provisions:

- A comprehensive plan to reduce youth smoking, including tough penalties if targets are not met.
- An end to the tobacco industry's practice of marketing and promoting tobacco to children.
- Broad document disclosure by the industry (especially documents pertaining to marketing tobacco products to children).
- Progress toward other tobacco related public health goals such as reducing environmental tobacco smoke (ETS), expanding tobacco cessation programs (programs designed to help addicted smokers to quit), strengthening efforts to control tobacco internationally, and providing funds for future health research.
- Protection for tobacco farmers and their communities.
- Full authority for the FDA to regulate tobacco products.[26]

The United States Senate considered a number of draft bills for potential use in legislating the June 20, 1997 settlement proposal. In March 1998, Senate Bill 1415 was introduced by Senator John McCain and became the focus of all settlement-related congressional actions. The McCain Bill was much stronger than the proposals in the 1997 settlement proposal. It contained the following provisions:

- Requirement that the tobacco industry pay $516 billion over twenty-five years to help states and the federal government bear the medical costs of smoking-related illnesses.

- Raise cigarette taxes by $1.10 per pack over five years.
- Drastically reduce cigarette marketing, advertising, and promotions.
- Preserve the FDA's ability to regulate the tobacco industry.[27]

An amendment to the bill would have created a very detailed regulatory scheme to be administered by the FDA. These amendments would have granted the FDA the authority to designate safer cigarettes as "reduced risk tobacco products," the FDA would be allowed to set performance standards such as lower yields of nicotine in tobacco products, and could require the elimination of other harmful constituents found in tobacco smoke. The FDA could also ban all cigarette products or require nicotine levels of zero, in which case the new standards would be delayed two years after the president notified Congress of the new provisions. Obviously, Senate Bill 1415 was vehemently opposed by the tobacco industry. The tobacco industry threatened to pull out of all negotiations. They also sponsored an advertising campaign that painted the McCain Bill as a tax-and-spend proposal. Eventually, Senate allies were emboldened to add amendments to the bill that gutted many of its provisions such as eliminating funds for tobacco use prevention. The only version of the bill that went before the Senate for a vote was eventually killed by filibuster, even though fifty-seven senators supported the bill. The forty-two senators that voted to kill the bill received four times more in political donations from the tobacco industry.[28] The McCain Committee Bill eventually died after four weeks of intense debate.

On November 23, 1998, 11 tobacco companies entered into a legal settlement with 46 states, the District of Columbia, and 5 commonwealths and territories. In the settlement agreement the tobacco industry agreed to pay states $206 billion over twenty-five years.[29] Another $40 billion will be paid to the initial states (Mississippi, Florida, Minnesota, and Texas) to settle their suits.

In addition to the payments from the tobacco industry to the states, the settlement provided for a number of other requirements and restrictions listed below.

Youth Access to Tobacco Products

- No free samples may be distributed to anyone except in an enclosed area where the retailer or operator can ensure that no minors are present.
- No gifts to youth such as t-shirts, bags, and hats in exchange for buying tobacco products.
- No gifts may be sent through the mail without proof of age.
- The sale, manufacture, or distribution of cigarettes in packages fewer than twenty (kiddie packs) is prohibited until December 31, 2001.

Marketing

- No brand name sponsorship of concerts, teams sporting events, or events with a significant youth audience are allowed.
- No industry sponsorship of events in which paid participants are underage.
- Tobacco brand names in stadiums and arenas are prohibited.
- Payments to promote tobacco products in entertainment settings, such as movies are illegal.
- The distribution and sale of merchandise with brand name tobacco labels are prohibited.

Lobbying

- Prohibits the tobacco industry from lobbying lawmakers to divert settlement funds to nonhealth uses.
- Restricts the tobacco industry from lobbying against advertising restrictions on or in school grounds.
- Prohibits new tobacco industry legal challenges to state and local tobacco control laws enacted before June 1, 1998.

Outdoor Advertising

- Prohibits tobacco advertising on billboards and on mass transit such as busses.
- At the expense of the tobacco industry, could substitute advertising that discourages youth from smoking.

Cessation and Prevention

- The tobacco industry is required to pay $25 million annually for ten years to support a charitable foundation (the American Legacy Foundation) to study programs to reduce teen smoking and to prevent diseases associated with tobacco use. This foundation is governed by a board of directors and conducts a sustained national advertising and education program to counter youth tobacco use and educate consumers about the dangers of smoking.
- The tobacco industry is required to pay $1.45 billion over five years to support the National Public Education Fund charged with carrying out a national sustained advertising and education program to counter youth tobacco use. The industry is required to contribute $300 million annually to the fund as long as the tobacco companies involved in the settlement continue to hold 99.05% of the market.[30]

One critical element was missing from the agreement: the authority of the FDA to regulate tobacco products in any way. Additionally, the National Governor's Association issued a policy statement concerning the settlement that stated that the federal government had no legitimate claim to settlement funds and instead asserted states' entitlement to the funds. The association committed to spending "a significant portion of the settlement funds on smoking cessation programs, health care, education, and programs benefiting children" but reserved the right to make funding decisions tailored to states' individual needs.[31] These have become prophetic words as the settlement funds are being used for many purposes, but only a small percentage is currently being used to prevent young people from smoking.

STATES' USE OF SETTLEMENT FUNDS

The Master Settlement Agreement provides an historic opportunity to do something positive about the devastating toll that tobacco has had on the American public. Approximately $246 billion dollars over twenty-five years will be allocated to the states as compensation for the costs states have incurred for the provision of medical services to sufferers of tobacco-related illnesses. By the year 2003, the states had already received $44 billion in Master Settlement Agreement payments. It was understood that the states would allocate at least part of their settlement funds in programs to prevent children from starting to smoke, and to treat those already addicted to tobacco products or suffering from tobacco-related illnesses.

Almost immediately, California and Maine developed comprehensive tobacco control programs. As a result of an evaluation of these programs, the Centers for Disease Control developed recommendations for each state on how much funding was required per capita population to have a significant impact on reducing tobacco use.[32] The formula was based on the population of each state and the extent of tobacco use in that state. The approximate annual costs to implement all the recommended program components were estimated to range from $7–$20 per capita in smaller states (population less than 3 million), $6–$17 per capita in medium sized states (population 3–7 million), and $5–$16 per capita in larger states (population more than 7 million). Table 4.1 lists the settlement funds available for each state in 2001, the low estimate for a comprehensive tobacco control program as computed by the CDC, the amount states actually allocated toward tobacco control programs in 2002, the per capita expenditure on tobacco control programs, and the percentage of program funding as compared to the CDC low estimate.[33]

The figures in the table tell a tragic story. Every state in the union readily has funds available for investment in new efforts to reduce and control tobacco use. Despite the availability of settlement funds, four years after the Master Settlement Agreement, 45 states and the District of Co-

Table 4.1
Tobacco Control Funding Among the States in 2002

State	2001 Tobacco Settlement Revenue	CDC Low Estimate for Total Program Cost	Total Tobacco Control Funding, 2002	Per Capita Funding, 2002	Percentage of CDC Low Estimate
Alabama	$96,961,493	$26,740,000	$2,226,923	$0.50	8%
Alaska	$21,176,139	$8,088,000	$4,899,804	$7.72	61%
Arizona	$87,669,615	$27,788,000			
Arkansas	$51,364,510	$17,906,000	$14,118,428	$5.30	79%
California	$759,225,833	$165,098,000	$137,816,465	$4.02	83%
Colorado	$85,026,250	$24,546,000	$14,924,792	$3.39	61%
Connecticut	$110,430,429	$21,240,000	$2,573,529	$0.75	12%
Delaware	$23,523,288	$7,479,000	$584,449	$1.03	8%
District of Columbia	Na	$8,631,000	$6,237,661	$7.85	72%
Florida	$731,300,000	$78,383,000	$30,603,004	$1.88	39%
Georgia	$152,235,170	$42,591,000	23,903,594	$2.86	56%
Hawaii	$35,800,091	$10,778,000	$23,903,594	$19.16	217%
Idaho	$22,531,022	$11,044,000	$2,669,888	$2.02	24%
Illinois	$288,674,835	$64,909,000	$50,821,349	$4.06	78%
Indiana	$106,515,675	$34,784,000	$6,692,125	$1.09	19%
Iowa	$53,940,181	$19,347,000	$11,127,313	$3.78	58%
Kansas	$51,707,586	$18,052,000	$2,771,608	$1.02	15%
Kentucky	$104,957,133	$25,090,000	$4,912,696	$1.21	20%
Louisiana	$139,997,812	$27,132,000	$2,339,851	$0.52	9%
Maine	$47,268,164	$11,189,000	$14,018,672	$10.96	125%
Maryland	$140,202,664	$30,301,000	$32,299,397	$6.04	107%
Massachusetts	$240,246,288	$35,244,000			
Michigan	$258,862,265	$54,804,000	$6,334,605	$0.63	12%
Minnesota	$336,997,000	$28,624,000	$30,191,558	$6.07	105%
Mississippi	$211,149,286	$18,788,000	$22,594,439	$7.87	120%
Missouri	$142,110,326	$32,767,000	$23,542,752	$4.17	72%
Montana	$26,248,117	$9,355,000	$1,904,621	$2.09	20%
Nebraska	$36,903,219	$13,308,000	$8,643,236	$5.01	65%
Nevada	$37,830,589	$13,477,000	$5,116,564	$2.46	38%
New Hampshire	$43,303,862	$10,888,000	$4,406,545	$3.53	40%
New Jersey	$239,846,695	$45,073,000	$32,461,666	$3.53	72%
New Mexico	$36,989,850	$13,711,000	$6,935,009	$3.75	51%

Table 4.1 (*continued*)

State	2001 Tobacco Settlement Revenue	CDC Low Estimate for Total Program Cost	Total Tobacco Control Funding, 2002	Per Capita Funding, 2002	Percentage of CDC Low Estimate
New York	$754,339,700	$95,830,000	$46,479,998	$2.44	49%
North Carolina	$142,728,818	$42,591,000	$3,848,940	$0.47	9%
North Dakota	$22,701,724	$8,161,000	$3,385,534	$5.27	41%
Ohio	$312,446,299	$61,735,000	$121,630,988	$10.67	197%
Oklahoma	$64,265,818	$21,825,000	$3,799,907	$1.09	17%
Oregon	$68,264,932	$21,131,000	$13,052,416	$3.75	62%
Pennsylvania	$341,834,697	$65,568,000	$43,162,000	$3.50	66%
Rhode Island	$44,589,359	$9,888,000	$4,499,819	$4.27	46%
South Carolina	$72,961,122	$23,905,000	$3,248,862	$0.80	14%
South Dakota	$21,642,999	$8,688,000	$4,487,556	$5.90	52%
Tennessee	$151,394,114	$32,233,000	$1,876,736	$0.33	6%
Texas	$974,220,834	$103,288,000	$16,746,521	$0.79	16%
Utah	$27,593,646	$15,230,000	$1,718,829	$0.75	11%
Vermont	$24,458,081	$7,905,000	$7,772,084	$12.67	98%
Virginia	$126,823,184	$38,866,000	$16,939,129	$0.79	44%
Washington	$127,351,202	$33,341,000	$20,642,290	$3.44	62%
West Virginia	$54,981,783	$14,160,000	$7,986,893	$4.41	56%
Wisconsin	$123,248,769	$31,158,000	$7,469,595	$1.38	24%
Wyoming	$14,772,038	$7,381,000	$2,073,302	$4.16	28%

Source: Investment in Tobacco Control: State Highlights 2001 (Atlanta: USDHHS, 2001).

lumbia have failed to make even the minimum investment in comprehensive tobacco control programs recommended by the Centers for Disease Control and Prevention. Overall, just 5% of the tobacco settlement funds received by the states were actually used to prevent and reduce tobacco use in 2002.

Hawaii invests the most funding per capita of any state. It invests over twice the CDC minimum recommendation of $10.7 million with a $23.3 million investment in tobacco control. Ohio, Maine, Mississippi, Maryland, and Minnesota also make the minimum investment recommended by the CDC. Tennessee makes the smallest per capita investment in tobacco control. It spent just $1.8 million on tobacco control despite receiving $151.3 million in settlement funds the previous year. To make matters worse, none of the revenue from the settlement in Tennessee was allocated for tobacco control purposes. The vast majority of the $1.8 million spent on tobacco control came from the CDC and a private foundation. Tennessee has a higher youth smoking rate than the national average, thus it critically needs the investment in tobacco control. Other states that invest less than 10% of their settlement funds toward the CDC minimum are Alabama, Delaware, Louisiana, and North Carolina.

In my own state of Texas, only $16.7 million was invested in tobacco control in 2002 and only $12.5 million of that investment came from settlement funds. The state received $974.2 million in tobacco settlement funds in the previous year. As a result of the shortfall in tobacco prevention programming, the Texas Department of Health (TDH) made a strategic decision to implement comprehensive programs in the only way that they would be effective in reducing tobacco use. With the knowledge that $16.7 million could not provide comprehensive tobacco control programs to the entire state, TDH provides these comprehensive programs only in the Houston area.

Commitment to tobacco control programs is an investment in the lives of youth and others who suffer from tobacco-related illness. It also represents tremendous potential savings to taxpayers. Miller and colleagues developed a complex statistical model to estimate 2001 Medicaid costs attributable to smoking and the potential savings from reducing the prevalence of smoking by investing in tobacco control programs.[34] The overall cost savings for all states that could manage to reduce their smoking prevalence by 5 to 50%, would range from $110 million to $1.1 billion per year. One might think that a smoking prevalence reduction of that magnitude is unrealistic, but California reduced its youth smoking rate by 25% after implementing comprehensive tobacco control programs. This Medicaid cost-savings estimate does not include the cost savings in private insurance premiums, out-of-pocket medical expenditures, costs of purchasing cigarettes, and lost productivity due to illnesses caused by cigarettes. A U.S. Department of Treasury report estimated that nonhealth costs, including lost productivity, totals at least $40 billion per year.[35]

However, it's sometimes difficult for policy makers and decision makers to think of the significant short-term and long-term benefits of investing in tobacco control. State legislatures in recent years have had to confront budget shortfalls, and for some states, using the settlement funds to offset budget problems or for other purposes has proven too difficult to resist. Some states have set aside their settlement funds as "rainy day" funds. Several states, including Ohio and New Hampshire, have set aside large portions for their public schools. Louisiana, Michigan, and Nevada used settlement funds to provide scholarships for state residents to attend state colleges and community colleges.[36]

It was already mentioned that California has been one of the model states for developing comprehensive tobacco control programs that have had a significant impact on lowering tobacco use. In the 2002–2003 budget, Governor Gray Davis proposed to securitize a portion of the state's tobacco settlement revenues to provide $2.4 billion to help balance the upcoming year's budget. A state securitizes its settlement payments by issuing bonds that are backed by future tobacco settlement revenues. These debt service payments funded by future tobacco settlement revenues were $62 million in 2002–2003 and $190 million annually for twenty-two years thereafter, for a total cost of $4.2 billion.[37] Thus, California mortgaged $4.2 billion of its future tobacco settlement funds to gain $2.4 billion to help offset their budget deficit. This one-time solution to the state's budget woes cost a model tobacco prevention program hundreds of millions of dollars.

This is not an isolated incident but a growing trend. In 2003, the General Accounting Office estimated that only 24% of that year's settlement funds were being used for any type of health-related initiatives, while 36% were used to fix budget shortfalls. The news is even worse in 2004. Only 17% of tobacco settlement funds will be used for health-related programs, while 54% will be used to offset budget problems. For three straight years, the mayor of Washington D.C. diverted $58.7 million in tobacco settlement funds to balance the general budget.[38] Kentucky spent $130 million of its tobacco funds to fix budget problems. It spent only 36% of its settlement funds on health programs of any kind, and spent 43% of their funds on economic development in tobacco farm areas. Tennessee plans to count the settlement funds it receives in 2004 as general revenue, meaning that it will not be allocated for any specific purpose such as health initiatives.[39] Colorado, Idaho, Ohio, and other states are strongly considering making the same moves.

Florida presents one of the more interesting cases concerning the use of settlement funds. In 1996, Florida developed a tobacco control program oriented around reducing youth tobacco use. It became a model program for the rest of the nation and will be discussed in more detail in the following chapter. In December 2001, Governor Jeb Bush commissioned a blue-ribbon panel to review the progress of the state's youth tobacco prevention program. A 2002 survey of 250 Florida schools revealed that smoking declined 57% among middle-school students since 1998 and 36% among high school students.[40] The panel concluded that the program was a roaring success. Governor Bush vowed to make "the program, and the funding to support it, a permanent part of Florida's Department of Health."[41] In the early years of the program it received approximately $70 million a year, but that figure fell significantly by 2001. The panel recommended returning the program's funding from $39 million in 2002 back to $70 million. The panel's report was nowhere to be found when the Florida legislature discussed the program and its funding. Instead of an increase to $70 million, the Republican-controlled House and Senate attempted to eliminate *all* funding for the program. State senator Ron Klein managed to win back $1 million to keep the program going.[42]

CONCLUSION

Former Food and Drug Commissioner David Kessler was asked to participate in the initial negotiations that resulted in the Master Settlement Agreement. He declined because he felt negotiating in secret without involving a wide range of important constituents was an incorrect strategy. After the settlement agreement had been completed, Henry Waxman asked Kessler and former Surgeon General C. Everett Koop to chair a committee of public health representatives to review the proposed settlement and report back. Kessler reviewed the proposal and became convinced that it would confer legitimacy on tobacco as a product. The settlement would assure financial predictability, stable stock prices, and a less controversial working environment for the tobacco industry. Later, Kessler believed that states' attorneys general top priority was to protect the flow of settlement funds to state coffers after they publicly commented that they did not want the tobacco industry to go bankrupt. The success of lawsuits and a Master Settlement Agreement against the most powerful industry on earth has proven, thus far, to have been a missed opportunity.

5

Comprehensive Tobacco Control Programs

INTRODUCTION

I was at a criminal justice conference not long ago and attended a panel on illicit drug use and delinquency. The panel was discussing drug prevention programs. I was surprised to hear someone mention that criminal justice policy makers in the area of drug prevention needed to take a long look at the tobacco prevention programs going on around the country. He stated that tobacco control programs were achieving success unlike any type of prevention programs he had ever seen, and that a model for tobacco prevention programs had been developed and replicated throughout the country. Having worked with the tobacco prevention programs in Texas, I was aware of this fact, but was surprised that the word was getting out.

BEST PRACTICES

In 1999 the Centers for Disease Control and Prevention published a manual titled *Best Practices for Comprehensive Tobacco Control Programs.* This manual has become something of a Bible for public health officials working in tobacco prevention. In this manual, the CDC suggests that the

> goal of comprehensive tobacco control programs is to reduce disease, disability, and death related to tobacco use by: preventing the initiation of tobacco use among young people; promoting quitting among young people and adults; eliminating nonsmokers' exposure to environmental tobacco smoke (ETS); and identifying and eliminating disparities related to tobacco use and its effects among different population groups.[1]

The *Best Practices* recommendations were based on the analysis of comprehensive state tobacco control programs. These recommendations came from two different sources of information. The first source was published evidence-based practices such as tobacco prevention education, enforcement of youth access laws, and mass media campaigns. The second source of information came from the evidence of the effectiveness of the tobacco control programs in California and Massachusetts. As mentioned in the previous chapter, the CDC recommended that states fund these programs at a range between $5 and $20 per capita based on the population size of the state, tobacco use prevalence, and other factors. The best practices address nine different components of comprehensive tobacco control programs that include community programs to reduce tobacco use; chronic disease programs to reduce the burden of tobacco-related diseases; school programs; enforcement; statewide programs; counter-marketing; cessation programs; surveillance and evaluation; and administration and management.

Community Programs

The CDC recommends that community programs[2] attempt to achieve all of the goals listed above by developing programs that

> increase the number of organizations and individuals involved in planning and conducting community-level education and training programs; use state and local counter-marketing campaigns to place pro-health messages that inform, educate, and support local tobacco control initiatives and policies; promote the adoption of public and private tobacco control policies; and measure outcomes using surveillance and evaluation techniques.[3]

Effective community programs must attempt to change the attitudes and behavior that supports tobacco use. In order to accomplish that, effective communities change the way tobacco is promoted, sold, and used. They also attempt to change the knowledge, attitudes, and practices of young people. Community-based organizations require funding for full-time staff, for operating expenses, to purchase resource and educational materials, to provide education and training programs, to support communication campaigns, establish local plans of action, and enlist other community leaders into the process. Most states are funding local health departments or health-related nonprofit community organizations that represent each county or large cities in the state.

Properly implemented, community programs such as those in California and Massachusetts have produced measurable progress toward tobacco control objectives.[4] In both states, community action has led to an increase in the number of local ordinances that restrict public smoking. This has led to a steady decline in the percentage of nonsmoking adults reporting exposure to secondhand smoke. Also, in both states community youth programs have produced tremendous declines in the number of underage youth who are successful in attempts to purchase tobacco products.

Oregon is another state that has made impressive strides in reducing youth tobacco use, and much of this success has to do with effective community coalitions and activities. Examples of these activities include engaging young people to actually plan and conduct their own community tobacco prevention and education events and campaigns; working with judges and tobacco retailers to develop education and diversion programs; strengthening tobacco use policies in schools and daycare centers; conducting youth-led countywide assessments of tobacco advertising (e.g., Operation Storefront discussed in Chapter 2); developing plans to reduce tobacco industry sponsorship of public events; offering smoking cessation programs by drug and alcohol prevention agencies; and using Native American tribal newspapers and community presentations by reservation youth to educate members of tribes about tobacco use and the tobacco industry's advertising and promotion of its products on reservations (Native Americans have one of the highest rates of tobacco use among any racial and ethnic groups in the nation).[5]

Chronic Disease Programs

One of the primary goals of the Master Settlement Agreement was to offset the costs incurred due to tobacco-related diseases. Tobacco use increases the odds for several diseases, and even if all current tobacco use stopped today, there would continue for a long time to be a residual burden of disease among those who have previously used tobacco products. The CDC also recommends incorporating tobacco prevention and cessation messages into broader public health activities to increase the circulation of these messages. State-based comprehensive tobacco prevention and control programs can address tobacco-related diseases such as cancer, cardiovascular disease, asthma, oral cancers, and stroke. Few states have had the necessary financial resources to effectively link tobacco control activities to other activities to reduce the burden of these diseases.[6]

Examples of activities that states have developed include implementing community interventions that coordinate tobacco control initiatives with cardiovascular disease prevention; developing marketing campaigns to increase the awareness of the impact of environmental tobacco smoke (ETS) as a trigger for asthma; providing training to dentists to talk to their patients about the dangers of smokeless tobacco in the development of mouth and throat cancers; and expanding cancer registries to monitor tobacco-related cancers.[7]

School Programs

As mentioned in Chapter 1, most people who start smoking do so in adolescence. School-based tobacco education programs are therefore critical in preventing youth tobacco use. The earliest tobacco education programs made the simple assumption that adolescents are completely rational people who would simply choose not to smoke if given information concerning the health risks. Educational techniques using films, lectures, posters, and books did increase knowledge about tobacco use, but were ineffective in actually persuading young people no to smoke. As a result of past failures, new approaches began to be developed in the 1970s and 1980s based on new theories about adolescent tobacco use. Eventually, much of the research pointed to the influences of smoking peers, smoking by others in the immediate social environment, and other social and psychological factors. Programs were developed in an attempt to resist social influences that encourage smoking.

Successful school-based tobacco prevention programs help identify the direct and indirect social influences that promote tobacco use among youth and teach youth the skills needed to resist those influences. Specifically, these programs have a number of goals including teaching the short-term and long-term negative social and health consequences of smoking and the advantages to not smoking; informing youth that only a small proportion of young people and adults are regular smokers (many youth believe that almost everyone smokes); teach youth to recognize the social influences in the immediate environment, the community, and the culture that promote smoking; and teach specific skills to resists pressures to smoke from peers, adult modeling, the mass media, and tobacco industry marketing.[8]

Differences in smoking rates between groups receiving programs versus those that do not have been found and range between 25 to 60%. And, although some evaluations suggest that the effectiveness of these programs may dissipate over time, the effects have lasted from one to five years.[9] These programs frequently differ in length, format, delivery methods, and community setting, but seem to focus on teaching youth how to resist the pressures to smoke.

The effectiveness of school-based tobacco prevention programs is strengthened by other antitobacco messages coming from parents, school policies, the mass media, and restrictions on youth access. Experimentation with tobacco often develops in middle school and sometimes even earlier, thus most school-based tobacco prevention programs start in middle school and continue through high school. In many cases tobacco education starts as early as grade school.

The CDC's *Guidelines for School Health Programs to Prevent Tobacco Use and Addiction* is an excellent resource for communities in the process of developing school-based tobacco prevention programs.[10] It contains information concerning tobacco-free, policies, evidence-based curricula, teacher training, parental involvement, and services to help youth stop smoking. The CDC has also identified other effective school-based programs that are now considered the state of the art in youth tobacco prevention.

Project Towards No Tobacco Use

Project Towards No Tobacco Use (Project TNT) has become one of the most popular youth tobacco prevention programs and is based on the social influences model.[11] The program consists of four different sets of curricula, each with ten lessons, and its target audience is seventh-grade students. Trained health educators employed by the project deliver the curricula on ten consecutive school days. The first curriculum set provides social skills to help students more easily refuse direct offers to smoke from peers. The second curriculum set provides methods or skills to counter the indirect pressures to smoke such as smoking by peers and adults, tobacco industry advertising, and exaggerated notions of the actual prevalence of smoking among peers and adults. The third set is designed to improve the knowledge of the short-term and long-term negative impacts of smoking. Finally, the fourth curriculum set addresses all three of these areas simultaneously.[12]

Sussman and colleagues conducted an evaluation of the program in forty-eight southern California schools.[13] Students from eight schools were assigned to receive one of each of the four curricula while the remaining sixteen schools were assigned to receive the standard programs already in place. Self-reported smoking by the youth was measured immediately after the end of the program and one year later in the eighth grade. The TNT curricula that combined all three of the main objectives resulted in 64% less weekly smoking than the control group. By the end of the eighth grade the group that received the TNT curricula still had a 55% lower incidence of weekly smoking than the control group.

Know Your Body

The Know Your Body (KYB) program is a school-based effort to reduce multiple risk factors for chronic disease among adolescents. This comprehensive program addresses not only cigarette smoking, but also dietary behaviors and physical fitness, and its target audience include youth in grades 4 through 9.[14] The program was designed to meet the rapidly changing educational needs of young people in this age group. The six-year curriculum progresses from a focus on knowledge and beliefs to a focus on decision-making skills.[15] Health beliefs about smoking were addressed in grades 4 and 5. In grades 6 through 8 the direct and indirect social influences to smoking were addressed. In the ninth grade, psychological factors such as stress and self-image were addressed.

Students' usual classroom teachers were specially trained to deliver the program. The entire curriculum was delivered in approximately two hours per week throughout the school year; the smoking component was about twenty-four total hours. There is a parent education component of the program that included asking parents to participate in students' homework assignments, attend meetings on the program, sending newsletters to parents, and a self-assessment of risk factors for chronic disease.[16]

Fourth grade students in fifteen New York elementary schools were followed through the ninth grade. Students in eight schools received the KYB program while students in the remaining seven schools received no health education programs. The follow-up survey in the ninth grade included 593 students, or 65% of the original cohort. The program had a dramatic impact as the smoking rate among students receiving the KYB program was 73% lower than the comparison group. The program had a positive impact on other types of health behaviors as well.[17]

Minnesota Heart Health Program: Class of 1989 Study

Because the social influences for smoking exist outside of the school and because not all youth at risk for smoking actually attend school, a small number of programs have expanded traditional school-based programming to also include the positive influences of parents, community organizations, and the mass media. Evaluations of a few of these programs suggest that they can achieve a substantial effect on youth smoking that persists throughout the high school years.[18]

The Class of 1989 Study of the Minnesota Heart Health Program (MHHP) is another multifaceted community health education program focused primarily around reducing the risk of cardiovascular disease. The program includes a smoking prevention component provided in grades 7 through 9. The Class of 1989 Study used a seven-session program delivered in weekly sessions during the seventh grade by peer leaders and assisted by teachers.[19] This program was followed by a two-session unit in the eighth grade that addressed smoking and exercise, and by an eight-session unit in the ninth grade focused on preventing smoking and drug abuse. Other components focused on diet and exercise behaviors.

In addition to the school-based education programs, students participated in other projects related to the overall community theme of cardiovascular disease risk reduction. This work was conducted within school-supported health councils. In all, students participated in five years of educational programs provided within their schools and focused on smoking and other health behaviors.

These school-based programs were supported over the entire program period by community education and organization activities designed to reduce cigarette smoking, high levels of serum cholesterol, and elevated blood pressure. All three health problems are tied to cardiovascular disease.[20] The community activities included individual risk factor screening and education, direct education sessions, food labeling education conducted in grocery stores, intensive mass media education, education of health professionals, and community organization to engage citizens, health professionals, and community leaders in developing and carrying out annual community education plans.

Perry and colleagues assessed the impact of these programs on youth smoking behavior.[21] Students from one community that received these direct and indirect interventions were compared to a matching community that did not receive these messages. The baseline target population included all sixth graders from thirteen elementary schools in both communities. There were no significant differences in smoking behavior between youth in the two communities at grade 6. Within one year, smoking rates were 40% lower in the community with the program. These results persisted through the twelfth grade, three years after the school-based programs ended and one year after the community programs were concluded. By the twelfth grade, there was still a 39% difference in smoking rates between youth in the two communities. Evaluators believed that the community component of the program was a key factor in sustaining the lower levels of youth tobacco use.

University of Vermont School and Mass Media Project

The University of Vermont School and Mass Media Project (VSMM) evaluated the effects of combining a school-based tobacco prevention program with an intensive mass media campaign. Both programs were based on the social influence model and stressed developing social skills to resist smoking along with the belief that most people their age did not smoke. Other components of the program included smoking cessation (helping youth quit smoking) and developing awareness of the influence of tobacco industry marketing.

Curriculum content covered key elements of the social influences model described above and were delivered by classroom teachers. Students received the program over a four-year period. The study cohort was divided into grades 5 through 8, 6 through 9, and 7 through 10 to examine the effects of the program at different grade levels.[22]

The mass media campaign was developed with the aid of youth identified as being at a high risk of smoking (defined as youth who had already experimented with smoking or knew at least two people in their immediate social environment who smoked). High-risk girls and boys provided diagnostic information used to tailor the media campaign to this group of youth.[23] Pilot mass media advertisements were developed and tested on small samples of high-risk students.

Mass media advertisements that addressed the common social influences themes and were rated as attractive to their target audience were produced for 30 and 60 second television and radio spots. These advertisements were broadcast on television and radio programs that were rated as popular among youth. On the average, 190 television, 350 cable, and 350 radio broadcasts were purchased per year over a span of four years.

Flynn and colleagues evaluated the program and the design included four geographically separate but demographically matched metropolitan areas from three states.[24] In two communities, students received the mass media and school programs for four years. Students in the other two communities received only the school programs during these four years. The initial cohort included all students from the fourth through sixth grades from fifty elementary and middle schools. About 99% of the students or 5,458 students participated in the initial survey. Annual follow-up surveys were conducted over the next four years. Also, a classroom and telephone follow-up survey was attempted to reach all original cohort members during grades 10 through 12.

Findings from the program concentrated on the 47% of the original cohort who were fully exposed to program components, or 2,540 students. By the end of the four-year program, students in the mass media communities reported 34–41% less smoking than students in the school-only communities. Importantly, two years later when the study cohort was in the tenth through twelfth grades, differences in reported smoking behavior between the two groups was still significant and of similar magnitude.[25]

Enforcement of Tobacco Laws

Because some tobacco control policies have been enacted into federal, state, and local laws, active enforcement of these laws has gained in importance. Supporters of enforcement of tobacco laws believe that active enforcement sends a message to the public that community leadership values these policies and that tobacco control laws will deter potential violators. Some states have enacted laws concerning tobacco advertising and promotions, but the most frequent areas of legislation and enforcement are restrictions on minors' access to tobacco and the enforcement of clean indoor air regulations.

There have been a small number of studies that suggest that the combination of enforcing laws that restrict tobacco sales to minors and educating tobacco retailers can reduce illegal sales to minors.[26] Generally, these laws are enforced by conducting sting operations using minors.

In Texas, these stings are conducted in the following manner. Youth about 16 years in age are asked to accompany two plain-clothes police officers to convenience stores and other stores licensed to sell tobacco where kids have legal access. One officer enters the store and browses magazines, candy, or soft drinks. The youth enters the store and attempts to purchase a specific brand of tobacco. The undercover officer is close enough to overhear the transaction. If the clerk asks the youth for identification, the youth is instructed to tell the clerk that they do not have an ID and leave the store. If the clerk sells tobacco to the minor, the undercover officer purchases something (candy or a beverage) and makes a mental note of the clerk's name and physical appearance. After completing all sting operations for the day, the officers return and cite the clerk for selling tobacco to a minor (a $500 fine in Texas). The officers wait until the end of the day to cite retailers to prevent them from calling other retailers to warn them about the stings. Sting operations are only one component of a comprehensive program developed that trains and educates Texas police officers about the state's tobacco laws.

The Texas Statewide Tobacco Education and Prevention (S.T.E.P.) program was developed by Texas State University to train law enforcement officers regarding tobacco laws, effective enforcement methods, retailer, youth, and community education, and health issues related to tobacco use.[27] While state laws require that all law enforcement departments enforce youth possession and tobacco retailer laws, the Texas legislature did not provide funding for enforcement. This is a common a scenario among all states. It's unrealistic to expect widespread and frequent enforcement of these laws without a funding source. Thus, the Texas Department of Health entered into contracts with several law enforcement departments to enforce Texas tobacco laws in areas where they were attempting to provide comprehensive youth tobacco prevention services. We were asked to evaluate the effectiveness of the training and the overall enforcement of tobacco retailer laws.

S.T.E.P. staff included full-time trainers from Texas State University who discussed tobacco health issues and federal and state tobacco laws. S.T.E.P. also utilized regional trainers, most of whom were licensed peace officers with years of experience in enforcing tobacco laws. These officers shared their experiences in enforcing the laws and trained officers on conducting compliance education, compliance inspections, and controlled buys or stings.[28]

Contracts with the departments required that officers frequently conduct compliance inspections, controlled-buy/sting operations, and compliance education for retailers, children, parents, community members, and municipal judges and justices of the peace. Thus, S.T.E.P. staff spent much of their time discussing the tobacco laws, how to enforce them, and how to conduct tobacco education.

Officers were introduced to the Synar Amendment, an antitobacco bill passed by Congress in 1989.[29] Some of the key provisions of this bill include the following:

- States must have laws which ban the sale of tobacco to persons under 18 years of age.
- States must enforce these laws in a manner that can be expected to reduce the availability of tobacco to minors.
- States must use "random, unannounced inspections" of retailers selling tobacco products to determine if the laws are being adhered to.
- States must develop a strategy and time frame for achieving an inspection failure rate of less than 15% of outlets accessible to youth.
- Health and Human Services is authorized to withhold up to 40% of a state's federal substance abuse funds if it is determined that states are not enforcing their laws regarding tobacco sales to minors.

In addition to the Synar Amendment, officers are expected to enforce the provisions of Texas State Senate Bill 1.[30] It restricts tobacco use on school property and includes the following provisions:

- Smoking or using tobacco products at a school-related or school-sanctioned activity on or off school property is prohibited.
- Students are prohibited from possessing tobacco products at a school-related or school-sanctioned activity on or off school property.
- School personnel must enforce these policies on school property.

Finally, officers going through S.T.E.P. training were introduced to the major provisions of Senate Bill 55, commonly called the Texas Tobacco Law, which took effect in 1997 and 1998.[31] This law mandates the following:

- Minors are prohibited from buying, using, or possessing tobacco products except in the presence of the minor's parent, guardian, or adult spouse.
- Minors that violate the law are required to attend an eight-hour tobacco awareness program, perform tobacco-related community service, or pay a fine of up to $250.
- Minors that fail to attend the tobacco awareness program or perform tobacco-related community service may have their driver's license suspended.
- Parents of minors may also be required to attend a tobacco awareness program.
- The sale of "kiddie packs" containing fewer than 20 cigarettes is prohibited.
- Free samples and coupons to anyone under 18 years of age is prohibited.
- Outdoor advertising of tobacco products within 1,000 feet of a church or school is prohibited.

- Cigarette vending machines and other self-service sales are prohibited in all places open to minors.
- Retailers who sell tobacco products are required to ask for proof of identification from anyone purchasing tobacco who appears to be under 27 years of age.
- Retailers that sell tobacco products to minors are guilty of a Class C misdemeanor punishable by a fine up to $500.
- Tobacco retailers are subject to penalties upon failure to adequately inform employees of the current law ($500 fine for the first offense, $750 fine for the second offense, $1000 fine for the third offense, and permit revocation for a fourth offense).
- Existing signage is amended to include that it is both illegal to sell to minors and illegal for minors to buy tobacco products (the state comptroller sends an official warning sign to tobacco retailers to be posted when they pay their tobacco permit fee).

It was clear to us during the training sessions attended by Prairie View staff that most officers were unaware of the existence of the vast majority of these tobacco laws. Officers were most aware of youth possession of tobacco laws, and least aware of tobacco merchant laws.

S.T.E.P. staff defined compliance education as "a prevention process consisting of presentations, training, events, and activities that are provided to the community-at-large and tobacco retailers, regarding youth access to tobacco issues and laws."[32] A long list of different types of activities and youth educational presentation suggestions were included in training materials. A sample of these educational activities includes media coverage by local news media during inspections, public service announcements, television interviews, school lectures, D.A.R.E. lessons on tobacco, Boys and Girls Scouts meetings, Citizens Police Academy Training, and Regular Police Academy. S.T.E.P. staff also enlisted the Texas Department of Health, the Texas Commission on Alcohol and Drug Abuse, the American Cancer Society, the American Lung Association, and the American Heart Association for distribution of brochures and other educational materials.

S.T.E.P. staff emphasized the importance of bringing retailers together in a classroom setting to educate them about the tobacco laws and to inform them that officers will be conducting compliance inspections and sting operations. Finally, the training discussed the importance of providing in-service training to other officers in their agency so that they might also become involved in enforcing tobacco laws.

In addition to sting operations, law enforcement officers who received this training were expected to conduct "compliance inspections." S.T.E.P. training staff defined compliance inspections as "an enforcement process consisting of law enforcement officers conducting inspections of retail es-

tablishments, checking for display of appropriate warning signs, possession and display of tobacco permits, checking methods of access to tobacco products, and display of outdoor advertising."[33] Trainers covered a
number of different scenarios and had officers complete inspection reports based on the information they received.

We conducted a survey of all the officers who received the S.T.E.P.
training as well as a random sample of officers throughout the state to
assess their attitudes concerning tobacco issues and the extent to which
the officers enforced tobacco laws. It was expected that officers who received the S.T.E.P. training would be actively engaged in tobacco law
enforcement because their departments were contracted by the Texas
Department of Health to enforce those laws. The random sample of officers throughout the state were surveyed as a comparison group and
to gauge the extent to which the state's tobacco laws were being enforced. Some of the more important results of our survey are listed
below:[34]

- S.T.E.P. program officers actively engaged in tobacco law enforcement were
  28% more likely than the comparison group of officers to believe that tobacco use in their community was a serious or very serious problem (86%
  compared to 58%). The belief that youth tobacco use is a problem in the
  community increased among S.T.E.P officers from 75% in 2000 to 86% in
  2002.

- S.T.E.P. officers were about twice as likely than the comparison group to believe that the settlement will have a great deal or some impact on reducing
  Texas smoking (51% compared to 26%).

- S.T.E.P. officers were 12% more likely than the comparison group of officers
  to state that enforcing the state's tobacco laws was an important function
  within their department (81% compared to 69%).

- S.T.E.P. officers were over two times more likely to be involved in educating parents and community members about the state tobacco laws than the
  comparison group (49% compared to 19%).

- S.T.E.P. officers were over two times more likely to be involved in conducting compliance inspections of tobacco retailers than the comparison group
  (64% compared to 23%).

- S.T.E.P. officers were over three times more likely to be involved in conducting sting operations using minors than the comparison group (59%
  compared to 17%).

- About 40% of S.T.E.P. officers issued six or more citations to youth in the
  last year compared to 27% of the comparison group. This was an increase
  of 12% from 2000.

- About 18% of S.T.E.P. officers issued six or more citations to tobacco retailers in the last year compared to only 1% of the comparison group. This was
  an increase of 3% from 2000.

- From June 2000 to May 2001 there were 2,448 inspections of tobacco retailers with minor-led stings and 4,426 inspections without minors (compliance checks). There were a total of 167 citations issued to tobacco retailers during this time period.

I think that what made the largest impact on us concerning the officers' attitudes toward tobacco law enforcement was a general recognition, over a rather short period of time, that youth tobacco use is a very serious problem that was worthy of their time and effort. However, it is also clear that S.T.E.P. officers are not issuing a large number of citations to tobacco retailers, despite the fairly large number of inspections. I believe that tobacco retailers in these areas are better informed about tobacco laws and the active enforcement program, and as a result are in greater compliance with the laws than retailers in areas without active enforcement programs. Finally, our survey also revealed that unless specifically contracted (or paid) to enforce these laws, the vast majority of law enforcement departments generally ignore them. In Texas, this means that the vast majority of law enforcement departments in the state do not enforce the state's tobacco retailer laws. Thus, contracting with departments or otherwise designating an enforcement authority to enforce retailer laws is an essential component to comprehensive programs.

In addition to retailer laws, *Best Practices* has identified the enforcement of clean indoor air regulations as an important element to comprehensive tobacco control programs.[35] There has been much less resistance to the regulation of environmental tobacco smoke than tobacco advertising or the regulation of tobacco products. This is probably because there has been a long history of grassroots efforts to reduce ambient tobacco smoke, especially in public settings. Also, there is considerable evidence of the negative health effects of environmental tobacco smoke. Since 1971, a consistent stream of rules, regulations, and laws have created smoke-free environments in an increasing number of settings including government offices, public places, restaurants, worksites, military establishments, and on airplanes flying domestically. As of December 31, 1999, environmental tobacco smoke was regulated in public places in forty-five states and the District of Columbia.[36] Additionally, there are at least 820 local ordinances restricting public smoking in place, and that number is growing daily.[37]

The effectiveness of these laws and regulations is an area of intensive study. Most studies suggest that smoke-free policies are extremely popular, and are even generally supported by smokers. Studies have also shown that these regulations are effective in protecting nonsmokers from environmental tobacco smoke and they have the added benefit of reducing the number of cigarettes that employees smoke during the day.[38]

The problem with both minors' access and environmental tobacco smoke laws is not popular appeal, but an active enforcement mechanism. While most states have enacted both of these types of laws, only fifteen states have identified an enforcement authority for minors' access violations. Among states that do define an enforcement authority such as Texas (local law enforcement are required to enforce tobacco retailer laws), generally there is no funding allocated specifically for enforcement activities. As a result, active enforcement of these laws is quite rare. The enforcement of public smoking violations is also generally passive. Complaints by the public are investigated by state or local officials who use a range of graduated fines to enforce these regulations.

Statewide Programs

One of the most important elements of the CDC's *Best Practices* is the recommendation that funding be provided for statewide tobacco control and prevention programs.[39] Local programs have obvious limits on the scope of their activities. Statewide programs in California, Massachusetts, Minnesota, and Oregon have increased the capacity of local programs by providing technical assistance on the evaluation of programs, promoting media advocacy, and implementing environmental tobacco smoke and minor's access laws. These statewide programs have funded multicultural organizations and networks to collect data and develop and implement culturally appropriate interventions. They have also sponsored local, regional, and statewide training, conferences, and technical assistance on the most effective practices for tobacco use prevention and cessation. More specific examples of innovative and effective statewide programs are discussed below.

California

California's tobacco control program has a longer history than other state programs because it was not funded by master settlement funds. California's program was the result of a proposition.[40] Propositions are laws developed by grassroots movements and voted upon directly by the public without going through the legislative process. The program was funded by an increase in cigarette taxes (from $0.10 to $0.37) and is the largest and most comprehensive effort by any state to reduce tobacco use. The long-term goals of the program were extremely ambitious:

1. reduce the initiation of cigarette smoking by children and youth under age 19 from the 1987 rate of 26.4% to 6.5% by 1999;
2. reduce cigarette smoking among adults aged 20 years and older from the 1987 rate of 26.0% to 6.5% by 1999; and
3. reduce smokeless tobacco use among males aged 12–24 years from the 1987 rate of 8.9% to 2.2% by 1999.

Funding was directed to the California Department of Health Services and the Department of Education at the level of $126.8 million ($3.90 per capita) starting in July 1989.[41]

From the start, community mobilization has been a critical element of California's statewide program for reducing tobacco use. The community-based programs were developed and directed by the Department of Health Services and the sixty-one local health departments within their agency. These local units were advised by area coalitions and established multiple subcontracts with community-based organizations to conduct tobacco prevention events, programs, and presentations for diverse racial and ethnic groups.[42] These units have also been instrumental in mobilizing communities to eliminate exposure to environmental tobacco smoke, reducing minors' access to tobacco, and by advising local politicians. Local departments have received about 20% of the funding allocated for education programs.

Like most tobacco prevention programs, the most visible element in the California program is a statewide media campaign. The media campaign began in 1990 and has focused primarily on changing public opinion about tobacco use from being normative or widely accepted behavior to being unacceptable and dangerous. In particular, the media campaign has developed messages aimed at exposing the public to the tobacco industry's manipulative and deceptive marketing practices as well as educating the public about the dangers of environmental tobacco use. Most media campaigns target young people. While the California campaign includes messages directed toward youth, much of their focus has been on changing social norms and reducing adult tobacco use. The hope is that these messages will have an indirect effect on youth because they often smoke to appear more like adults. Funding for the media campaign has varied considerably over the years but got a good start in 1998 at $24 million or 12% of the funds.[43]

Approximately 16% of education funds have been spent on competitive grants to community-based organizations. The vast majority of these grants have gone to fund programs to serve racial and ethnic minority communities. Several statewide projects have been developed from these grants including the Tobacco Education Clearinghouse of California that distributes library and video materials. The California Tobacco Control Resource Partnership provides technical assistance and training to local lead agencies. About 24% of the education funds are directed toward school-based tobacco education programs, and these programs are headed by the California Department of Education. The California school-based program reached approximately 350,000 students between 1994 and 1996.[44]

The largest share of the education funds (59% through 1996) is directed toward medical care programs. This funding allocation has been the result of political decisions made at the executive level and was strongly supported by the California Medical Association and the tobacco industry.[45] Originally, the state legislature specified the funding level to be 45% with 20% directed toward reducing tobacco use. That 20% level has yet to be reached as funding for these programs ranged from 16.5% in the first year to 10% three years later. The organization, Americans for Nonsmokers' Rights, sued the state due to this reallocation of funds and won in both state court and on appeal.[46]

Begay and colleagues have tracked the influence of the tobacco industry in California politics since the passage of Proposition 99.[47] The tobacco industry's political financing increased from $790,050 in the 1985–1986 election to $7,615,091 in the 1991–1992 election. During this time, the industry spent more on political contributions to California state legislators than to candidates for the United States Congress. Some of the industry tactics in California have included using front groups to conceal their involvement, organizing local referenda to defeat or suspend local ordinances, and financing local election campaigns to repeal ordinances by popular vote.[48] Glantz and Begay found a strong relationship between the amount of money received from tobacco sources and pro-tobacco positions among state legislators.[49]

By 1993, California revised and refocused their tobacco control program around four broad priorities that include (1) protecting people from exposure to environmental tobacco smoke, (2) revealing and countering tobacco industry influence, (3) reducing young people's access to tobacco products, and (4) providing cessation services. The organizational structure has remained largely the same with a statewide office and several statewide and regional programs.[50]

By all accounts, the California Tobacco Control Program had been a resounding success when it was fully funded. Before implementation of the program, California's monthly per capita cigarette consumption was declining at a rate of 0.42 packs compared to a national decline of 0.36 packs for the rest of the nation. By 1993, the decline in cigarette consumption increased significantly to 0.65 packs (that is a reduction of 1.05 million packs of cigarettes), while the decline for the rest of the country increased less significantly to 0.45 packs. Between 1993 and 1996 the rate of decline of consumption of tobacco products decreased significantly to 0.17 packs, but the decline for the rest of the nation virtually halted at 0.04 packs.[51]

There is a reason for the reduced effectiveness of the California program between 1993 and 1996; their original funding level had been reduced by over 50% during that period. In contrast, spending on advertising and promotions by the tobacco industry in California exceeded spending on tobacco control by a ratio of 5 to 1 from 1989 to 1993. From 1993 to 1996, this ratio increased to 10 to 1.[52] Despite this tremendous imbalance in spending, the California Tobacco Control Program has managed to significantly reduce both adult and youth tobacco use.

Florida

The Florida Tobacco Pilot Program was initially developed in the Governor's Office under the leadership of Governor Lawton Chiles, who was a party to the state's lawsuit. The program is now managed by the Florida Department of Health, Office of Tobacco Control. As mentioned earlier, this program is unique in the sense that is entirely focused on youth. The program's goals include: (1) changing youth attitudes about tobacco use, (2) increasing youth empowerment through community involvement, (3) reducing youth access to tobacco products, and (4) reducing the exposure of youth to environmental tobacco smoke.[53] Another unique and perhaps critical feature of this program is that Florida youth were heavily involved in the planning and implementation of this program.

One important element of the Florida program was the development of countermarketing to offset the influence of the tobacco industry. A commercial advertising firm was hired to work directly with Florida youth. The result was the "Truth Campaign," perhaps the most original and innovative antitobacco media campaign ever developed. This campaign was developed to expose the tobacco industry's practices and to attack the image of smoking as cool and rebellious. After Governor Jeb Bush eliminated funding for this campaign, the American Legacy Foundation picked it up and funded the program at the national level.[54]

A Teen Tobacco Summit was held in 1998 in Florida to advise the Florida Department of Health on the overall development of the state's antitobacco program. This led to the creation of chapters of Students Working Against Tobacco, which have been active in all sixty-seven Florida counties. In addition, tobacco education and training curricula were developed and implemented as a result of the collaboration of schools, voluntary agencies, professional organizations, and universities. This program component has resulted in tobacco prevention education in middle and high schools, and additional strategies for tobacco prevention for youth in grades K–12.[55]

The Florida Department of Business and Professional Regulation's, Division of Alcoholic Beverages and Tobacco actively enforces youth access to tobacco laws, and provides other marketing and educational initiatives to ensure compliance with all tobacco laws.

The Florida Department of Health, in conjunction with the University of Miami, is responsible for evaluating the effectiveness of each of these programs in meeting their goals and objectives. The program had its greatest impact among middle school kids (grades 6–8). The prevalence of current cigarette use declined from 18.5% in 1998 to 8.6% in 2000, or an overall 54% decline. During the same period, high school students (grades 9–12) current cigarette use declined for 27.4% to 20.9%, or an overall 24% decline. There was also a 46% and 21% decrease in cigar use among middle school youth and high school kids respectively. Smokeless tobacco use decreased by 54% among middle school youth, and by 19% for high school youth. Not all Florida youth were exposed to all elements of the tobacco control program, but those who were, experienced more significant decreases in tobacco use. As mentioned in the previous chapter, these encouraging results may not continue as funding for this inventive program has dropped from a high of $70 million in 1998 to $1 million in 2003.[56]

Countermarketing

Countermarketing consists of a wide range of efforts that generally include paid television, radio, billboard, and print counteradvertising at the state and local level. It can also include media advocacy and other public relations techniques such as press releases, local events, and health promotion activities. Countermarketing efforts can be effective in a number of ways; it can promote smoking cessation, decrease the incidence of the initiation of tobacco use, increase public support for tobacco control efforts, complement school and community efforts, and counter pro-tobacco influences.[57]

Countermarketing campaigns are fighting an uphill battle for consumer attention with the tobacco industry. As mentioned in Chapter 2, tobacco advertising and promotions appear to promote adult use and increase youth experimentation with tobacco products. Children, in particular, are vulnerable to tobacco advertising. Youth buy the most heavily advertised brands (Marlboro, Camel, and Kool) and are three times more affected by advertising than adults. In fact, today's average fourteen-year-old has already been exposed to more than $20 billion in tobacco industry advertising and promotion images beginning at age six.[58]

Despite the flood of pro-tobacco images, there is considerable evidence that intensive and sustained media campaigns can produce significant declines in both adult and youth smoking. To date, the statewide public education and media campaigns in California and Massachusetts have had the greatest success in reducing youth tobacco use. Additionally, multifaceted prevention programs such as the Minnesota Heart Health Program and the University of Vermont School and Mass Media Project demonstrate that combining media campaigns with school-based and community-based activities can postpone or prevent smoking in 20–40% of adolescents. In a single year, the Florida tobacco control program anchored by an aggressive and imaginative media campaign produced significant declines in tobacco use among middle and high school youth in Florida.

The relative effectiveness of specific messages and strategies is being debated, but in general, previous effective media campaigns all had sufficient reach, frequency, and duration. The Centers for Disease Control also suggest that countermarketing efforts should combine messages on prevention, cessation, and protection from secondhand smoke.[59] They should also target both youths and adults. Countermarketing should also maximize the number, variety, and novelty of messages and production styles rather than communicate a few messages repeatedly. Finally, these messages should not appear paternalistic with simple refrains such as not to smoke.

Cessation

According to the Centers for Disease Control *Best Practices*, programs that are successful in helping adults and young people quit using tobacco products can produce a quicker and larger short-term public health benefit than any other component of comprehensive programs discussed in this chapter.[60] Smokers who quit before the age of fifty will cut in half their risk of dying in the next fifteen years. There is also a tremendous cost benefit from the reduced tobacco use produced by cessation programs. A moderately priced and effective cessation program will pay for itself within three to four years. One smoker who succeeds in quitting reduces the anticipated medical costs from heart disease and stroke by approximately $853 over the next seven years. In fact, smoking cessation programs have demonstrated larger cost savings than other clinical prevention services such as mammography, colon cancer screening, PAP tests, and treatment of high cholesterol.

Best Practices has identified a number of effective strategies to help people quit smoking. One approach is simply to have healthcare professionals advise patients to quit and give suggestions about how to go about it. The Public Health Service-sponsored Clinical Practice Guideline *Treat Tobacco Use and Dependence* recommends that clinicians use the "five A's' approach: (1) *ask* patients about smoking, (2) *advise* all smokers to quit, (3) *assess* willingness to make a quit attempt, (4) *assist* those who want to quit, and (5) *arrange* follow-up visits with those trying to quit.[61] These simple recommendations can be completed by doctors within two to three minutes and have been associated with helping 5 to 8% of smokers quit.

More expensive, but more effective approaches to helping smokers quit are organized cessation treatments that involve multisession counseling programs and more extensive contact with healthcare providers. These counseling programs use a variety of approaches. One approach is problem-solving training, which involves helping people who have recently quit smoking identify high risk situations such as alcohol use and the presence of others smoking and learn how to cope with them.[62]

Another approach called rapid smoking requires the smoker to inhale deeply from a cigarette about every six seconds until they become nauseated. This is a form of aversive therapy that transforms the smoking experience from a perception of pleasure to one of unpleasantness. Other approaches include the use of motivational rewards for not smoking, the use of social support systems, and the use of acupuncture.[63]

A number of pharmacological interventions have been developed that have proven quite effective in reducing tobacco use. Most use some form of nicotine replacement that gives the smoker just enough nicotine to break the cycle of dependence by relieving withdrawal symptoms. The oldest form of nicotine replacement is Nicotine polacrilex or nicotine gum. Nicotine gum comes in doses of 2mg and 4mg and is now approved as an over-the-counter medication for adults only. Several studies have found that the gum is an effective aid for smoking cessation. A recent review of nicotine replacement devices by Fiore and colleagues found that users of the 2mg nicotine gum had a quit rate of about 24% compared to a quit rate of 17% for those using a placebo.[64]

Nicotine patches have been approved for use since 1991 and for over-the-counter sales since 1996. The patch is attached to the skin much like a band-aid and contains a reservoir of nicotine that diffuses through the skin and into the wearer's bloodstream at a constant rate. Generally, people wearing the patch are instructed to apply one patch each day. Most patches are intended for 24-hour use and deliver 21–22mg of nicotine. Overall, the nicotine patch has been found to be effective in helping users to stop smoking by reducing cravings and other withdrawal symptoms. The review by Fiore and colleagues found that users of the nicotine patch had a quit rate of about 18% compared to 10% of smokers receiving a placebo.[65]

Nicotine nasal sprays have been approved as a nicotine replacement since 1996. The spray looks very much like any nasal spray, consisting of a pocket-sized bottle and pump fitted to a nozzle that is inserted in the nose. Each spray delivers about 0.5mg of nicotine to the mucus membranes of each nostril of the nose. The user is instructed to use the nicotine spray as needed as withdrawal symptoms appear. In the review of nicotine replacement devices, users of the nicotine nasal spray had a quit rate of almost 31% compared to almost 14% of those smokers using a placebo.[66]

Bupropion is a drug developed to treat depression. It is the only pharmacological approach discussed that does not involve nicotine replacement. Interest in this drug to treat nicotine addiction has increased due to reports of patients spontaneously quitting smoking when using it to treat symptoms of clinical depression. Clinical investigations of a sustained-release form of bupropion began in the mid-1990s. Symptoms of depression and depressed mood have been associated with attempts to

quit smoking, thus use of an antidepressant as an aid for smoking cessation makes sense. This drug is available by prescription only and is taken
for approximately two weeks before a quit attempt and for three months
afterwards. Fiore and colleagues found that 31% of smokers prescribed
buproprion were successful in their quit attempts compared to 17% taking a placebo.[67]

Surveillance and Evaluation

The effectiveness of each of the elements of a comprehensive tobacco
control program discussed above can only be assessed through independent evaluations and surveillance. This is important in order to make programs accountable to state policy makers and to insure that programs are
achieving their goals and objectives. Surveillance is the monitoring of tobacco-related behaviors, attitudes, and health outcomes at regular inter-
vals of time and usually involves the use of surveys. Examples of
surveillance measures include the prevalence of tobacco use among adolescents and adults, per-capita tobacco consumption, exposure to environmental tobacco smoke, exposure of individuals and communities to
statewide and local tobacco programs, and exposure to tobacco industry
advertising and promotions.[68]

Evaluations are used to track the progress of each program element in
meeting specific performance goals. They also compliment tobacco-related surveillance by linking statewide and local program efforts to
progress toward outcome objectives. A necessary first step in surveillance
and evaluation activities is to collect baseline data in order to assess the
extent of tobacco use and other tobacco program-related measurements.
The baseline measurements are than compared to subsequent measurements after the development and implementation of tobacco control programs. Tobacco use should decrease after the implementation of tobacco
control programs.[69] It's critical that agencies (such as a state health department) responsible for the development of tobacco control programs
contract with surveillance and evaluation researchers from entities (such
as universities) that are independent of the agency and that have little or
no stake in the results of the evaluation in order to meaningfully assess
the outcomes of their efforts.

Administration and Management

To be effective, state tobacco control programs must have a strong management structure. Comprehensive programs often involve multiple state
agencies (e.g., health, education, and law enforcement) and require coordination with different local governments, health-related volunteer agencies, and community coalitions. In addition to the complex structure of

these programs, the effectiveness of program activities also requires the coordination and integration of programs such as countermarketing and telephone "Quitlines" so that programs may have their greatest effect. As an early innovator in the development of comprehensive programs, California has documented the challenges regarding organizational issues and the need for adequate staffing and management structures.[70]

Comprehensive tobacco control program administration and management activities include recruiting qualified technical, program, and administrative staff; awarding contracts and grants; coordinating implementation across program areas; creating an effective internal and external communication system; and developing a fiscal management system with the ability to minimize start-up delays.

CONCLUSION

State lawmakers face many unpopular decisions in the process of allocating scarce public dollars for education, welfare, public health and other services. It would be hard to argue with these policy makers that in times of recession and tax revolts, using tax dollars to fund comprehensive tobacco control and prevention programs is a difficult sell to their constituents. However, the necessary funding has already been allocated in the form of the Master Settlement Agreement. It's more a matter of having the political will to use the funds as intended—to develop tobacco prevention, education, cessation, and enforcement programs. The real tragedy is that an effective model to reduce youth tobacco use exists and works.

6

Youth Tobacco Prevention Organizations

INTRODUCTION

Formed in the 1960s, Action on Smoking and Health (ASH) was one of the first organizations developed for the purpose of taking on the tobacco industry and attempting to lobby public officials for meaningful tobacco control policies. It was ASH that submitted the fateful letter to FDA Commissioner David Kessler requesting that the agency regulate tobacco as a drug. Since that time, there has been tremendous growth in youth tobacco prevention programs. Most of these programs share the goals of attempting to prevent youth tobacco use and to expose the more despicable practices of the tobacco industry. Some of the more innovative and effective organizations are profiled in this chapter.

THE AMERICAN LEGACY FOUNDATION

The American Legacy Foundation was developed as part of the Master Settlement Agreement (MSA) between the tobacco industry and the attorneys general of the forty-six states and five U.S. territories. Their slogan is "Building a world where young people reject tobacco and anyone can quit."[1] This independent public health foundation is national in scope and develops programs that address the health effects of tobacco use through grants, technical training and assistance, youth activism, strategic partnerships, counter-marketing and grass roots marketing campaigns, public relations, and community outreach to populations disproportionately affected by the toll of tobacco. The two overriding goals of Legacy are: (1) "to arm all young people with the knowledge and tools to reject tobacco, and (2) to eliminate disparities in access to tobacco prevention and cessation services."[2]

Cessation

The American Legacy Foundation promotes a range of smoking cessation programs. The foundation developed a partnership with QuitNet, which is one of the Internet's most visited quit-smoking sites and is operated in association with Boston University School of Public Health. QuitNet helps the smoker map out a plan to quit using tobacco products tailored just for them. It offers expert advice to the smokers that need or want it and also provides the smoker with educational resources. Finally, QuitNet links the smoker to a larger community of smokers and ex-smokers ready to help them quit. This telephone service is available any time of the day or night. The QuitNet web site can be visited at http://www.quitnet.com.

The foundation developed the Great Start campaign, which is the first national media and quitline campaign to help pregnant women quit smoking. The Great Start Quitline links pregnant women who call in to the quitline with counselors who understand the special needs and concerns of pregnant smokers. The Great Start Quitline service is a joint effort of the American Legacy Foundation and the American Cancer Society. Similarly, the foundation developed the Circle of Friends: Uniting to be Smoke-Free program. This is a national grassroots social movement to show support for women struggling to quit smoking. The organization also discusses the toll of tobacco-related diseases on American women, their families and communities.

Grants

The American Legacy Foundation provides grants to support innovative tobacco control programs. The foundation realizes that changing social behaviors takes a sustained effort and cannot occur due to the efforts of one public awareness campaign. They believe that creating smoke-free generations in America will only occur when national and grassroots programs work in tandem over time. The American Legacy Foundation's Grants Initiatives are part of the plan to identify new and better tobacco control programs.

The foundation's grants typically fall into two major categories: national calls for proposals and small innovative grants. Since 2000, the foundation has awarded more than $150 million in grants and commitments.

Priority Populations

The American Legacy Foundation has developed and funded programs designed to reduce tobacco use among priority populations. These pop-

ulations are groups believed to be vulnerable to or targeted by the tobacco industry and have been disproportionately impacted by tobacco.
Through the Priority Populations Initiative, the foundation awarded more
than $24 million in grants over three years to organizations that work to
reduce tobacco use among one or more of the following underserved populations: African Americans, Asian American/Pacific Islanders, gay/
lesbian/bisexual/transgendered, Hispanic/Latinos, low socioeconomic,
and Native American/Alaska Natives.

Part of the rationale behind the Priority Populations Initiative is the fact
that low-income Americans and members of racial, ethnic, and cultural
minority groups bear the greatest burden of smoking-related death and
disease. For example, Americans below the poverty line are more than
40% more likely to smoke than others, and a disproportionate number of
the poor in this country are also minorities. Finally, low-income Americans, regardless of race or ethnicity have less access to smoking cessation
programs and other related health services.

The Foundation also believes that a high smoking rate among these priority populations is not an accident, but the specific intention of the industry. As mentioned in the previous section, the tobacco industry
aggressively targets these populations with heavy advertising and community outreach. The Foundation strongly believes that helping those
populations who have the fewest resources to fight the influence of the
tobacco industry is a matter of social justice. In the first two years of the
organization's operation, they organized several forums to gain a better
understanding of the issues from leading minority organizations and
community activists. These efforts actually led to the development of the
foundation's Priority Populations grants program. The grants are given
over three years to a broad range of groups that research and employ effective, innovative approaches to decreasing tobacco use.

Research

The American Legacy Foundation has developed an ambitious and impressive research agenda built around the goals to build effective initiatives and contribute to and expand upon the body of knowledge about
tobacco control. Their Research and Evaluation Coordinating Center is located at the Research Triangle Institute (RTI). They also consult researchers from some of the most prestigious colleges and universities
across the country.

The foundation's research and evaluation team conducts two national
surveys—the National Youth Tobacco Survey (NYTS) and the Legacy
Media Tracking Survey (LMTS)—to document the tobacco-use beliefs, attitudes and behaviors of American youth, and the effectiveness of the
Truth Campaign. These surveys and reports developed from the surveys

may be accessed for free on the Foundation's web site. The Foundation's research team is also conducting a comprehensive evaluation of the truth campaign that includes multiple study methodologies.

Prevention

Perhaps the most visible and well-known aspect of the work of the American Legacy Foundation is the Truth Campaign. This national prevention and education program conducts grassroots and promotional events, and has an interactive web site with the goals of arming kids with the facts about tobacco use and industry marketing, and encourages youth to get involved in efforts to inform their peers.

The Truth Campaign has become famous for its edgy and hard-hitting approach. The concept behind the campaign is that by telling the truth about the tobacco industry and its products and exposing their marketing tactics, teens are allowed to make informed choices about tobacco use. The campaign is purposely not preachy or judgmental; characteristics of media campaigns that are not terribly effective with youth.

Since 2000, the Truth Campaign has become the largest youth smoking prevention campaign in the country and has helped reduce youth smoking rates. The Monitoring the Future study reported dramatic declines in smoking rates among eighth, tenth, and twelfth graders, and they cited the truth campaign as a factor in this public health success story.

The Truth advertising campaign attempts to reach teens through print, radio, the Internet and television. Their commercials are targeted to youth-oriented channels such as MTV, the WB, and UPN. In one particularly memorable ad, teens piled 3,000 simulated body bags outside the building of an American tobacco company as company executives gazed down and passersby watched in curiosity. The body bags were meant to represent the daily death toll due to tobacco use. The Truth grassroots initiative gives teens the opportunity to spread the word about big tobacco in peer-to-peer settings. In 2003, Truth "crewmembers" went on the road for six weeks and to forty-five cities in twenty-five states.

In 2003, the Truth Campaign was the recipient of the Gold and Grand EFFIE advertising awards due to the effectiveness of its "Infect Truth" campaign, and for its tremendous success in helping to drive down youth smoking prevalence to the current historic lows. The foundation was just the second nonprofit organization to earn this top honor in the EFFIE's 35-year history. The Truth web site receives thousands of hits each day and provides detailed information about tobacco and the tobacco industry in a unique manner. The Truth web site is found at http://www.thetruth.com.

CAMPAIGN FOR TOBACCO-FREE KIDS

The Campaign for Tobacco-Free Kids is one of the largest and most innovative nonprofit antitobacco organizations. Their primary goals are to "alter the public's acceptance of tobacco by deglamorizing tobacco use and countering tobacco industry marketing to youth and other practices; change public policies at federal, state and local levels to protect children from tobacco; and increase the number of organizations and individuals fighting against tobacco.[3] Their 130-plus partners include health, education, medical, civic, corporate, youth, and religious organizations that are dedicated to reducing tobacco use among children and adults. They rely on funding from private foundations such as the Robert Wood Johnson Foundation, other nonprofit organizations such as the American Cancer Society, and from the general public.

They have partnered with over 130 other organizations and racially diverse communities and with assistance from the areas of health, education, medicine as well as from, civic, corporate, youth, women's and religious organizations. They believe they can have much greater success by working toward a common goal with other like-minded organizations and produce a greater change than by working alone. They inform their partners with "action alerts," issue briefs, and legislative updates. The hope is that members of these other organizations can put political pressure on policy makers on key tobacco issues. Anyone can join the Campaign's online action network without cost. Those who join will be informed of news concerning the industry and provide straightforward methods of telling policy makers how they feel about specific tobacco issues. They have a federal initiatives link on their web site that provides information concerning a number of issues including: a federal tobacco lawsuit filed by the justice department, Internet tobacco sales, FDA authority over the tobacco industry, cigarette smuggling, fire-safe cigarettes, and increased federal taxes on tobacco products.

One issue they are passionate about is a lawsuit filed by the federal government in September 1999 against the nation's major tobacco companies. The lawsuit specifically attempts to hold the industry legally accountable for decades of public deception concerning the health risks of smoking, the addictiveness of nicotine and marketing practices to children. The suit seeks to stop these practices and recover damages from the industry. The Campaign for Tobacco-Free Kids makes it clear that they believe that the public health community supports the lawsuit, while the tobacco industry has made it a top priority to cut off funding for the lawsuit and kill it.

The Campaign believes that the second Bush Administration initially failed to provide adequate funding for the lawsuit and then sought to enter into premature settlement talks with the industry. Congress stepped in and subsequently has provided the necessary funding for the suit to continue.

Since then, the Justice Department has prepared a document disclosing the government's proposed remedies in the lawsuit. Their proposal asks for many of the changes sought by the Food and Drug Administration under Dr. Kessler. They are asking for restrictions on tobacco marketing; large, graphic health warnings on cigarette packs; disclosure of all ingredients, additives and other chemicals in cigarettes; and other measures. The government also has indicated it will seek to recover $289 billion in industry profits from illegal sales to children. The case has gotten even stronger with the discovery of recent evidence of industry wrongdoing. Several recent studies and reports have shown that after signing the 1998 legal settlement with the states in which they promised to stop marketing to kids, tobacco companies increased their marketing expenditures by 66% to a record $11.2 billion, with much of the increase in ways effective at reaching kids. A trial date of September 15, 2004 has been set on the case.

In the state initiatives link on their web site, the Campaign discusses the Master Settlement Agreement with the states. They include a report concerning how the states have spent their settlement funds (the subject of Chapter 4), how the states rank in funding tobacco prevention programs, and information concerning the effectiveness of state tobacco prevention funding. On the main page of their web site, they have a detailed, updated link that provides information on the rate of tobacco use in the state by kids and adults, death rates from smoking, and the financial costs of smoking to the state and state taxpayers.

The Campaign for Tobacco-Free Kids also has a global initiatives page. They point out that while tobacco use has attracted much attention in United States, fewer than 5% of the world's smokers live in the United States. The larger market for the industry is other nations, especially developing nations that have yet to develop tobacco control laws. According to the Campaign, worldwide more than four million people die each year from tobacco use, and if current trends continue, tobacco will kill ten million people a year by 2020. About 70% of those deaths will occur in developing countries. The Campaign discusses how the tobacco industry increases their marketing efforts to addict more smokers around the world, focusing especially on the "untapped markets" of women and children in the developing world.

The Global Initiatives section is a guide to global tobacco issues, including links to fact sheets, tobacco use data, country case studies, and information on the negotiation of an ongoing international treaty on tobacco control. Their intent is to raise awareness of the global tobacco epidemic.

The youth action section of the Campaign's web site is extremely in-novative. This section provides youth with ideas about how to get more involved in tobacco control efforts. Currently, their web site provides in-formation on how kids can get funding to attend the World No Tobacco Day events held throughout the country. They also provide information to kids on how they might attend the Sixth Annual International Anti-Smoking Youth Festival in Athens.

They have information and activities for youth interested in tobacco ad-vocacy at different levels of involvement. They provide basic information and ideas for those just getting started that included the activities or youth advocates in other states. For those who have already been in-volved they discuss what the tobacco industry has been doing recently in the United States and abroad, encourage involvement in a new national youth led collation with the goal of holding the industry accountable for its behavior, and present ways that kids can influence the policy process concerning tobacco control.

The youth action section also points potential youth advocates to anti-tobacco organizations within their own states that are already organized around tobacco control efforts. These organizations are an important source of information and resources. They also provide links to twenty-one different web sites that provide information and resources to youth ready to get involved in tobacco control efforts. The "idea market place" is a section where kids across the country can share youth advocacy ideas concerning tobacco control. The campaign keeps a running gallery of these ideas.

ACTION ON SMOKING AND HEALTH (ASH)

Action on Smoking and Health (ASH) is one of the oldest antismoking organizations in the country. This nonprofit group has been fighting on behalf of nonsmokers and antismoking advocates for over thirty-six years. Currently, much of its work is legal in nature. ASH describes itself as the legal action arm of the nonsmoking community, and has involved itself in many types of tobacco-related lawsuits. It was ASH's petition to the Food and Drug Administration in May 1977 that led to the FDA's in-vestigation of big tobacco.

ASH's mission is to "protect nonsmokers from the clearly-established dangers of secondhand tobacco smoke; reduce the deadly toll of smok-ing by banning the advertising and promotion of cigarettes, and by keep-ing them out of the hands of children; force those who use or profit from tobacco to pay the enormous costs of smoking which are now borne largely by nonsmokers; end all government support of the tobacco in-dustry; and serve as a clearinghouse of information and ideas for all people concerned about smoking, both here and abroad."[4]

The executive director of ASH is John F. Banzhaf III. This well-known antismoking advocate has been compared to Ralph Nader in terms of his passion on the subject of smoking and the tobacco industry. Banzhaf is a professor of public interest law at George Washington University. He makes frequent appearances on news shows, has been a featured speaker at many conferences on tobacco, and has testified numerous times on topics related to smoking.

ASH provides nonsmokers with legal forms and other information to help them protect their rights and to learn more about the problems and costs of smoking to nonsmokers. Included in the legal advice they give is how to join class action suits against the tobacco industry, how to file a complaint if smoking is allowed at work or in your apartment or condo, and even how to bring up the issue of smoking in child custody cases.

ASH has been a major force in the cause of tobacco control for many years. Their first notable contribution occurred in 1966 when Banzhaf filed a complaint with the Federal Communications Commission (FCC), arguing that stations broadcasting cigarette commercials should be required to provide free time for the opposing view. In response, the FCC ruled that the "Fairness Doctrine" applies to cigarette commercials, and that radio and television stations must devote hundreds of millions of dollars worth of broadcast time to antismoking messages. In 1972, the tobacco industry stopped broadcasting cigarette commercials as a result.

In 1971, United Airlines became the first airline to adopt smoking and no-smoking sections on airplanes as a result of a request made by ASH. The same year, ASH published the first major report concerning the health hazards of ambient tobacco smoke, titled *Tobacco and the Nonsmoker: Hazards of Smoke in the Air.* The next year, ASH trustee Betty Carnes led a successful crusade for a comprehensive law protecting nonsmokers in Arizona.

In 1975, an ASH petition sparked an investigation by the National Institutes of Health into the dangers of carbon monoxide in cigarette smoke. Later that year ASH reported to the Third World Conference on Smoking and Health that major antismoking organizations permitted smoking in their own offices and meetings. Also, in response to a petition by ASH, the Federal Trade Commission sued the six major cigarette manufacturers concerning their billboard ads.

In 1977, ASH requests resulted in a ban on smoking aboard mobile lounges at Dulles International Airport and strong warnings about the dangers of smoking while taking birth control pills. In 1981, ASH requested that major air carriers protect nonsmoking passengers from exposure to tobacco smoke while in airports. All the major carriers, except Eastern, eventually complied to the request. Also that year, an ASH-inspired lawsuit brought by the FTC against the six major cigarette manufacturers was settled with the companies agreeing to increase the size of warning notices on cigarette billboards.

In 1985, ASH helped persuade the National Association of Health Commissioners (NAIC) to call for higher health insurance premiums for smokers, a move which eventually resulted in this change by several companies. The same year, ASH held the First World Conference on Nonsmokers' Rights in Washington, D.C.

In 1987, ASH joined the American Public Health Association and the Public Citizen Health Research Group in asking the Occupational Safety and Health Administration (OSHA) to ban smoking in common workplaces. In 1989, ASH helped to defeat a "smokers' rights" bill in Maryland. This bill was widely viewed as the first step in a new tobacco industry strategy to give smokers the right to sue on the basis of alleged discrimination. The same year, ASH followed its legal petition to OSHA with a lawsuit seeking to require the agency to ban or severely limit smoking in all United States workplaces. Finally, ASH aided Congressman Tom Luken in documenting how tobacco companies paid producers to feature cigarettes and smoking in movies.

In 1991, ASH filed a request through the Freedom of Information Act requesting that the Environmental Protection Agency (EPA) release the technical component to its report on environmental tobacco smoke (ETS). The released document claimed that ETS kills more than 50,000 Americans each year. The same year, ASH attorneys provided new information and documents to the National Institute for Occupational Safety and Health (NIOSH). In its final report NIOSH concluded that ETS met the criteria of OSHA for classification as a potential occupational carcinogen.

By 1993, the EPA officially determined that secondhand tobacco smoke is a "Group A carcinogen" which kills an estimated 3,000 Americans each year from lung cancer alone, and creates widespread and very serious risks for children. Also in 1993, as a direct result of ASH pressure, several fast-food restaurant chains either experimented with or completely banned smoking in their outlets. Finally, responding to information provided by ASH, the Clinton Administration recommended a 75-cents-per-pack increase in the cigarette excise tax to help finance health care reform.

In 1995, ASH successfully defended Maryland's Occupational Safety and Health rules banning smoking in the workplace, which were the strongest state smoking regulations in the nation. Also, following a complaint by ASH to the Department of Justice, Philip Morris agreed to remove ads from sports stadiums.

In 1996 a federal investigation into smoking in movies was launched due to ASH complaints to the U.S. Department of Justice. The same year, ASH organized a kids' contest supporting the Food and Drug Administration's announcement that they were investigating whether it could regulate nicotine in tobacco. The result was the largest regulatory filing in American history ever made by children.

The following year, ASH helped to persuade President Clinton to ban smoking in virtually all federal buildings. Also, the Advisory Committee on Tobacco Policy and Public Health, of which ASH is a member, issued a report condemning the proposed Master Settlement Agreement by the states attorneys' general.

In 1998, ASH helped to form "Save Lives, Not Tobacco." This is a coalition of over 300 antismoking, public health and other organizations that played a major role in denying immunity to the tobacco industry. In 1999, ASH received the support of U.S. Surgeon General David Satcher, M.D., the Department of Health and Human Services (DHHS), and the Federal Trade Commission (FTC) for its proposal to require health warnings for cigars. The health warnings went into effect in 2000. It also persuaded several major restaurant chains to review their policies regarding smoking, helped to formulate the legal theories behind the government's suit against the tobacco industry, and discovered a key legal precedent that may result in persuading the U.S. Supreme Court to restore the FDA's jurisdiction over cigarettes.

In 2003, the Framework Convention on Tobacco Control was unanimously adopted at the World Health Assembly in Geneva, Switzerland. ASH was identified as playing a crucial role during the development of this first legally binding tobacco treaty. ASH helped to promote and support a global network for coordinated international campaigning against tobacco. ASH staff was appointed to lead the Framework Convention Alliance, an international coalition of over 200 nongovernmental organizations from over 100 countries. It is effectively carrying out a watchdog function for the Framework Convention on Tobacco Control. Later that same year, ASH helped New York, Massachusetts, and Connecticut pass statewide smoke free workplace legislation.

BADvertising

In 1986 an artist named Bonnie Vierthaler began developing what she calls "honest ads."[5] She changes the appearance of traditional tobacco ads, spoofing them in a way that makes them an antitobacco image. In fact, this is an early example of the graphic and in-your-face counteradvertising that has made the Truth Campaign so successful. One popular example is the image of Joe Camel as the grim reaper. The ad is called the Smooth Reaper. Another ad features Merit cigarettes in a "New Crush-Proof Box." The box is an open coffin with a few cigarettes on the inside poking out. She began displaying these ads in a traveling exhibition to schools, hospitals, libraries, parks, and shopping malls. She developed the BADvertising Institute (a spoof on the Tobacco Institute) as a means to reproduce and distribute the images through posters and slide shows.

In 1987, Vierthaler enlisted a group of doctors, students, and community members in Lancaster, Pennsylvania to mail BADvertising posters to every school in the nation. Hundreds of people worked for two days to send 120,000 posters to 30,000 schools. Within a short time her images were also displayed on billboards, bus cards, national magazines, and professional journals. The images Vierthaler creates are intended to change attitudes and behaviors by graphically exposing the truth behind tobacco advertising; revealing the deceitful tactics used by the tobacco industry; reversing the imagery in tobacco ads to make smoking seem "uncool"; and getting people angry at the tobacco industry for the deception and manipulation used in tobacco advertisements.

Vierthaler developed a "Train the Trainer Seminar" and "BADvertising Workshops" to teach youth tobacco prevention specialists how to employ the same right-brain techniques used in traditional advertising to develop antitobacco messages. Her work has been widely used in tobacco prevention programs throughout the nation, and was more recently on display at the World Conference on Tobacco or Health in Beijing, China.

In the workshops, antitobacco advocates are instructed to create "honest ads" in the following way. First, participants are asked to gather a large number of popular magazines with tobacco advertisements inside. The ads are cut out and the participants are asked to think about who is being targeted in the ad, what is the message, and how it is it being communicated. During the search process for tobacco ads, BADvertisers are asked to look for pictures that communicate a more honest image of what really happens when one uses tobacco. In some cases, these "honest images" come from medical journals. The dishonest ads are spread out in one area, and the honest ads in another. The participants then mix and match honest images with dishonest ads through the message, colors, and size of the ads. The honest ads are cut out and glued on top of the dishonest ads. In the end, the new advertisement should look good and communicate a strong, honest statement about tobacco use.

California's youth tobacco prevention program, Stop Teenage Addiction to Tobacco (STAT), started using BADvertising images in their counteradvertising campaign as far back as 1986. The posters and slide kits continue to have a strong presence in California health education programs. BADvertising went on to impact the antitobacco campaigns in both Massachusetts and Florida. In fact, the Truth Campaign in its beginning stages consulted the BADvertising Institute.

THE FOUNDATION FOR A SMOKEFREE AMERICA

The Foundation for a Smokefree America was founded by Patrick Reynolds in 1989. Patrick is none other than the grandson of the founder of R.J. Reynolds Tobacco Company. His views on smoking began to change after seeing his father, oldest brother, and other relatives die from cigarette-induced emphysema and cancer. This led to an overall concern about the widespread death, disease, and economic hardship caused by tobacco use. Reynolds is a former pack-a-day smoker himself. He quit smoking, divested his R. J. Reynolds stock, and became an antitobacco advocate and spokesman. His unique story and famous name gives him instant credibility, and Reynolds has used this credibility to speak to over one million American youth, distribute educational videos concerning tobacco industry practices, and to advocate for tougher laws concerning tobacco advertising and youth tobacco use. He has testified before Congress as well as several state and municipal legislatures. The Foundation for a Smokefree America has become Reynolds' full-time job and the organization actually runs out of his modest home.

The mission of Smokefree America is to motivate youth to remain tobacco free and empower current smokers to give up the habit. The goals of the foundation are to:

1. establish in-house programs to fight tobacco use at the local, regional, and national levels;
2. educate children through smoking prevention activities, and interactive educational programs;
3. continue offering smokers online cessation resources;
4. enact peer teaching programs designed to help youth defend themselves against the onslaught of peer pressure and tobacco advertising;
5. implement programs to remind physicians to take a more proactive role with their smoking patients, to intervene and ask them to quit; and
6. raise youth awareness of smoking by stars in the movies, and to view point-of-sale tobacco displays as paid advertising.

In Patrick Reynolds' speeches, he tells a story to audiences about his own experiences with tobacco. In one assembly, he began by revealing that his parents divorced when he was three years of age. After six years of not seeing his father at all, he decided to try to contact him to set up a meeting. His dad sent for him, but Patrick's elation was replaced by grief and sadness when he discovered that his father was slowly dying of cigarette-induced emphysema. He went on to educate youth in the audience about the extreme addictiveness of tobacco and his own seventeen-year effort to quit smoking. He emphasized that the choice to smoke is no longer involved or available once addiction sets in, and tobacco addiction can occur within a very short period of time. Next, he attacked tobacco industry advertising by discussing the pervasiveness of cigarette smoking in Hollywood films and by showing slides of antismoking images. In one antismoking image, the beautiful panoramic scenes of Marlboro Country are replaced by an image of office workers standing outside the building in the cold, getting their nicotine fix. The ultra-cool "Joe Camel" is replaced by "Joe Chemo" hooked up to an IV on a hospital bed.

He also discussed the internal memos of tobacco executives that revealed their full intent to advertise directly to kids. A discussion of how advertising impacts the unconscious mind, and conveys the message that tobacco use is acceptable, widespread and the norm follows. Reynolds makes it clear to the audience that three out of four people do not smoke and that most people, including teens, do not like to be around smokers.

He goes on to roleplay with young audience members about how to talk to their parents about tobacco, and how to try to get them to quit. Reynolds points out that he often gets the important question as to why tobacco advertisements are legal if they are so bad. He discusses the First Amendment right to advertise and how that has been interpreted in a way to allow advertising. He also discusses the important role of tobacco industry contributions to legislators who make decisions about tobacco legislation. As a result, according to Reynolds, the United States Congress has done almost nothing to regulate tobacco as a product and tobacco advertising.

Reynolds emphasizes the critical role of storefront and countertop advertising by telling the audience that chew or spit tobacco had almost vanished as a tobacco product by the 1950s and 1960s. As part of the effort to reintroduce chew tobacco to American consumers, United States Smokeless Tobacco Company paid retailers to keep chewing tobacco displays on countertops. This conveys the false message that chew tobacco was a popular and widely accepted product. This type of advertising was extremely effective and by the 1970s and 1980s, chewing tobacco became increasingly more popular among youth. He tells the sad story of Sean Marsee to bring home the point about the deadliness of chewing tobacco. Sean began using chew tobacco as a teen, following the lead of many of his track teammates. He made several attempts to quit without success. By age eighteen he was diagnosed with oral cancer. The cancer was on his tongue and it had to be removed. He was never able to talk again after the surgery. Shortly afterwards the cancer spread to his jaw and neck muscles. Surgeries to remove the cancer left him terribly disfigured. Just before his death at the age of nineteen, he allowed a friend to take a picture of him in an effort to persuade others not to use chew tobacco. Sean put on all of his twenty-eight track ribbons and wrote the simple message to other teens, "Don't dip snuff."

TAR WARS

Like all other youth tobacco prevention programs, Tar Wars was founded by the American Academy of Family Physicians in response to the growing, yet preventable, health crisis caused by tobacco use.[6] This award-winning program targets fourth- and fifth-grade students through an innovative approach to youth tobacco-free education. The program also features a very popular poster contest. The educational portion of the program focuses on the short-term, image-based consequences of tobacco use and how to think critically about tobacco advertising. A follow-up poster contest at the school, state, and national levels is conducted to reinforce the Tar Wars message.

In 1988, Jeffrey Cain, a medical doctor, met Glenna Pember during a meeting of the Coalition for a Tobacco-Free Colorado. Dr. Cain was chief resident of the Mercy Family Medicine Residency Program in Denver and an active member of the local chapter of DOC (Doctors Ought to Care, another popular antitobacco organization). Ms. Pember was a health educator with the Denver Museum of Natural History. The two decided to launch a project to prevent adolescent tobacco addiction and help fifth-grade students understand the tactics employed by tobacco companies to persuade them to use tobacco products.

During its first year in operation, the newly formed Tar Wars program was able to reach over 7,000 children in the Denver area. In its second year, the program was offered to schools throughout Colorado with the support of the Colorado Academy of Family Physicians and St. Anthony Health Corporation.

The American Academy of Family Physicians (AAFP) formally endorsed Tar Wars as a national program in 1993. The endorsement was the critical ingredient in promoting Tar Wars to AAFP members locally, nationally, and internationally. With representation from throughout the United States, a national board was formed the same year to help expand the program's effectiveness, goals, and vision. In 1995, formal, nonprofit status was granted.

In June 1997, the AAFP signed a license agreement with national Tar Wars to operate the program for the next four years. Tar Wars continued to grow and succeed since that time. An estimated 335,000 children were exposed to the program during the 1998–1999 academic year, and more than 400,000 children participated during the 1999–2000 academic year. Tar Wars continues to focus on improving the quality of the program, increase the educational value, and focus on developing an interactive approach to making healthy lifestyle choices.

Since the development of Tar Wars in 1988, the program has been implemented in all fifty states as well as internationally and has been able to reach more than seven million children worldwide, with volunteer presenters delivering the Tar Wars message to students. In June 2000, the AAFP acquired full ownership and operation of the Tar Wars program. Tar Wars staff at the national office, located at AAFP headquarters in Leawood, Kansas provide support to approximately eighty state and regional coordinators who implement Tar Wars in their areas.

Currently, primarily healthcare professionals and educators present the Tar Wars lessons to approximately 500,000 fourth- and fifth-grade students each year. Coalitions composed of healthcare professionals, school personnel, and community members are commonly formed that share the same goal of discouraging tobacco use among children. Tar Wars strongly encourages community members to volunteer their time as a presenter, a coordinator for their state or region, or as a corporate sponsor.

The mission of Tar Wars is to educate students about being tobacco-free, provide them with the tools to make positive decisions regarding their health, and promote personal responsibility for their well being. By utilizing a community-based approach to mobilize family physicians, educators, and other healthcare professionals, Tar Wars can accomplish its mission. To accomplish this mission, Tar Wars has the following goals: (1) educate and motivate students to be tobacco-free; (2) mobilize healthcare professionals to become proactive in their community's health education; and (3) encourage community involvement in support of the Tar Wars program.

Tar Wars Tobacco prevention efforts rely on an integrated, multifactorial approach to achieve the program's goals. The organization views other types of complementary school tobacco-free education programs as not independent from, but rather, interlocking pieces of a puzzle that require repetition and reinforcement to be successful. Any of these pieces alone cannot be the single answer to the problem. Collectively, however, their tobacco-free messages are each delivered in a different manner, thus reaching and appealing to more children than one program alone can affect.

How does Tar Wars know it has been successful in achieving its desired outcomes of increasing students' understanding of the short-term, image-based consequences of tobacco use and the deceptive tactics found in tobacco advertising? Unlike many other organizations, Tar Wars has gone through a rigid program evaluation to test its effectiveness. Publications of the evaluations reveal that it is consistent with the guidelines for youth tobacco prevention programs as outlined by the Centers for Disease Control (CDC). Tar Wars currently addresses five of the seven implementation guidelines recommended by the CDC: instruction, curriculum, training, family involvement, and evaluation. Through coalitions and community-wide efforts, some state Tar Wars programs meet all seven.

Conclusions drawn from a quantitative evaluation of the longitudinal impact of Tar Wars showed sustained improvements in students' knowledge and attitudes related to tobacco use. Students exhibited greater recognition of the health effects, cost, and image distortion associated with tobacco use compared to their peer control group. Findings also indicated positive and sustained effects among students following exposure to the program in comparison to peers who had not heard of the program.

A qualitative evaluation of Tar Wars based on student, teacher, and presenter perspectives found a high level of satisfaction with the program and positive, short-term changes in knowledge of tobacco use. Students indicated an understanding of key program elements, and classroom teachers believed the program was worthwhile and presented unique information. Presenters exhibited enthusiasm for the ease of use and future opportunities for presentation. Constituent chapters involved with Tar Wars were highly satisfied with the program as well.

Evaluations conducted by the Tar Wars national office utilizes pre- and post-test data to measure knowledge and attitude changes regarding tobacco use. More than 63,000 pre- and post-tests were collected for the 2001–2002 academic year. Overall results from this evaluation showed a 90.9% satisfaction rate with the Tar Wars program. Nearly 90% correctly answered the knowledge-based questions, and 98.9% responded that they would not use tobacco in the coming year. State Tar Wars Coordinators are provided with state-specific results for use in their grant applications and other funding opportunities.

Based on AAFP Practice Profile Survey results, the number of family physicians participating in Tar Wars nearly doubled between 1997 and 1999. A survey conducted at the 1999 Annual Conference of the National Association of School Nurses showed that, of all available tobacco prevention programs, Tar Wars was the most recognized.

Who may become a Tar Wars instructor? Family physicians, family practice residents and medical students, school nurses and nurse practitioners, physician assistants, other healthcare providers, dental hygienists, health education professionals, community leaders, and even parents can present Tar Wars. Thus, anyone can become involved and no special training or background is needed to get involved.

Tar Wars is a one-time, one-hour classroom presentation requiring minimal preparation and follow-up. The program can be implemented at any time during a school year, and the scripted lesson plan can easily be incorporated into a classroom curriculum. During the classroom presentation, students engage in a series of six interactive activities designed to increase their knowledge of the short-term effects of tobacco use, help them identify reasons why people use tobacco products, and prompt them to think critically about tobacco advertising. Guest speakers, such as family physicians and other healthcare professionals from the community, can be invited to present Tar Wars.

Tar Wars sponsors an annual poster contest for fourth- and fifth-grade students at both the state and national levels. Judges of the contest look for original art work that incorporates positive messages about being tobacco free. State poster contest winners and their families are eligible to attend the annual Tar Wars National Poster Contest, sponsored by the American Academy of Family Physicians. The poster contest concludes with an awards ceremony, during which the national winners are announced. All state winners in attendance receive a prize packet that includes a Certificate of Appreciation, a ribbon, a color copy of their poster, and a savings bond. Amounts of the savings bonds vary, depending on placement. The First Place Winner receives a Grand Prize trip to Disney World in lieu of a savings bond.

The National Poster Contest is a once-in-a-lifetime opportunity for students to receive recognition for their tobacco-free efforts, voice their opinions about tobacco use to their congressional leaders, participate in tobacco-free workshops, and meet other state winners who share their tobacco-free views.

CONCLUSION

The revelations of tobacco industry practices coupled with the tremendous toll of American tobacco use has led to an escalation of popular antitobacco organizations and programs. These organizations can be fairly small in scope like BADvertising or large and multinational like the American Legacy Foundation and the Campaign for Tobacco-Free Kids. The oldest organization is ASH, which has a long and impressive history of tobacco control activism. Tar Wars and the Foundation for a Smokefree America are more recent organizations that are growing in popularity. One of the greatest challenges in reducing youth tobacco use is changing the popular mindset that smoking is normative, popular, and cool—especially among young people. These programs have developed innovative approaches using classroom presentations, sponsored contests, and the Internet that effectively deliver the opposite message. However, these organizations face tremendous challenges in reaching their goals because they all rely heavily on volunteers and public donations to remain in operation.

7

The Future of Tobacco Control

INTRODUCTION

This book has documented the extraordinary changes in the landscape of
tobacco control, especially over the last decade. Only ten years ago the
tobacco industry had enormous public and political support. They successfully argued in civil courts and the court of public opinion that to the
best of their knowledge, their products posed no serious health risks.
Since that time, the Food and Drug Administration investigation and subsequent revelations by tobacco industry insiders and internal industry
documents have proven that the industry has purposely deceived the
American public for decades concerning the health risks of their products. Among the many salacious findings, what is particularly disturbing
is that the industry has been aware of the health effects of tobacco use
from their own research findings for decades, the industry has specifically manipulated nicotine levels in their products to maintain addiction,
and they have purposely advertised and promoted their products to children in an attempt to find replacement smokers for those who quit or die.
This knowledge has led to successful lawsuits against the industry and
ultimately to $240 billion in settlement funds directed to all fifty states
and the District of Columbia. Several states have developed comprehensive tobacco control programs that have made impressive strides in reducing youth and adult tobacco use. Not only do we have the financial
resources to make substantial reductions in youth tobacco use, we have
the scientific knowledge concerning which interventions are most effective.

Despite these gains, tobacco use remains the single leading cause of
preventable death in the United States. Only a small fraction of the $240
billion in settlement funds are being used toward youth tobacco preven-

tion efforts. In many cases, these funds are being siphoned off to offset state budget problems. Also, while the tobacco industry does not have the public image it once had, it has survived. The industry continues to market their products (much of this marketing makes its way to kids) and expand their markets to populations that have yet to be ravaged by the effects of tobacco.

TOBACCO AND MINORITY POPULATIONS

Cigarette smoking has generally declined among adult African Americans, Asian Americans and Pacific Islanders, and Hispanics. In fact, the prevalence of cigarette smoking decreased substantially among these racial and ethnic groups between 1978 and 1995. Nevertheless, rates of tobacco use are still quite high among American Indians and Alaska Natives, who use tobacco products at the highest rate among all racial and ethnic groups. An additional concern is that since 1978, the prevalence of cigarette smoking has remained remarkably high among American Indian and Alaska Native women of reproductive age. Meanwhile tobacco use has declined considerably among African American, Asian American and Pacific Islander, and Hispanic women of reproductive age.[1]

One of the great successes in tobacco control has been the trend of lower smoking rates among African American adolescents starting in the 1970s and continuing into the 1980s. The rate of cigarette use was more than cut in half among African American male and female high school students. One possible explanation for this trend is that the attractiveness of cigarette smoking has decreased more rapidly among African American high school seniors than white seniors. Also, African American seniors have been more willing to acknowledge the health risks of cigarette smoking, to claim that cigarette smoking is a dirty habit, and to claim that they prefer to date nonsmokers.[2] Additionally, African American parents may be more likely than white parents to express clear antismoking messages according to findings from recent focus groups.[3] Finally, in contrast to white female adolescents, African American female adolescents tend to believe that cigarette smoking has a negative impact on their image.[4]

However, by the mid-1990s the decline in tobacco use among both African American and Hispanic adolescents reversed and tobacco use among these youth is now on the rise. The increase is particularly conspicuous among African American youth, who experienced the greatest decline of cigarette smoking among all racial and ethnic groups in the 1970s. The prevalence of those admitting to previous-month smoking among African American male high school students increased from 14.1% in 1991 to 27.8% in 1995. In addition to the recent increases in tobacco use among African American high school students, the Monitoring the Future surveys found that "previous-month smoking" increased among eighth-grade African American students from 5.3% in 1992 to 9.6% in 1996. Similarly, the prevalence of cigarette smoking increased from 6.6% to 12.2% among African American ninth-graders.[5]

Tobacco use among African Americans may be of particular concern because health data indicate that they may be particularly susceptible to certain tobacco-related diseases. For instance, death rates from lung cancer per 100,000 population among Hispanic men were 25.2, compared to 53.7 for white men, and 80.5 for African American men.[6] Many researchers believe that African American men, especially between the ages of forty to fifty-four, may be especially susceptible to lung carcinogens, perhaps because African American men detoxify carcinogens differently.[7] The rates of other types of tobacco-related cancers are also highest among African American men. Finally, levels of serum cotinine, which is a biomarker of tobacco exposure, are higher among African American smokers in comparison to white smokers who use similar amounts of tobacco products. Thus, the need for tobacco control programs in African American communities is especially great.

However, the development of tobacco control programs in minority communities, especially African American neighborhoods, is problematic because the tobacco industry has provided longtime economic support. The tobacco industry supports African American communities in five ways: (1) direct employment; (2) supporting community agencies and organizations; (3) providing economic support for educational programs; (4) supporting political, civic, and community campaigns; and (5) supporting cultural activities.[8]

Direct Employment

Around the turn of the century, the tobacco industry faced a tremendous demand for tobacco products and took advantage of black labor to increase productivity. By the 1930s, African Americans made up about half of all employees involved in the process of taking tobacco from its leafy state to a finished product.[9] Mechanization in tobacco factories and migration of African Americans to northern cities has resulted in a decline in the number of African Americans in tobacco factories. However, the industry has hired increasing numbers of African Americans to conduct marketing and promotional activities within African American urban neighborhoods. Ad agencies employed by the tobacco industry have also used a large number of African American models and athletes to endorse and promote tobacco products.[10]

Tobacco companies have become extremely important advertising revenue contributors to African American publications. Many racial and ethnic minority community-oriented newspapers and national magazines rely heavily on tobacco industry revenues. In fact, the publisher of *Target*

Market News, an African American consumer marketing publication, suggested, "reducing cigarette ads could deprive the inner city of much needed revenues."[11] The president of a prominent African American ad agency claimed, "if they kill off cigarette and alcohol advertising, black papers may as well stop printing."[12] As recent as 1988, the *National Black Monitor* published a three-part tribute to the tobacco industry, and defended its relationship with the tobacco industry by stating, "black newspapers . . . could not have survived without the past and continuing support from the tobacco industry."[13]

Funding of Community Agencies and Organizations

The tobacco industry has been providing significant financial contributions to various racial and ethnic community organizations. Maxwell and Jacobson[14] describe these relationships as marriages of convenience. These diverse organizations receive a much-needed financial boost and the tobacco industry gains some amount of name recognition and good will. In fact, industry publications suggest that these investments in minority communities are "effective . . . devices to augment minority advertising efforts and throw some water on any hot spots."[15] The list of national minority organizations receiving tobacco industry support include; the Congressional Hispanic Congress, the National Black Caucus of State legislators, the National Urban League, and the United Negro College Fund.[16] The tobacco industry has seemed to especially target African American organizations. For example, Philip Morris alone has contributed to the Leadership Conference on Civil Rights; the National Association of Black Social Workers; the National Black Police Association; 100 Black Men of America, Inc.; the National Coalition of 100 Black Women; the National Conference of Black Lawyers; and National Minority AIDS Council.[17]

Other promotional materials further document the incursion of the tobacco industry in racial and ethnic communities. In 1986 R. J. Reynolds published a booklet titled *A Growing Presence in the Mainstream*.[18] The booklet proudly documents the company's involvement and support of racial and ethnic communities. It contained quotes from Martin Luther King Jr., Booker T. Washington, Maya Angelou, and the *New Testament*. A list of accomplishments were reported in the book that included R. J. Reynolds' record for employing minorities, contracts with African American–owned insurance firms resulting in the provision of life insurance for more than 25% of company employees, R. J. Reynolds advertising in over 200 racial and ethnic magazines and newspapers, and recognition by the United Negro College Fund as the largest single contributor to the fund's schools since 1983.

The tobacco industry also makes their presence felt at the local community level. In African American and Hispanic communities, tobacco companies have been known to sponsor street fairs, jazz festivals, little league baseball teams, soccer teams, symphony orchestras, auto races, and art exhibits.[19]

Support for Education

The tobacco industry has a long legacy of supporting minority educational programs at all levels. Philip Morris has made contributions to a nonprofit organization called Teach for America that trains teachers from predominantly minority and urban areas. Both Philip Morris and R.J. Reynolds donate funds to public school systems in racial and ethnic minority communities.[20]

The tobacco industry has a long legacy of providing funding to historically and predominantly African American colleges and universities. This tradition dates back to the 1890s when Richard Joshua Reynolds, the founder of R.J. Reynolds, donated substantial funds to a historically African American school that eventually became Winston-Salem State University.[21]

As previously mentioned, the tobacco industry has been a strong supporter of the United Negro College Fund (UNCF). The UNCF formed in the 1940s to provide much needed financial support to a small number of African American private colleges and universities. A former president of UNCF defended the acceptance of tobacco industry support with the following rationale: the tobacco industry had been longtime supporters of higher education for African Americans at a time when the cause was not popular; the tobacco companies that donated funds had factories in communities where the colleges and universities were located; and the contributions were too large to reject and were needed for the very survival of these institutions.[22]

In more recent years, the tobacco industry has supported adult literacy programs. Philip Morris joined with the Pew Charitable Trusts and the Philadelphia Mayor's Commission on Literacy to start the Gateway Program. This adult literacy program was to serve as a national model and received at least $3 million from Philip Morris.[23]

Support for Political Campaigns

The tobacco industry has provided financial contributions to racial and ethnic politicians, particularly at the local level, though contributions to white legislators far outweigh contributions to African American politicians. This is especially true at the national level, however, two African

American politicians ranked fourteenth and sixteenth on a list of tobacco industry campaign contributions received from 1985 to 1995.[24]

At the state and local levels of government, the tobacco industry tends to be big donors to all politicians, particularly those in a position to vote on increases in tobacco taxes and public and worksite smoking restrictions. With respect to tobacco excise taxes, state and local politicians also determine how the tax is spent. For example, they determine how much of the tax is spent on tobacco control and education programs. Many of these politicians are racial and ethnic minorities. After Proposition 99 raised cigarette taxes in California by 25 cents a package, political contributions in that state increased from $800,000 in the 1985–1986 election to $7.6 million in the 1991–1992 election.[25]

Support for Cultural Activities

A growing trend has been the support and sponsorship of cultural events by the tobacco industry. While the industry sponsors cultural events for the full spectrum of society, many of these activities are directed at racial and ethnic communities. Cultural events designed to enhance racial and ethnic pride and sponsored by the industry include Hispanic rodeos; American Indian powwows; racial and ethnic minority dance companies; racial and ethnic parades and festivals; Tet festivals; Chinese New Year events; Cinco de Mayo festivities; and activities related to Black History Month, Asian/Pacific American Heritage Month, and Hispanic Heritage Month.[26]

Specific tobacco products have been associated with cultural events through sponsorships and even store promotions. For example, Skoal Bandit smokeless tobacco was involved in Miami's Calle Ocho festival through live radio broadcasts from several 7-Eleven stores in the area.[27] Skoal Bandit also promoted a Hispanic festival in Corpus Christi the same year. More recently, Marlboro and a British brand of cigarettes (555 State Express) sponsored the Little Saigon Tet Festival in Orange County, California. Both brands distributed promotional items at booths at the event.[28]

The tobacco industry has a long history of sponsoring racial and ethnic musical events. African American jazz artists had advertised cigarette products in *Ebony* magazine as early as the 1950s. The industry has continued this practice by heavily sponsoring jazz, rap, blues, rhythm and blues, salsa, gospel, and world music concerts. In many cases, these events are associated with specific tobacco brands. The tobacco industry promotes these concerts on racial and ethnic minority radio stations, in the press, and through magazines that have large minority circulations.[29] At the concerts, the industry frequently promotes their products by naming events after the brands, placing promotional signs on and around stages, and by distributing free cigarettes and other promotional items.

The promotion of tobacco products at cultural events is not yet illegal because there are no federal laws prohibiting these activities, and few states have enacted such laws. The Master Settlement Agreement prohibitions on tobacco promotions concern youth only, and tobacco industry officials would argue these cultural events are not directed toward youth. The tobacco industry is also legally able to advertise and promote their products at sporting events such as auto racing and rodeos.

At first glance, one might ask the question, what's the problem with industry sponsorship of minority businesses, publications, education, and cultural events? The tobacco industry is providing much needed financial resources for a worthwhile purpose, and other sources of funding are largely unavailable. Minority community leaders are generally split in their opinions on the matter. This is because they know that acceptance of tobacco money and support is at least an indirect endorsement of tobacco use. Additionally, as already discussed, tobacco industry advertising in minority publications and tobacco product promotions at cultural events and concerts provide direct access to minority populations—especially young minorities. Industry documents suggest that such investments in minority communities are not meant to simply improve public relations, but to gain access and legitimacy in a market that currently uses tobacco products at a relatively low level. The industry is also aware that many minority communities tend to feel politically powerless and thus are among the least likely to complain about tobacco advertising and promotions to community political leaders.

Advertising and Targeted Tobacco Products in Minority Communities

The effect of tobacco industry advertising on minority populations is not well-known. What is known is that adolescents of all races and ethnicities smoke those cigarette brands that are most heavily advertised. The three most heavily advertised brands are Marlboro, Camel, and Newport, and these are the three most popular brands among adolescent smokers. While these three brands make up 35% of the adult market share, they make up 86% of the adolescent market share. Marlboro is by far the most popular cigarette brand among white youth, but African American youth prefer Newport. Newport is a mentholated cigarette that is heavily advertised in African American communities.[30]

The tobacco industry has blatantly targeted their products to specific racial or ethnic groups. For example, Japan Tobacco Inc. has begun to market its top brand, Mild Seven, in America. This brand is marketed as a cigarette manufactured by Asians for Asians. Full-page advertisements of Mild Seven have appeared in Asian American magazines. Before the billboard ban took effect, Mild Seven billboards appeared in Koreatown and Little Tokyo in Los Angeles.[31]

One of the more infamous examples of target marketing is the cigarette Uptown. R. J. Reynolds developed this cigarette in the 1980s to compete with Lorillard's Newport brand. R. J. Reynolds apparently didn't even attempt to disguise their intentions. The company stated that African Americans were the primary market for the new brand, stating, "We expect Uptown to appeal most strongly to black smokers. Our research led us to believe that Uptown's blend . . . will be an appealing alternative to smokers currently choosing a competitive brand. We have developed a product based on research that shows that a significant percentage of black smokers are currently choosing a brand that offers a lighter menthol flavor than our major menthol brand, Salem."[32] Despite the claim that Uptown would have a "lighter" menthol taste, the brand yielded tar levels at 19 milligrams per cigarette. This was a higher tar level than any other R. J. Reynolds brand other than unfiltered Camel cigarettes. The marketing plan for Uptown cigarettes was designed to use media effective at reaching African Americans, including billboards, transit advertising, bus shelters, point-of-purchase signs, and advertisements in racial and ethnic newspapers and magazines.

Also, R. J. Reynolds planned to introduce Uptown in February 1990 to coincide with Black History Month activities. R. J. Reynolds sponsored many of these activities and the company intended to distribute free samples of Uptown at these events. They selected Philadelphia as a test site for a number of reasons. Philadelphia had a high percentage of African Americans in 1990 (40%), a number of newspapers that served the African American population of the city, and African Americans tended to live in distinct neighborhoods that could easily be reached through billboards and transit advertising.[33]

R. J. Reynolds completely underestimated the resistance to the Uptown campaign. A coalition of community members, civic and religious leaders, healthcare professionals, and even the Secretary of Health and Human Services at the time, Louis Sullivan, quickly formed to oppose the introduction of Uptown. The negative national publicity led to R. J. Reynolds canceling their plans to test-market Uptown in Philadelphia, and they ultimately decided to withdraw the brand from the market entirely. Only five years later, R. J. Reynolds attempted to introduce a brand of cigarettes called "X." This appears to be a fairly obvious appeal to African Americans because of the red, green, and black packaging and the association with the civil rights leader Malcolm X. Many youth at the time wore t-shirts and hats with the symbol X after the film *Malcolm X* was released. This time R. J. Reynolds denied any attempts to market to

African Americans. Despite their claims, opposition to the brand quickly developed and R. J. Reynolds withdrew the brand from the market.[34]

TOBACCO CONTROL AS A GLOBAL MOVEMENT

The death toll in America from tobacco use is approximately 400,000 people per year. But the global death toll is about five million people per year. Furthermore, tobacco use among developing nations has increased dramatically in recent years. The World Health Organization projects the number of tobacco-related deaths will double within two decades if current trends are not reversed, and will actually become the leading cause of death globally. Approximately 70% of these deaths will occur in developing nations.[35]

In 1999, World Health Organization Director, Gro Harlem Brundtland proposed the Framework Convention on Tobacco Control. This was the first ever attempt at a world public health treaty. Over 190 nations were involved in the negotiation process of the treaty and it enjoyed popular support around the world. In fact, the only real source of opposition to the treaty was the United States government. The United States used its influence to delay treaty negotiations and opposed several treaty provisions. The Secretary of Health and Human Services, Tommy Thompson, finally announced that the U.S. government would drop their efforts to renegotiate the terms of the treaty in May 2003. This was the last obstacle to adoption of the treaty.[36]

Provisions of the treaty include:

1. a total ban on tobacco advertising, promotion, and sponsorship;
2. health warning labels that cover 30% of the package (but, ideally the label should cover 50% of the package);
3. elimination of deceptive terms on packages such as "light," "low tar," and "mild";
4. a total ban on smoking in all public places, including workplaces;
5. establishment of guidelines concerning regulating the content of tobacco products;
6. disclosure of all ingredients in tobacco products; and
7. a commitment to search for sources of funding for tobacco control efforts.[37]

The treaty has had an immediate impact throughout the world. India is the most populated nation to ban all forms of direct and indirect tobacco industry advertising and has prohibited smoking in public places. At least twelve other nations have enacted total bans on tobacco advertising and promotions. The Canadian government has the authority to regulate tobacco products by prescribing the amounts of nicotine that can go into the cigarette. They can also specify that other ingredients be left out, as well as testing methods for tobacco products. In Brazil, the government requires that all tobacco companies register their products by brand name. They have to disclose the types of additives used and compounds present in the mainstream and sidestream smoke of cigarettes. In the European Union, all tobacco companies must list all ingredients on all tobacco brands, explain the reason for their inclusion, as well as the function of each additive. All of that information is made public to European consumers. None of these provisions exist within the United States.[38]

TOBACCO AND THE INTERNET

Reducing youth access to tobacco products is one of the primary goals of any youth tobacco prevention program. Legislation exists in every state that youth under age 18 cannot purchase tobacco products, and enforcement mechanisms are in place in many states in an attempt to deter retailers from selling tobacco to minors. However, to the extent these measures are successful, obtaining cigarettes illegally may actually be easier now than ever. Go to any large search engine web site such as Google or Yahoo! and type the words "cigarettes" and "online," or "tobacco" and "online," or "cheap cigarettes." The search results will yield hundreds of web sites selling cigarettes and other tobacco products. There were only a handful of such web sites in the late 1990s, but there are over 400 such sites selling tobacco products at this time. In fact, Internet tobacco sales are growing so rapidly, they will make up 14% of the total U.S. market by 2005.[39]

There are at least two looming problems with Internet tobacco sales. First of all, many of these web sites do not conduct adequate age verification checks. One study found that kids as young as eleven were successful more than 90% of time in purchasing cigarettes over the Internet. Age verification at the time of purchase was usually limited to checking off a box that the buyer was old enough to buy cigarettes, and more than 86% of the cigarettes purchased were either left at the recipients' door or accepted by the youth purchasers without any age verification.[40] Another study tested the effectiveness of Internet filtering programs in blocking youth access to Internet tobacco venders. They examined twenty-eight programs available for blocking access and selected four that included tobacco as a category for blocking: Bess/N2H2, Cyber Patrol, CYBERsitter, and iWay Patrol. They tested these filtering programs on 316 pro-tobacco web sites, including 154 that sold tobacco products. The only program to block more than half of the web sites was Bess/N2H2, which blocked 65% of the web sites. Also, the filtering programs tended not to agree on which web sites to block. The authors concluded that filtering programs are not very effective in blocking youth access to online tobacco messages and products.[41]

The second major problem with Internet tobacco sales is that they offer smokers a way to avoid paying state tobacco and sales taxes, thereby keeping cigarette prices down and smoking levels up. Three-quarters of all Internet tobacco sellers explicitly say that they will not report cigarette sales to tax collection officials, thus violating federal law, according to the U.S. General Accounting Office. States lose as much as $200 million annually in uncollected tobacco taxes through Internet sales, according to a study by Forrester Research Inc.[42]

The Senate Judiciary Committee recently approved legislation, the Prevent All Cigarette Trafficking Act, known as the PACT Act, introduced by Senators Orrin Hatch and Herb Kohl. The PACT Act faced a major obstacle. Native American Indian tribes make up a large percentage of Internet tobacco venders and believe that the bill infringes on tribal sovereignty rights. After the PACT Act passed the Senate Judiciary Committee, representatives of Native American Tribes raised concerns regarding the bill's impact on tribal sovereignty rights. These concerns prompted substantial additional changes to the PACT Act. After these changes, and some others, were made, the PACT Act passed the full Senate by unanimous consent on December 9, 2003. This bill addresses the growing problem of tobacco excise tax evasion caused by Internet sales of tobacco products by:

1. requiring that Internet sellers ensure that all state excise taxes have been paid on any cigarettes or smokeless tobacco they send into a state, with all required tax stamps affixed;
2. requiring all Internet sellers to register with those states to which they are making sales and to comply with all state tobacco tax laws as if the Internet seller were based in the state;
3. allowing states to block the delivery of cigarettes and smokeless tobacco sold by Internet sellers that fail to register with the state or otherwise fail to comply with federal or state law; and
4. giving state officials the right to bring elusive Internet sellers into federal court and to collect comprehensive injunctive and equitable relief, including monetary damages.[43]

The only real problem with this bill is that it does not directly address the problem of age verification of tobacco purchases. Thus, more recently, Representative Meehan introduced House Bill 3047 that would protect kids by requiring effective age verification both at the point of purchase and the point of delivery for Internet tobacco sales.[44] However, most experts agree that enforcing these new laws will prove to be a challenge.

THE CHANGING TOBACCO INDUSTRY

In the Waxman Congressional hearings of 1994, seven CEOs of the largest tobacco companies in America testified on national television and under oath that they did not believe that smoking caused cancer. Tobacco industry documents reveal that they not only knew of tobacco's cancer causing properties, but they had this knowledge from their own sponsored research as early as the 1960s and did nothing about it. The damage to the industry's credibility cannot be overstated, and the industry has mounted an enormous public relations campaign meant to improve their image. If you go to the Philip Morris web site, (http://www.philipmorrisusa.com) you will not find tobacco advertisements or promotions. Instead, you find evidence of a very sophisticated public relations campaign intended to transform the image of the company.

For instance, in their mission and values section, they discuss developing new technologies to reduce the harm of smoking, communicating openly about the health effects of their products, and marketing responsibly only to adults. They now list all of the ingredients in each of their tobacco products including the tar and nicotine yields. Philip Morris also states that they agree with the overwhelming medical and scientific evidence that cigarette smoking causes lung cancer, heart disease, emphysema, and other serious diseases. They provide links to former foes such as the U.S. Centers for Disease Control, the American Cancer Society, and the U.S. Surgeon General Reports. They admit to the addictive nature of smoking and the difficulty in quitting. They link to resources on getting help to quit. Philip Morris points out that descriptors such as mild, light, and ultra light do not necessarily equate to low tar or low nicotine levels and there is no such thing as a safe cigarette. They actually cite public health officials' statements concerning the health effects of secondhand smoke and state that they support regulating smoking in public places. The company has developed a Youth Smoking Prevention department within their organization and distributes information to kids concerning peer pressure and to parents concerning how to keep their kids from smoking. Perhaps the most striking turnaround is that Philip Morris now publicly supports the regulation of tobacco products by the Food and Drug Administration.

The change in tone and position is dramatic, striking, and encouraging. Why have Philip Morris and other tobacco companies changed their positions on all of these issues? Because they have little choice in the matter. The truth is

1. they deceived the American public into purchasing a product that they knew was deadly;

2. conducted their own experiments demonstrating the addictive nature of smoking and its cancer-causing potential while hiding this information from the public;

3. manipulated nicotine levels in their products to increase their addictive potential;

4. developed technology to make cigarettes much safer and then hid this knowledge to protect themselves from liability; and

5. marketed their deadly products to kids to obtain the necessary replacement smokers to keep their revenues coming in.

The industry has not suddenly developed a sense of ethics and a corporate conscious. They're trying to survive. What other product in America is allowed to exist where we know tremendous harm will occur to the consumer if used as intended? In Dr. David Kessler's book, *A Question of Intent*, a tobacco company executive admitted confidentially that they knew that the FDA would attempt to regulate tobacco at some time. They were surprised that it took as long as it did (and it has yet to occur). The industry knows that they are living in a house of cards. It's all about making as much money as possible, for as long as possible, before the house of cards collapse.

THE FUTURE

The Supreme Court made the decision in 2000 that only the United States Congress can grant the Food and Drug Administration the authority to regulate tobacco products.[45] Previous proposed congressional bills failed despite overwhelming public support for FDA regulation. In May 20, 2004, Senators Mike Dewine (Republican from Ohio) and Edward Kennedy (Democrat from Massachusetts) introduced bipartisan legislation that would provide the FDA authority to regulate cigarettes and other tobacco products.[46] Representatives Henry Waxman (Democrat from California) and Tom Davis (Republican from Virginia) introduced a companion bill in the House of Representatives. The bill would provide limited regulatory authority to the FDA. For instance, the FDA could not ban nicotine or the sale of cigarettes to adults, require a prescription for nicotine, or regulate tobacco farmers. If the bill were passed, the FDA would have the authority to set limits on the concentration of nicotine and other harmful ingredients and smoke constituents in tobacco products. In this way, the harm from smoking could be greatly reduced and would help to wean American smokers off cigarettes over time. The FDA would have to consider whether reducing nicotine levels would create a black market for cigarettes. If it did, the FDA would also have the authority to combat counterfeit, contraband, and other illicit tobacco products. The bill would also require new and larger health warnings on tobacco packaging. Finally, it would allow the FDA to regulate the time, place, and manner of cigarette advertising and promotion.

However, at the time of this writing, this bill is currently in danger. The only way that legislators who support FDA regulation of tobacco could gain the necessary support of their colleagues was to couple the FDA bill with another bill to buyout tobacco farmers. This bill would end the subsidy system that has been in place that compensates tobacco farmers for limiting the amount of tobacco that they grow, and pay tobacco farmers a one-time $10 billion payout. In the Kennedy-DeWine Bill, the tobacco industry would pay for the buyout. However, the House Ways and Means Committee Chairman, Bill Thomas (Republican from California) added the tobacco buyout to an unrelated tax bill through an amendment. In this version, U.S. taxpayers pay for the buyout. Kennedy, DeWine, Waxman, and Davis believe that the FDA regulation bill cannot pass on its own.

Food and Drug Administration authority to regulate tobacco is a critical step to reduce the deadly toll of tobacco use. The United States has no national tobacco control and prevention program, despite the fact that it is the single most preventable cause of American deaths and costs tax payers about $50 billion per year in lost productivity and healthcare costs. Many tobacco control activists believe that the $27.7 million in political contributions to federal candidates, national political parties, and nonparty political action committees since 1997 have much to do with the inactivity of the federal government.[47]

Virtually all state governments have some type of tobacco control legislation, but the strength of these laws varies considerably. Also, in many cases there is either no designated enforcement authority or funding for enforcement. Virtually every state has a tobacco prevention program established from the Master Settlement Agreement with the tobacco industry. However, only seventeen states have contributed a significant amount of their settlement funds to provide tobacco education, prevention, and cessation services. Almost 99% of the $246 billion settlement went into each state's general fund, without any requirement that the money be used for tobacco education and prevention. This will certainly go down as one of the greatest wasted opportunities in the history of public health, if not reversed.

Local levels of government are where the tobacco wars are being waged and won. Hundreds of new smoke free ordinances are being passed each year. The *Journal of the American Medical Association* published a very revealing discussion with a former Tobacco Institute lobbyist who was dying of throat cancer. Victor Crawford stated:

> We could never win at the local level. The reason is, all the health advocates, the ones that unfortunately I used to call health Nazis, they're all local

activists who run the little political organizations. They may live next door to the mayor, or the city councilman may be his or her brother-in-law, and they say, who's this big-time lobbyist coming here to tell us what to do? When they've got their friends and neighbors out there in the audience who want this bill, we get killed. So the Tobacco Institute and tobacco companies' first priority has always been to preempt the field, preferably to put it all on the federal level, but if they can't do that, at least on the state level, because the health advocates can't compete with me on a state level. They never could. On the local level, I couldn't compete with them. And that's why all your antismoking legislation without exception has started at the local level, all across the country. The Congress itself has done virtually nothing. Even the states are just starting to act. But back in the 1980s it was the little counties, municipalities, townships, where your antismoking legislation was coming from. And that's what was driving the tobacco guys crazy, because they had to pay people like me to run around and fight the damn things. And every time I'd put out a fire one place, another one would pop up somewhere else.[48]

Tobacco control legislation is critical to reversing the deadly toll of tobacco use, but its effectiveness will be limited if we are not successful in also reversing the way people, especially young people, view tobacco. The tobacco industry has been very successful in depicting smoking as normative, widespread, socially acceptable, and a matter of individual choice. But once addiction sets in, the choice is gone. Despite all that is known about the dangers of tobacco, 3,000 U.S. teens continue to become addicted each day and over 1,000 of those teens will later die from the habit.

Resources for Parents, Teachers, and Students

Action on Smoking and Health (ASH)
http://ash.org/
This is an antismoking organization that focuses on legal and other actions to fight smoking and to protect the rights of nonsmokers. The site contains a wealth of information regarding tobacco, including health, legislation, current news, and quitting guidelines.

The Advocacy Institute
http://www.advocacy.org/
The Advocacy Institute is a U.S. based global organization dedicated to strengthening the capacity of political, social, and economic justice advocates to influence and change public policy. The Institute has a Tobacco Control Project, which provides strategic guidance and on counseling to tobacco control advocates. The site has links to their various issues, including public health.

American Cancer Society
http://www.cancer.org/docroot/home/index.asp
A voluntary health agency, the American Cancer Society is dedicated to eliminating cancer as a major health problem by preventing cancer, saving lives, and diminishing suffering from cancer through research, education, advocacy, and service. The site offers an array of information from statistics and tobacco to treatment options, prevention, and alternatives.

American Heart Association
http://www.americanheart.org
The American Heart Association is a nonprofit organization working to fight heart disease and stroke. The site contains links to symptoms and

warning signs, family health, scientific and professional resources, and a reference guide.

American Legacy Foundation
http://www.americanlegacy.org/americanlegacy/skins/alf/home.aspx
Established as a result of the Master Settlement Agreement with the tobacco industry, the American Legacy Foundation's purposes are to conduct a comprehensive, coordinated program of public education and study, and to fund cutting-edge research and marketing programs that tell the truth about tobacco use. The site contains an overview of the Foundation, an information center, links to research, education and programs, and ways to speak out against tobacco. They also sponsor the site "Truth," which offers the unvarnished truth about big tobacco companies and the effects of smoking on the human body.

American Lung Association
http://www.lungusa.org
This organization works against lung disease, with special emphasis on asthma, tobacco control, and environmental health. The site provides links to data and statistics on lung related diseases. The site also has information in Spanish.

Americans for Nonsmokers' Rights (ANR)
http://www.no-smoke.org/
ANR is a lobbying organization dedicated to nonsmokers' rights. The ANR site contains information on the tobacco industry, campaigns to reduce/eliminate smoking, advocacy, and secondhand smoke facts.

BADvertising Institute
http://www.badvertising.org/
The BADvertising Institute's mission is to immunize kids against tobacco, inspire smokers to quit, and equip advocates and educators with the tools for doing the same. They do this by powerful counteradvertising messages in the form of exhibits, posters and billboards, slide presentations, workshops, and their web site.

Campaign for Tobacco-Free Kids
http://www.tobaccofreekids.org/
The campaign fights to free America's youth from tobacco and to create a healthier environment. The site contains information on research, advertising campaigns, recent Supreme Court Decisions, programs for action, and special reports.

Community Intervention: Tools to Help Youth

http://www.communityintervention.org/

Community Intervention conducts training and publishes information concerning youth advocacy in a number of different areas, including teenage tobacco prevention and cessation. Community Intervention works with many types of professionals including, teachers, counselors, and social workers in all fifty states to be more effective with children ages 5–18. Community Intervention has conducted more than 1,000 seminars and publishes a catalog, *Tools to Help Youth*, which contains hundreds of books, games, posters, videos, and other resources related to the well-being of children.

Economics of Tobacco Control

http://www1.worldbank.org/tobacco/

This site from the World Bank provides information, analyses, reviews, and links to help researchers and policy makers, and to assist governments to choose and implement effective tobacco control measures. The site contains links to country data, myths and facts, additional links, and tobacco videos.

Health Policy Coach

http://www.healthpolicycoach.org

Health Policy Coach is part of the California Center for Health Improvement (CCHI). The Coach is a resource for people seeking to improve community health through prevention-focused policy change. The site provides peer-reviewed, searchable health policies, and "how-to" information and coaching resources of individuals and groups interested in effecting policy change in their communities. Policies include such topics as childcare, tobacco, firearms, environmental toxins, illegal drugs, alcohol, and infectious disease.

Institute for Global Tobacco Control

http://www.jhsph.edu/IGTC

The mission for the Institute is to prevent death and disease from tobacco use around the world through research, education, and policy development. Their site contains news and information, ongoing research projects, and a chapter on environmental tobacco smoke.

Legacy Tobacco Documents Library

http://legacy.library.ucsf.edu/

The Legacy Tobacco Documents Library (LTDL) contains seven million documents related to advertising, manufacturing, marketing, sales, and scientific research of tobacco products. Visitors can search, view, and download these documents from this web site.

March of Dimes (MoD)
http://www.marchofdimes.com/
The mission of the March of Dimes is to improve the health of babies by preventing birth defects and infant mortality. The March of Dimes web site contains information on programs of research, community services, education, and advocacy, including materials about the effects of smoking on pregnancy. There are also resources in Spanish.

National Center on Addiction and Substance Abuse (CASA)
http://www.casacolumbia.org/
CASA's mission is to (1) inform Americans of the economic and social costs of substance abuse and its impact on their lives; (2) to assess what works in prevention, treatment, and law enforcement; (3) to encourage every individual and institution to take responsibility to combat substance abuse and addiction; (4) to provide those on the frontlines with the tools they need to succeed; and (5) to remove the stigma of abuse and replace shame and despair with hope. The CASA web site contains information and links to publications, news, research and programs, family and youth information, and additional resources and links.

National Tobacco Control Program (NTCP) State Exchange
http://www.cdc.gov/tobacco/ntcp_exchange/index.htm
This site, from the Centers for Disease Control and Prevention, allows users to access and share information on state tobacco control programs, training, documents, and activities. There is a calendar of events, state information, and links for states to register to exchange documents and report control activities.

SmokeFree Educational Services, Inc.
http://www.smokefree.net/
The SmokeFree web site facilitates letter writing between smoke free advocates and key decision makers. Their site offers links to letters, people, smoke free events, other web pages, a discussion group, and available smoke free documents.

Smoke-Free Kids and Soccer
http://www.cdc.gov/tobacco/sports_initiatives_splash.htm
A collaborative efforts between the DHHS (including the National Cancer Institute and the Centers for Disease Control and Prevention), the President's Council on Physical Fitness and Sports, and the United States Women's National Soccer Team, Smoke-Free Kids and Soccer uses the women's team members to encourage adolescent girls to participate in soccer to maintain physical fitness and resist the pressures to smoke. The

web site contains information about the program, including banners, posters, and additional links.

SmokeLess States National Tobacco Policy Initiative
http://www.ama-assn.org/ama/pub/category/3229.html
The SmokeLess States National Tobacco Policy Initiative is a private sector effort that supports activities of statewide coalitions working to improve the tobacco policy environment with the goal of reducing tobacco use. The Initiative is a collaborative effort among the Robert Wood Johnson Foundation (the nation's largest philanthropy devoted exclusively to health and healthcare), the American Medical Association (the nation's largest physician group), and statewide coalitions receiving the grants.

Society for Research on Nicotine and Tobacco (SRNT)
http://www.srnt.org/
The Society's mission is to stimulate the generation of new knowledge concerning nicotine in all its manifestations, from molecular to societal. They offer a newsletter, message board, abstracts to their journal (*Nicotine and Tobacco Research*), a training directory, publications, event information, and other resources. The information is also available in German and French.

STAT: Stop Teenage Addiction to Tobacco
http://www.stat.org
Devoted to stopping childhood and teenage addiction to tobacco, the STAT site contains links to resources that will help end underage smoking.

Tar Wars
http://www.tarwars.org/
This program, from the American Academy of Family Practitioners targets fourth- and fifth-grade students for the tobacco-free education program. The site provides information about the program and how to become a participant in the program.

Tobacco Control Research Branch (TCRB) at the National Cancer Institute
http://dccps.nci.nih.gov/tcrb/
The TCRB plans, develops, implements, and maintains a broad spectrum of basic and applied research in the behavioral, social, and population sciences on the prevention and cessation of tobacco use among both youth and adults.

Tobacco Control Resource Center, Inc.

http://www.tobacco.neu.edu/

This site contains valuable legal resources on tobacco legislation and lawsuits, as well as links to other sites and tobacco resources.

Tobacco Etiology Research Network (TERN)

http://www.tern.org/

TERN promotes health by reducing the harm caused by substance abuse, especially tobacco. The Network is a collaborative and intense effort for scientists and researchers to work on tobacco and other substance abuse issues in a transdisciplinary way.

Tobacco Information and Prevention Source

http://www.cdc.gov/tobacco/

This web site from the Centers for Disease Control and Prevention contains a wealth of tobacco related information, prevention, statistics, and includes tobacco industry documents.

Tobacco.org

http://www.tobacco.org/

This site contains information about tobacco, including daily news and quotes. It is a great resource for keeping up on the daily events of tobacco control. It also contains resources for other Internet sites, quitting smoking, timelines, and an activism guide.

Truth Campaign

http://www.thetruth.com

Funded by the American Legacy Foundation, the "Truth" site offers an unvarnished and graphic look at the effects of smoking on the human body, the ways that big tobacco influence public perceptions, and ways to make antismoking/antitobacco attitudes known. Their main goal is to alert everyone to the lies and hidden practices of the cigarette companies, while giving people the tools to have a voice in changing that. The Truth Campaign is dedicated to educating people to understand the truth about nicotine addiction, how cigarettes and smokeless tobacco products are sold, and what these products can really do to the body.

Notes

Chapter 1

1. U.S. Dept. of Health and Human Services (hereafter USDHHS), *Reducing the Health Consequences of Smoking*.

2. Chinnock, "The Family Courts' Mandatory Duty," 801–820.

3. USDHHS, *Reducing the Health Consequences of Smoking*.

4. American Psychiatric Association (hereafter APA), *Diagnostic and Statistical Manual of Mental Disorders*.

5. USDHHS, *The Health Benefits of Cessation*; Pierce, et al., "Trends in Cigarette Smoking in the United States," 61–65.

6. West and Evans, "Lifestyle Changes in Long Term Survivors," 103–109.

7. Henningfield, Clayton, and Pollin, "Involvement of Tobacco in Alcoholism," 279–292.

8. Giovino, et al., "Surveillance for Selected Tobacco-Use Behaviors," 1–43.

9. Ibid., 6–7.

10. Ibid.

11. Ibid., 11 and 19.

12. Ibid., 19.

13. Ibid., 34.

14. Ibid., 33.

15. Centers for Disease Control and Prevention (CDC), "Trends in Cigarette Smoking Among High School Students," 409–412.

16. Ibid., 409.

17. Allen, et al., "Tobacco Use Among Middle and High School Students," 1096–1098.

18. Ibid.

19. USDHHS, *Reducing the Health Consequences of Smoking*.

20. Public Health Service (PHS), *Smoking and Health: Report of the Advisory Committee*.

21. Leventhal, "Experimental Studies Of Anti-Smoking Communications,"

95–121; Bandura, *Social Learning Theory*; McAlister, Perry, and Maccoby, "Adolescent Smoking: Onset and Prevention," 650–658.

22. Conrad, Flay, and Hill, "Why Children Start Smoking Cigarettes," 1711–1724.
23. Flay, "Youth Tobacco Use," 365–384.
24. Perry, Murray, and Klepp, "Predictors of Adolescent Smoking," 41.
25. McNeill, "The Development of Dependence," 589–592.
26. Evans, et al., "Deterring the Onset of Smoking in Children," 126–135.
27. Conrad, Flay, and Hill, "Why Children Start Smoking Cigarettes," 1711–1724.
28. Semmer, et al., "Psychosocial Predictors of Adolescent Smoking," 35–105.
29. Perry, Kelder, and Komro, "The Social World of Adolescents," 73–96.
30. Alexander, et al., "Cigarette Smoking and Drug Use in School Children," 59–66.
31. Kandel and Logan, "Patterns of Drug Use," 660–666.
32. Konopka, "Adolescence, Concept of, and Requirements."
33. Sussman, et al., "Psychosocial Predictors," 11S–16S.
34. Fiore, et al., "Trends in Cigarette Smoking in the United States," 49–55.
35. Clayton, "Gender Differences," 115–120.
36. Gritz and Crane, "Use of Diet Pills and Amphetamines," 33–35.
37. American School Health Association, et al., *The National Adolescent Health Survey*.
38. CDC, "Accessibility of Cigarettes to Youths," 485–488.
39. Semmer, et al., "Adolescent Smoking from a Functional Perspective," 387–401.
40. Lawrence and Robinson, "Self-Efficacy as a Predictor," 367–382.
41. Chassin, et al., "Changes in Peer and Parent Influence," 327–334; see also Fiore, et al., "Trends in Cigarette and Smoking in the United States."
42. Botvin, "Correlates and Predictors of Smoking," 97–103; Mittelmark, et al., "Predicting Experimentation," 206–208.
43. Conrad, Flay, and Hill, "Why Children Start Smoking Cigarettes."
44. Chassin, et al., "Predicting the Onset of Cigarette Smoking," 224–243.
45. Swan, Cresser, and Murray, "When and Why Children First Start to Smoke," 323–330.
46. Hunter, et al., "Psychosocial Influences on Cigarette Smoking," 17S–25S.
47. Flay, et al., "Cigarette Smoking," 132–183.
48. O'Connell, et al., "Cigarette Smoking and Drug Use," 223–231; Ogawa, et al., "Smoking among Junior High School Students," 814–820.
49. Hahn, et al., "Adolescents' First and Most Recent Use Situations," 439–448.
50. Newcomb, McCarthy, and Bentler, "Cigarette Smoking, Academic Lifestyle," 251–281.
51. Gerber and Newman, "Predicting Future Smoking," 191–201.
52. Leventhal, Fleming, and Glynn, "A Cognitive-Developmental Approach to Smoking Intervention," 79–109.
53. Collins, et al., "Psychosocial Predictors," 554–573.
54. Klepp, Halper, and Perry, "The Efficacy of Peer Leaders," 407–411.
55. Hahn, et al., "Adolescents' First and Most Recent Use Situations."
56. Chassin, et al., "Changes in Peer and Parent Influence."
57. Hunter, et al., "Psychosocial Influences on Cigarette Smoking."
58. Mittelmark, et al., "Predicting Experimentation."

59. Swan, Cresser, and Murray, "When and Why Children First Start to Smoke."

60. Borland and Rudolph, "Relative Effects of Low Socioeconomic Status," 27–30.

61. Brunswick and Messeri, "Origins of Cigarette Smoking," 353–370; Sussman, et al., "Psychosocial Predictors."

62. Ahlgren et al., "Antecedents of Smoking," 325–340.

63. Conrad, Flay, and Hill, "Why Children Start Smoking Cigarettes."

64. Newcomb, McCarthy, and Bentler, "Cigarette Smoking, Academic Lifestyle."

65. Fleming, et al., "Role of Cigarettes," 261–272; Newcomb and Bentler, "Frequency and Sequence of Drug Use," 101–118.

66. Brunswick and Messeri, "Causal Factors," 35–52.

67. Leventhal, Fleming, and Glynn, "A Cognitive-Developmental Approach to Smoking Intervention"; Collins, et al., "Psychosocial Predictors"; Sussman, et al., "Psychosocial Predictors."

68. Conrad, Flay, and Hill, "Why Children Start Smoking Cigarettes."

69. Swan, Cresser, and Murray, "When and Why Children First Start to Smoke."

70. McCaul, et al., "Predicting Adolescent Smoking," 342–346.

71. Hahn, et al., "Adolescents' First and Most Recent Use Situations."

72. Sussman, et al., "Psychosocial Predictors."

73. Lawrence and Robinson, "Self-Efficacy as a Predictor."

74. Conrad, Flay, and Hill, "Why Children Start Smoking Cigarettes."

75. Conrad, Flay, and Hill, "Why Children Start Smoking Cigarettes"; Collins, et al., "Psychosocial Predictors."

76. McNeill, et al., "Prospective Study," 72–78.

77. Perry, Murray, and Klepp, "Predictors of Adolescent Smoking."

78. Castro, et al., "A Multivariate Model," 273–289.

79. Hahn, et al., "Adolescents' First and Most Recent Use Situations."

80. Chassin, et al., "Predicting the Onset of Cigarette Smoking."

81. Young and Werch, "Relationship Between Self-Esteem and Substance Use," 31–44.

82. Conrad, Flay, and Hill, "Why Children Start Smoking Cigarettes."

83. Sussman, et al., "Psychosocial Predictors."

84. Chassin, Presson, and Sherman, "Social Psychological Contributions," 133–151.

85. De Vries, Kok, and Dijkstra, "Self-Efficacy as a Determinant of the Onset of Smoking," 209–222.

86. Conrad, Flay, and Hill, "Why Children Start Smoking Cigarettes."

87. Covey and Tam, "Depressive Mood," 1330–1333.

88. Newcomb, McCarthy, and Bentler, "Cigarette Smoking, Academic Lifestyle."

Chapter 2

1. CDC, "Cigarette Advertising," 261–265.

2. Jeffrey Wigand, former Brown & Williamson Executive, Retrieved from American Lung Association of Washington, http://www.alaw.org/tobacco _control, January 2004.

3. USDHHS, *Preventing Tobacco Use Among Young People.*

4. CDC, "Cigarette Advertising"; Smee, "Effect of Tobacco Advertising"; Pierce and Gilpin, "A Historical Analysis," 500–508.

5. P. G. Hollie, "Segmented Cigarette Market," *New York Times,* March 23, 1985, Business Day Section; Warner, et al., "Promotion of Tobacco Products," 367–392; Ernster, "Women and Smoking."

6. CDC, "Smoking Cessation," 504–507; CDC, "Smoking-Attributable Mortality," 444–451.

7. Wigand, http://www.alaw.org/tobacco_control.

8. Evans, et al., "Influence of Tobacco Marketing," 1538–1545.

9. American Medical Association House of Delegates, *Report of Reference Committee D.*

10. Tollison and Wagner, *The Economics of Smoking.*

11. Federal Trade Commission (hereafter FTC), "Advertising and Labeling of Cigarettes."

12. Ibid.

13. *Public Health Cigarette Smoking Act,* Public Law 91 (1969), 222.

14. Ibid., sect. 4.

15. *Capital Broadcasting Co. v. Mitchell,* 333 F. Supp. 582 (D.D.C. 1971).

16. Myers, et al., *Staff Report Cigarette Advertising Investigation.*

17. Ibid., 2–13.

18. Banzhaf, *Comprehensive Smoking Prevention.*

19. Ibid., 262.

20. Ibid.

21. Ibid., 263.

22. Ibid.

23. *Capital Broadcasting Co. v. Mitchell.*

24. Tucker, "Memo from Vice President of Marketing for R. J. Reynolds."

25. Philip Morris, *Young Smokers.*

26. Banzhaf, *Comprehensive Smoking Prevention.*

27. *Smokeless Tobacco Health Education Act of 1986,* Public Law 99 (1986), 252.

28. *Virginia State Board of Pharmacy v. Virginia Citizens Council, Inc.,* 425 U.S. 748 (1976).

29. *Ohralik v. Ohio State Bar Assn.,* 436 U.S. 447, 462 (1978).

30. *Oklahoma Telecasters Association v. Crisp,* 699 F.2d 490, 500 (10th Cir. 1983).

31. Bureau of National Affairs, "Cigarette Maker Settles," 964.

32. *Settlement Agreement Between States and Brooke Group LTD,* 13.1 TPLR 3.11 (1998).

33. See for example, *Penn Advertising of Baltimore, Inc. v. Mayor and City Council of Baltimore,* 862 F. Supp. 1402 (Md. 1994); *Oklahoma Telecasters Association v. Crisp,* 699 F.2d 490 (10th Cir. 1983).

34. CDC, "Changes in the Cigarette Brand," 469–472.

35. Pierce, Lee, and Gilpin, "Smoking Initiation," 608–611.

36. National Association of Attorneys General, *Master Settlement Agreement.*

37. *Boston Globe,* March 1, 2000, A6.

38. Campaign for Tobacco-Free Kids, "Special Report."

39. Ibid.

40. Ibid.

41. Turner-Bowker and Hamilton, *Cigarette Advertising Expenditures.*

42. Ibid., 1.

43. Ibid., 2.

44. Massachusetts Department of Public Health, *Smokeless Tobacco Advertising.*

45. Campaign for Tobacco-Free Kids, "Special Report."

46. Campaign for Tobacco-Free Kids, "Two New Studies."

47. FTC, *Cigarette Report for 2000.*

48. Ibid.

49. Ibid.

50. Wakefield, et al., *Changes at the Point of Purchase.*

51. Cummings and Sciandra, "Tobacco Advertising," 570–575.

52. Ibid.

53. "Study Finds C-Store," 12.

54. Feighery, et al., "Seeing, Wanting, Owning," 123–128.

55. Biener and Siegel, "Tobacco Marketing," 407–411.

56. Ibid.

57. Gallup International Institute, *Teen-age Attitudes and Behaviors Concerning Tobacco,* September 1992.

58. Altman, et al., "Tobacco Promotion and Susceptibility," 1590–1593.

59. USDHHS, *Preventing Tobacco Use Among Young People.*

60. Florida Department of Health, *Florida Youth Tobacco Survey,* 1999.

61. Schooler, Feigher, and Fora, "Seventh Graders' Self-Reported," 1216–1221.

62. Fishman, et al., *State Laws on Tobacco Control.*

63. Ibid.

64. Snell, Bailey, and Bailey, *Operation Storefront Texas.*

65. Campaign for Tobacco-Free Kids, "Special Report."

66. Minnesota Tobacco Document Depository, Brown & Williamson, no. 682349446-7.

67. Ibid.

68. Minnesota Tobacco Document Depository, R. J. Reynolds, no. 315229798.

69. Klein and St. Clair, "Do Candy Cigarettes Encourage," 362–365.

70. Minnesota Tobacco Document Depository, American Tobacco, no. 040707309-10.

71. Minnesota Tobacco Document Depository, Philip Morris, no. 2501300804-6.

72. J. Lipman, "Marlboro Just Says No On Logo," *Washington Post,* July 1990.

73. Minnesota Tobacco Document Depository, Philip Morris, no. 2501300804-6.

74. Ibid.

75. Smoke Free Movies, "How Movies Sell Smoke," http://www.smokefree movies.ucsf.edu (accessed February, 2004).

76. Ibid.

77. Ibid.

78. Ibid.

Chapter 3

1. Kessler, *A Question of Intent.*

2. *Ash v. Harris,* 655 F.2d 236 (D.C. Circuit, 1977).

3. Kessler, *A Question of Intent,* 34.

4. Ibid., 87.
5. Ibid., 93–94.
6. Ibid., 105.
7. Ibid., 114.
8. Ibid.
9. Ibid., 117.
10. Ibid., 133–137.
11. Ibid., 138.
12. Ibid., 110.
13. Ibid., 121–122.
14. Ibid., 140.
15. Ibid., 149.
16. Ibid., 154.
17. Ibid., 159.
18. Ibid., 160.
19. Ibid.
20. Ibid., 160–161.
21. Ibid., 161.
22. Ibid., 162.
23. Ibid.
24. Ibid.
25. Ibid.
26. Ibid.
27. Ibid., 164.
28. Ibid., 168–169.
29. Ibid., 169–170.
30. Ibid., 172.
31. Ibid., 185.
32. Ibid., 188.
33. Ibid., 186.
34. Ibid., 195.
35. Ibid., 197.
36. Ibid., 241.
37. Ibid., 237–238.
38. Orey, *Assuming the Risk*.
39. Legacy Foundation Library, University of California, San Francisco, http://legacy.library.ucsf.edu.
40. Kessler, *A Question of Intent*, 252.
41. Ibid.
42. Orey, *Assuming the Risk*.
43. Ibid.
44. Kessler, *A Question of Intent*, 256.
45. Ibid.
46. Ibid., 257.
47. Ibid., 248.
48. Ibid., 259–260.
49. Ibid., 279.
50. Ibid., 281.

51. Ibid., 331.

52. Ibid., 355–356.

53. *FDA et al. v. Brown and Williamson Tobacco Corporation et al.*, 120 S. Ct. 1291 (1999).

54. Kessler, *A Question of Intent*, 170.

Chapter 4

1. Rabin and Sugarman, *Smoking Policy*, 110–130.

2. Schwartz, "Tobacco Liability," 905–908.

3. *Lartique v. R. J. Reynolds Tobacco Co.*, 317 F.2d 19 (5th Cir. 1963), *cert. denied*, 375 U.S. 865 (1963).

4. USDHHS, "Regulatory Efforts," in *Reducing Tobacco Use*.

5. Ibid., 226.

6. Edell, "Risk Utility Analysis," 623–655.

7. Rabin and Sugarman, *Smoking Policy*, 131–160.

8. *Cipollone v. Liggett Group Inc.*, 505 U.S. 504, 112 S. Ct. 2608 (1992).

9. Kelder, "First Class Certification," 3–7.

10. Koepp, S., "Tobacco's First Loss," 48–50.

11. Daynard, "Tobacco Liability," 9–13.

12. *Haines v. Liggett Group Inc.*, 975 F.2d 81, 88 (3d Cir. 1992).

13. Ibid.

14. Ibid.

15. http://www.house.gov/commerce; http://www.mnbluecrosstobacco.com; and http://www.courts.state.mn.us/district, respectively.

16. Legacy Foundation Library, University of California, San Francisco, http://legacy.library.ucsf.edu.

17. Daynard, "Litigation by States," 3.

18. *Castano v. American Tobacco Co.*, No. 94-1044 (E.D. La. Feb. 17, 1995), *reviewed* 84 F.3d 734 (5th Cir. 1996).

19. *Engle v. R. J. Reynolds Tobacco Co.*, No. 94-08273 CA (20) (Fla., Dade Cty. Oct. 31, 1994), *cited in* 9.5 TPLR 2.147 (1994) (Order Granting Motion for Class Certification).

20. M. Janofsky, "Ailing Smokers Sue the Tobacco Industry," *New York Times*, May 7, 1994; Sect 1:11 (col 1).

21. M. Janofsky, "Mississippi Seeks Damages from Tobacco Companies," *New York Times*, May 24, 1994; Sect A:12 (col 5).

22. USDHHS, "Regulatory Efforts," in *Reducing Tobacco Use*, 239.

23. *Minnesota v. Philip Morris Inc.*, 13.2 TPLR 2.112, 1998.

24. USDHHS, "Regulatory Efforts," in *Reducing Tobacco Use*, 241.

25. Ibid.

26. USDHHS, "Regulatory Efforts," in *Reducing Tobacco Use*, 191.

27. Ibid., 192.

28. Campaign for Tobacco-Free Kids, "Buying Influence."

29. *Master Settlement Agreement*.

30. Ibid.

31. National Governor's Association, "Tobacco Settlement Funds."

32. U.S. General Accounting Office (hereafter USGAO), *Tobacco Settlement*.

33. USDHHS, *Best Practices.*
34. Miller, et al., "State Estimates," 140–151.
35. U.S. Department of the Treasury (hereafter USDT), *The Economic Costs.*
36. McGreary and Smith, *State Support.*
37. California Budget Project, "Borrowing Against the Future."
38. S.S. Hsu and Y. Woodlee, "Williams's Budget Would Boost Taxes," *Washington Post*, March 24, 2004.
39. N. Zuckerbrod, "States Rely on Tobacco Settlement to Fix Budgets," *The Courier Journal*, March 23, 2004.
40. H. Goodman, "Anti-Tobacco Campaign Vanishes Like a Puff of Smoke," *Sun Sentinel*, March 23, 2004.
41. J. Baime, "Governor Bush Flip Flops on Tobacco Control: Administration Stays Silent on Program Cuts, Says Ignite Florida," *U.S. Newswire*, March 22, 2004.
42. Goodman, "Anti-Tobacco Campaign."

Chapter 5

1. USDHHS, *Best Practices.*
2. See the following for more information on community programs: California Department of Health Services, Tobacco Control Section, 1998–2001, *Local Lead Agency Comprehensive Tobacco Control Guidelines*, January 1998; California Department of Health Services, Tobacco Control Section, *Program Policy Manual and Community Planning Guidelines for Community Programs*, February, 1998; Massachusetts Department of Public Health, *Massachusetts Tobacco Control Program: Community Health Network Request for Responses*, 1998; Oregon Health Division, *Oregon Tool Kit: Community-Based Best Practices to Reduce Tobacco Use*, September, 1997.
3. USDHHS, *Best Practices*, 12.
4. Ibid.
5. Ibid.
6. Ibid., 14.
7. Ibid.
8. USDHHS, "Effective Educational Strategies."
9. Ibid., 66–67.
10. USDHHS, *Guidelines for School Health Programs.*
11. Sussman, et al., "Project Towards No Tobacco," 1245–1250.
12. Sussman, "Curriculum Development," 339–351; Sussman, et al., "Project Towards No Tobacco," 109–123.
13. Ibid.
14. Walter, "Primary Prevention," 81–85.
15. Walter and Wynder, "The Development, Implementation," 59–71.
16. Ibid.
17. Walter, et al., "Modification of Risk Factors," 1093–1100.
18. Perry, et al., "Community-Wide Smoking," 1210–1260.
19. Ibid.
20. Mittelmark, et al., "Community-Wide Prevention," 1–17.
21. Perry, et al., "Community-Wide Smoking."
22. Flynn, et al., "Cigarette Smoking Prevention," S45–S51.
23. Worden, et al., "Development of a Smoking Prevention," 531–558.

24. Flynn, et al., "Long-Term Responses," 389–394.

25. Ibid.

26. Forster and Wolfson, "Youth Access," 203–235; Regotti, et al., "The Effect of Enforcing," 1044–1051.

27. Texas Statewide Tobacco Education and Prevention, *Community Law Enforcement*.

28. Ibid.

29. USDHHS, *Synar Regulation*.

30. Texas Department of Health, *State of Texas Tobacco Laws*.

31. Ibid.

32. Texas Statewide Tobacco Education and Prevention, *Community Law Enforcement*, 48.

33. Ibid., 56.

34. Snell, Bailey, and Bailey, *Law Enforcement Attitudes*; Snell, *Enforcement of Texas Tobacco Laws*.

35. USDHHS, *Best Practices*, 18–19.

36. USDHHS, "Regulatory Efforts," in *Reducing Tobacco Use*.

37. Ibid.

38. Ibid.

39. USDHHS, *Best Practices*, 20.

40. Proposition 99, Tobacco Tax and Health Promotion Act.

41. Tobacco Education Oversight Committee, *Toward a Tobacco-Free California*.

42. Ibid.

43. Ibid.

44. Ibid.

45. Novotny and Siegel, "California's Tobacco Control Saga," 317–326.

46. *Americans for Nonsmokers' Rights v. State of California*, 51 Cal. App. 4th 743 (1996).

47. Begay, et al., "The Tobacco Industry," 1214–1221.

48. Traynor, et al., "New Tobacco Industry Strategy," 479–486.

49. Glantz and Begay, "Tobacco Industry Campaign Contributions," 1176–1182.

50. Pierce, et al., *Tobacco Control in California*.

51. Ibid.

52. Ibid.

53. USDHHS, "Comprehensive Programs," in *Reducing Tobacco Use*.

54. Ibid.

55. Ibid.

56. Ibid.

57. USDHHS, *Best Practices*, 22.

58. Ibid.

59. Ibid.

60. Ibid., 24.

61. Houston, et al., *Guidelines for Diagnosis and Treatment of Nicotine Dependence*.

62. USDHHS, "Management of Nicotine Addiction," in *Reducing Tobacco Use*.

63. Ibid.

64. Ibid.

65. Fiore, et al., *Treating Tobacco Use*.

66. Ibid.

67. Ibid.
68. USDHHS, *Best Practices*, 27.
69. Ibid.
70. Ibid., 28; See also California Department of Health Services, *A Model for Change*.

Chapter 6

1. http://www.americanlegacy.org.
2. http://www.americanlegacy.org.overview.
3. http://www.tobaccofreekids.org/organization.
4. http://www.ash.org.
5. http://www.BADvertising.org.
6. http://www.tarwars.org.

Chapter 7

1. USDHHS, *Tobacco Use Among U.S. Racial/Ethnic Minority Groups*.
2. USDHHS, *Preventing Tobacco Use Among Young People*.
3. McIntosh, "Black Teens Not Smoking," 564.
4. Mermelstein, et al., "Explanations of Race."
5. Johnston, et al., *National Survey Results on Drug Use*.
6. USDHHS, *Tobacco Use Among U.S. Racial/Ethnic Minority Groups*.
7. Schwartz and Swanson, "Lung Carcinoma in African Americans," 45–52; Richie, et al., "Differences in the Urinary Metabolites," 783–790.
8. Blum, "The Targeting of Minority Groups."
9. Foner, *Organized Labor*.
10. Pollay, et al., "Separate, but Not Equal," 45–57.
11. Johnson, "Tobacco Stains," 27.
12. Ibid.
13. National Black Monitor, "The Black Press," 4.
14. Maxwell and Jacobson, *Marketing Disease to Hispanics*.
15. DiGiacomo, "Doing the Right Thing," 32.
16. Johnson, "Tobacco Stains."
17. D. Z. Jackson, "Cash from the Hand that Kills Them," *Boston Globe*, September 23, 1992.
18. RJR Nabisco, Inc., *A Growing Presence*.
19. Blum, "The Targeting of Minority Groups."
20. USDHHS, *Tobacco Use Among U.S. Racial/Ethnic Minority Groups*.
21. Ibid.
22. Ibid.
23. Ibid.
24. Ibid.
25. Ibid.
26. Maxwell and Jacobson, *Marketing Disease to Hispanics*.
27. A. E. Gross, "Skoal Rides Tobacco Road," *Promote*, September 1989.
28. Ibid.
29. Robinson, et al., "Smoking and African Americans," 123–181.

30. CDC, "Changes in the Cigarette Brand," 577–581.

31. Koeppel, "Japan's Mild 7 Cigarette Targets Asians in the U.S.," 4–5.

32. Philadelphia News Observer, "R. J. Reynolds to Test Market New Product in Philadelphia," *The Philadelphia News Observer*, January 3, 1990, 7.

33. USDHHS, *Tobacco Use Among U.S. Racial/Ethnic Minority Groups.*

34. Ibid.

35. Campaign for Tobacco-Free Kids, "Nations Rise to Global Challenge."

36. Campaign for Tobacco-Free Kids, "U.S. Decision to Support Tobacco Treaty."

37. Framework Convention Alliance, "Highlights of the Framework."

38. Campaign for Tobacco-Free Kids, "The United States: No Longer a World Leader."

39. USGAO, *Internet Cigarette Sales.*

40. Ibid.

41. Ibid.

42. Ibid.

43. Ibid.

44. Ibid.

45. *FDA et al. v. Brown and Williamson Tobacco Corporation et al.*, 120 S. Ct. 1291 (2000).

46. Campaign for Tobacco-Free Kids, "Kennedy-DeWine Bill."

47. Ibid.

48. Skolnick, "Interview with Victor Crawford," 199–202.

Selected Bibliography

Ahlgren, A., Norem, A. A., Hochhauser, M., and Garvin, J. "Antecedents of Smoking Among Preadolescents." *Journal of Drug Education* 12, no. 4 (1982): 325–340.

Alexander, H. M., Callcott, R., Dobson, A. J., Hardes, G. R., Lloyd, D. M., O'Connell, D. L., and Leeder, S. R. "Cigarette Smoking and Drug Use in School Children: IV-Factors Associated with Changes in Smoking Behavior." *International Journal of Epidemiology* 12, no. 1 (1983): 59–66.

Allen, J. A., Vallone, D., Haviland, M. L., Healton, C., Davis, K. C., Farrelly, M. C., Husten, C. G., and Pechacek, T. "Tobacco Use Among Middle and High School Students—United States, 2002." *Morbidity and Mortality Weekly Report* 52, no. 45 (2003): 1096–1098.

Altman, D. G., Carol, J., Chalkley, C., Cherner, J., DiFranza, J., Feighery, E., Forster, J., Gupta, S., Records, J., Slade, J., et al. "Tobacco Promotion and Susceptibility to Tobacco Use among Adolescents Aged 12 through 17 Years in a Nationally Representative Sample." *American Journal of Public Health* 86 (1996): 1590–1593.

American Medical Association House of Delegates. *Report of Reference Committee D.* American Medical Association, 1995.

American Psychiatric Association. *Diagnostic and Statistical Manual of Mental Disorders: DSM-IV-TR.* 4th ed., text revision. Washington, DC: American Psychiatric Association, 2000.

American School Health Association, et al. *The National Adolescent Health Survey: A Report on the Health of America's Youth.* Oakland, CA: Third Party Publishing, 1989.

Americans for Nonsmokers' Rights v. State of California, 51 Cal. App. 4th 743 (1996).

Bandura, A. *Social Learning Theory.* Englewood Cliffs, NJ: Prentice Hall, 1977.

Banzhaf, J. F. *Comprehensive Smoking Prevention Education Act.* 97th Congress, 2d Session 256, 1982.

Bauman, K. E., Foshee, V. A., Linzer, M. A., and Koch, G. G. "Effect of Parental Smoking Classification on the Association Between Parental and Adolescent Smoking." *Addictive Behaviors* 15, no. 5 (1990): 413–422.

Begay, M. E., Traynor, M., and Glantz, S. A. "The Tobacco Industry, State Politics, and Tobacco Education in California." *American Journal of Public Health* 83, no. 9 (1993): 1214–1221.

Biener, L., and Siegel, M. "Tobacco Marketing and Adolescent Smoking: More Support for a Causal Inference." *American Journal of Public Health* 90, no. 3 (1999): 407–411.

"The Black Press and the Tobacco Industry." *National Black Monitor* 15, no. 7 (1990): 4.

Blum, A. "The Targeting of Minority Groups by the Tobacco Industry," in *Minorities and Cancer*, edited by L. A. Jones, 153–163. New York: Springer-Verlag, 1989.

Borland, B. L., and Rudolph, J. P. "Relative Effects of Low Socioeconomic Status, Parental Smoking and Poor Scholastic Performance on Smoking among High School Students." *Social Science and Medicine* 9, no. 1 (1975): 27–30.

Botvin, E. M. "Correlates and Predictors of Smoking Among Black Adolescents." *Addictive Behaviors* 17, no. 2 (1992): 97–103.

Brunswick, A. F., and Messeri, P. A. "Causal Factors in Onset of Adolescents' Cigarette Smoking: A Prospective Study of Urban Black Youth." *Advances in Alcohol and Substance Abuse* 3, no. 1–2 (1983): 35–52.

———. "Origins of Cigarette Smoking in Academic Achievement, Stress and Social Expectations: Does Gender Make A Difference?" *Journal of Early Adolescence* 4, no. 4 (1984): 353–370.

Bureau of National Affairs, Inc. "Cigarette Maker Settles FTC Charges of False Ads Regarding Health Effects." *Antitrust and Trade Regulation Report* 58, no. 1471: 964.

California Budget Project. "Borrowing Against the Future: Is Securitizing California's Tobacco Settlement Revenues the Best Way to Close the Budget Gap?" http://www.cbp.org/bb020402.htm (accessed March 24, 2004).

California Department of Health Services. *A Model for Change: The California Experience in Tobacco Control.* Sacramento, CA: California Department of Health Services, 1998.

Campaign for Tobacco-Free Kids. "Buying Influence, Selling Death: Campaign Contributions by Tobacco Interests." http://tobaccofreekids.org/press office (accessed February 18, 2002).

———. "Kennedy-DeWine Bill to Grant FDA Authority Over Tobacco Products Will Protect Kids, Save Lives and End Special Protection for Big Tobacco." http://tobaccofreekids.org/global (accessed May 22, 2004).

———. "Nations Rise to Global Challenge by Adopting Historic Treaty." http://tobaccofreekids.org/reports/addicting (accessed May 5, 2004).

———. "Special Report: Big Tobacco Still Addicting Kids." http://tobaccofree kids.org/reports/addicting (accessed July 7, 2003).

———. "Two New Studies Confirm Tobacco Industry Has Increased Advertising Aimed at Children Since State Settlement." http://tobaccofreekids .org/pressoffice (accessed January 22, 2004).

———. "U.S. Decision to Support Tobacco Treaty is Step Forward if Without Conditions and Limitations." http://tobaccofreekids.org/reports/ addicting (accessed May 5, 2004).

————. "The United States: No Longer a World Leader in Tobacco Control." http://tobaccofreekids.org/global (accessed May 5, 2004).

Castro, F. G., Maddahian, E., Newcomb, M. D., and Bentler, P. M. "A Multivariate Model of the Determinants of Cigarette Smoking Among Adolescents." *Journal of Health and Social Behavior* 28, no. 3 (1987): 273–289.

Centers for Disease Control and Prevention, "Accessibility of Cigarettes to Youths Aged 12–17 Years—United States, 1989." *Morbidity and Mortality Weekly Report* 41, no. 27 (1992): 485–488.

————. "Changes in the Cigarette Brand Preferences of Adolescent Smokers— United States, 1989–1993." *Morbidity and Mortality Weekly Report* 43, no. 50 (1994): 577–581.

————. "Cigarette Advertising—United States, 1988." *Morbidity and Mortality Weekly Report* 39, no. 16 (1990): 261–265.

————. "Smoking-Attributable Mortality and Years of Potential Life Lost— United States, 1984." *Morbidity and Mortality Weekly Report* 46, no. 20 (1990): 444–451.

————. "Smoking Cessation During Previous Year Among Adults—United States, 1990 and 1991," *Morbidity and Mortality Weekly Report* 42, no. 26 (1993): 504–507.

————. "Trends in Cigarette Smoking Among High School Students—United States, 1991–2001." *Morbidity and Mortality Weekly Report* 51, no. 19 (2002): 409–412.

Chassin, L., Presson, C. C., and Sherman, S. J. "Social Psychological Contributions to the Understanding and Prevention of Adolescent Cigarette Smoking." *Personality and Social Psychology Bulletin* 16, no. 1 (1990): 133–151.

Chassin, L., Presson, C. C., Sherman, S. J., Montello, D., Corty, E., and Olshavsky, R. W. "Predicting the Onset of Cigarette Smoking in Adolescents: A Longitudinal Study." *Journal of Applied Social Psychology* 14, no. 3 (1984): 224–243.

Chassin, L., Presson, C. C., Sherman, S. J., Montello, D., and McGrew, J. "Changes in Peer and Parent Influence During Adolescence: Longitudinal Versus Cross-Sectional Perspectives on Smoking Initiation." *Developmental Psychology* 22, no. 3 (1986): 327–334.

Chinnock, W. F. "The Family Courts' Mandatory Duty to Restrain Parents and Other Persons from Smoking Around Children." *Arizona Law Review* 45 (2003): 801–820.

Clayton, S. "Gender Differences in Psychosocial Determinants of Adolescent Smoking." *Journal of School Health* 61, no. 3 (1991): 115–120.

Collins, L. M., Sussman, S., Johnson, C. A., Hansen, W. B., and Flay, B. R. "Psychosocial Predictors of Young Adolescent Cigarette Smoking: A Sixteen-Month, Three-Wave Longitudinal Study." *Journal of Applied Social Psychology* 17, no. 6 (1987): 554–573.

Conrad, K. M., Flay, B. R., and Hill, D. "Why Children Start Smoking Cigarettes: Predictors of Onset." *British Journal of Addiction* 87, no. 12 (1992): 1711–1724.

Covey, L. S., and Tam, D. "Depressive Mood, the Single-Parent Home, and Adolescent Smoking Behavior." *American Journal of Public Health* 80, no. 11 (1990): 1330–1333.

Cummings, K. M., and Sciandra, R. "Tobacco Advertising in Retail Stores." *Public Health Reports* 106, no. 5 (1991): 570–575.

Daynard, R. A. "Litigation by States Against the Tobacco Industry." *Tobacco On Trial* 3 (1997): 1–18.

————. "Tobacco Liability Litigation as a Cancer Control Strategy." *Journal of the National Cancer Institute* 80, no. 1 (1988): 9–13.

De Vries, H., Kok, G., and Dijkstra, M. "Self-Efficacy as a Determinant of the Onset of Smoking and Interventions to Prevent Smoking in Adolescents," in *European Perspectives in Psychology, Clinical, Health, Stress and Anxiety, Neuropsychology, Psychophysiology*, edited by P. J. Drenth, J. A. Sergeant, and R. J. Takens, 209–222. New York: John Wiley and Sons, Inc., 1990.

DiGiacomo, F. "Doing the Right Thing." *Marketing and Media Decisions* 25, no. 6 (1990): 32–45.

Edell, M. Z. "Risk Utility Analysis of Unavoidably Unsafe Products." *Seton Hall Law Review* 17 (1987): 623–655.

Ernster, V. L. "Women and Smoking." *American Journal of Public Health* (editorial) 83, no. 9 (1993).

Evans, N., Farkas, A., Gilpin, E., Berry, C., and Pierce, J. P. "Influence of Tobacco Marketing and Exposure to Smokers on Adolescent Susceptibility to Smoking." *Journal of the National Cancer Institute* 87, no. 20 (1995): 1538–1545.

Evans, R. I., Rozelle, R. M., Mittelmark, M. B., Hansen, W. B., Bane, A. L., and Havis, J. "Deterring the Onset of Smoking in Children: Knowledge of Immediate Physiological Effects and Coping with Peer Pressure, Media Pressure, and Parent Modeling." *Journal of Applied Social Psychology* 8, no. 2 (1978): 126–135.

Federal Trade Commission. "Advertising and Labeling of Cigarettes." *Federal Register* 29, no. 530 (1964).

————. *Cigarette Report for 2000*. Washington, DC: Federal Trade Commission, 2001.

Feighery, E. C., Borzekowski, D. L., Schooler, C., and Flora, J. "Seeing, Wanting, Owning: The Relationship Between Receptivity to Tobacco Marketing and Smoking Susceptibility in Young People." *Tobacco Control* 7 (1998): 123–128.

Fiore, M. C., Bailey, W. C., Cohen, S. J., Dorfman, S. F., Goldstein, M. G., Gritz, E. R., Heyman, R. B., Jaen, C. R., Kottke, T. E., Lando, H. A., et al. *Treating Tobacco Use and Dependence*. Rockville, MD: U.S. Department of Health and Human Services, Public Health Service, 2000.

Fiore, M. C., Novotny, T. N., Pierce, J. P., Harziandreu, E. J., Patei, K. M., and Davis, R. M. "Trends in Cigarette Smoking in the United States: The Changing Influence of Gender and Race." *Journal of the American Medical Association* 26, no. 1 (1989): 49–55.

Fishman, J. A., Allison, H., Knowles, S. B., Fishburn, B. A., Woollery, T. A., Marx, W. T., Shelton, D. M., Husten, C. G., and Eriksen, M. P. *State Laws on Tobacco Control—United States, 1998*. Atlanta, GA: Centers for Disease Control and Prevention, Office on Smoking and Health, National Center for Chronic Disease Prevention and Health Promotion, 48(SS03), 1999.

Flay, B. R. "Youth Tobacco Use: Risks, Patterns, and Control," in *Nicotine Addiction: Principles and Management*, edited by J. Slade and C. T. Orleans, 365–384. New York: Oxford University Press, 1993.

Flay, B. R., D'Avernas, J. R., Best, J. A., Kersell, M. W., and Ryan, K. B. "Cigarette Smoking: Why Young People Do It and Ways of Preventing It," in *Pediatric and Adolescent Behavioral Medicine*, edited by I. McGrath and P. Firestone, 132–183. New York: Springer-Verlag, 1983.

Fleming, R., Leventhal, H., Glynn, K., and Ershler, J. "The Role of Cigarettes in the Initiation and Progression of Early Substance Use." *Addictive Behaviors* 14, no. 3 (1989): 261–272.

Flynn, B. S., Worden, J. K., Secker-Walker, R. H., Badger, G. J., and Geller, B. M. "Cigarette Smoking Prevention Effects of Mass Media and School Interventions Targeted to Gender and Age Groups." *Journal of Health Education* 26, no. 2 (1995): S45–S51.

Flynn, B. S., Worden, J. K., Secker-Walker, R. H., Pirie, P. L., Badger, G. J., and Carpenter, J. H. "Long-Term Responses of Higher and Lower Risk Youths to Smoking Prevention Interventions." *Preventive Medicine* 26, no. 3 (1997): 389–394.

Foner, P. S. *Organized Labor and the Black Worker, 1619–1981*. New York: International Publishers, 1981.

Forster, J., and Wolfson, M. "Youth Access to Tobacco." *Annual Review of Public Health* 19 (1998): 203–235.

Framework Convention Alliance. "Highlights of the Framework Convention on Tobacco Control (FCTC)." http://www.who.int/gb/fctc/PDF/inb6/einb65.pdf (accessed May 22, 2004).

Gerber, R. W., and Newman, I. M. "Predicting Future Smoking of Adolescent Experimental Smokers." *Journal of Youth and Adolescence* 18, no. 2 (1989): 191–201.

Giovino, G. A., Schooley, M. W., Bao-Ping, Z., Chrismon, J. H., Tomar, S. L., Peddicord, J. P., Merritt, R. K., Husten, C. G., and Eriksen, M. P. "Surveillance for Selected Tobacco-Use Behaviors—United States, 1900–1994." *Morbidity and Mortality Weekly Report* 43 (1994): 1–43.

Glantz, S. A., and Begay, M. E. "Tobacco Industry Campaign Contributions are Affecting Tobacco Control Policymaking in California." *Journal of the American Medical Association* 272, no. 15 (1994): 1176–1182.

Gritz, E. R., and Crane, L. A. "Use of Diet Pills and Amphetamines to Lose Weight among Smoking and Nonsmoking High School Seniors." *Health Psychology* 10, no. 5 (1991): 33–35.

Hahn, G., Charlin, V. L., Sussman, S., Dent, C. W., Manzi, J., Stacy, A. W., Flay, B., Hansen, W. B., and Burton, D. "Adolescents' First and Most Recent Use Situations of Smokeless Tobacco and Cigarettes: Similarities and Differences." *Addictive Behaviors* 15, no. 5 (1990): 439–448.

Henningfield, J. E., Clayton, R., and Pollin, W. "Involvement of Tobacco in Alcoholism and Illicit Drug Use." *British Journal of Addiction* 85, no. 2 (1990): 279–292.

Houston, T. P., Eriksen, M. P., Fiore, M., Jaffe, R. D., Manley, M., and Slade, J. *Guidelines for Diagnosis and Treatment of Nicotine Dependence: How to Help Patients Stop Smoking*. Chicago: American Medical Association, 1994.

Hunter, S. M., Croft, J. B., Vizelberg, I. A., and Berenson, G. S. "Psychosocial Influences on Cigarette Smoking Among Youth in a Southern Community: The Bogalusa Heart Study." *Morbidity and Mortality Weekly Report* 26, no. 4 (1987): 17S–25S.

Johnson, D. R. "Tobacco Stains: Cigarette Firms Buy into African-American Groups." *The Progressive* 56, no. 12 (1992): 27–35.

Johnston, L. D., O'Malley, P. M., and Bachman, J. G. *National Survey Results on Drug Use from the Monitoring the Future Study, 1975–1995: Volume 1, Secondary School Students.* Rockville, MD: U.S. Department of Health and Human Services, Public Health Service, National Institutes of Health, National Institute on Drug Abuse, 1996.

Kandel, D. B., and Logan, J. A. "Patterns of Drug Use from Adolescence to Young Adulthood: Periods of Risk for Initiation, Continued Use, and Discontinuation." *American Journal of Public Health* 74, no. 7 (1984): 660–666.

Kelder, G. E. "First Class Certification in the Third Wave of Tobacco Litigation Herald the Beginning of the End for the Tobacco Industry." *Tobacco on Trial* 1 (1994): 3–7.

Kessler, D. *A Question of Intent: A Great American Battle with a Deadly Industry.* New York: Public Affairs, 2001.

Klein, J. D., and St. Clair, S. "Do Candy Cigarettes Encourage Young People to Smoke?" *British Medical Journal* 321 (2000): 362–365.

Klepp, K. I., Halper, A., and Perry, C. L. "The Efficacy of Peer Leaders in Drug Abuse Prevention." *Journal of School Health* 56, no. 9 (1986): 407–411.

Koepp, S. "Tobacco's First Loss." *Time* 131, no. 26 (1988).

Koeppel, D. "Japan's Mild 7 Cigarette Targets Asians in the U.S." *Adweek's Marketing Week* 31, no. 33 (1990).

Konopka, G. "Adolescence, Concept of, and Requirements for a Healthy Development," in *Encyclopedia of Adolescence, Vol. 1,* edited by R. M. Lemer, A. C. Petersen and J. Brooks-Gunn. New York: Garland Publishing, 1991.

Lawrence, L., and Robinson, L. "Self-Efficacy as a Predictor of Smoking Behavior in Young Adolescents." *Addictive Behaviors* 11, no. 4 (1986): 367–382.

Leventhal, H. "Experimental Studies Of Anti-Smoking Communications," in *Smoking, Health, and Behavior,* edited by E. F. Borgatta and R. R. Evans, 95–121. Chicago: Aldine, 1968.

Leventhal, H., Fleming, R., and Glynn, K. "A Cognitive-Developmental Approach to Smoking Intervention," in *Topics in Health Psychology: Proceedings of the First Annual Expert Conference in Health Psychology,* edited by S. Maes, C. D. Spielberger, P. B. Defares, and I. G. Sarason, 79–109. New York: John Wiley and Sons, Inc., 1988.

Massachusetts Department of Public Health. *Smokeless Tobacco Advertising Expenditures Before and After the Smokeless Tobacco Master Settlement Agreement.* Boston: Massachusetts Department of Public Health, 2002.

Maxwell, B., and Jacobson, M. *Marketing Disease to Hispanics: The Selling of Alcohol, Tobacco, and Junk Foods.* Washington, DC: Center for Science in the Public Interest, 1989.

McAlister, A. L., Perry, C. L., and Maccoby, N. "Adolescent Smoking: Onset and Prevention." *Pediatrics* 63, no. 4 (1979): 650–658.

McCaul, K. D., Glasgow, R., O'Neill, H. K., Freeborn, V., and Rump, B. S. "Predicting Adolescent Smoking." *Journal of School Health* 52, no. 8 (1982): 342–346.

McGreary, M., and Smith, P. M. *State Support for Health Research: An Assessment.* Washington, DC: A Report to the Mary Woodard Lasker Charitable Trust and Funding First, 2001.

McIntosh, H. "Black Teens Not Smoking in Great Numbers." *Journal of the National Cancer Institute* 87, no. 8 (1995): 564–565.

McNeill, A. D. "The Development of Dependence on Smoking in Children." *British Journal of Addiction* 86, no. 5 (1991): 589–592.

McNeill, A. D., Jarvis, M. J., Stapleton, J. A., Russell, M.A.H., Elser, J. R., Gammage, P., and Gray, E. M. "Prospective Study of Factors Predicting Uptake of Smoking in Adolescents." *Journal of Epidemiology and Community Health* 43, no. 1 (1988): 72–78.

Mermelstein, R., Robinson, R., Ericksen, M., Crosett, L., and Feldman, S. "Explanations of Race and Gender Differences in Teen Tobacco Use." Paper presented at the 124th annual meeting of the American Public Health Association, New York City, November 1996.

Miller, L. S., Zhang, X., Novotny, T., Rice, D. P., and Max, W., "State Estimates of Medicaid Expenditures Attributable to Cigarette Smoking, Fiscal Year 1993." *Public Health Reports* 113 (1998): 140–151.

Mittelmark, M. B., Luepker, R. V., Jacobs, D. R., Bracht, N. F., Carlaw, R. W., Crow, R. S., Finnegan, J., Grimm, R. H., Jeffery, R. W., Kline, F. G., et al. "Community-Wide Prevention of Cardiovascular Disease: Education Strategies of the Minnesota Heart Health Program." *Preventive Medicine* 15, no. 1 (1986): 1–17.

Mittelmark, M. B., Murray, D. M., Luepker, R. V., Pechacek, T. F., Pirie, P. L., and Pallonen, U. E. "Predicting Experimentation with Cigarettes: The Childhood Antecedents of Smoking Study (CASS)." *American Journal of Public Health* 77, no. 2 (1987): 206–208.

Myers, M. L., Iscoe, C., Jennings, C., Lenox, W., Minsky, E., and Sacks, A. *Staff Report on the Cigarette Advertising Investigation*. Washington, DC: Federal Trade Commission, 1981.

National Association of Attorneys General. *Master Settlement Agreement*. http://www.naag.org/settle.htm (accessed January 8, 2004).

National Governor's Association. *Tobacco Settlement Funds*. http://www.nga.org/Pubs/Policies/EC/ec06.asp (accessed November 12, 1999).

Newcomb, M. D., and Bentler, P. M. "Frequency and Sequence of Drug Use: A Longitudinal Study from Early Adolescence to Young Adulthood." *Journal of Drug Education* 16, no. 2 (1986): 101–118.

Newcomb, M. D., McCarthy, W. J., and Bentler, P. M. "Cigarette Smoking, Academic Lifestyle, and Social Impact Efficacy: An Eight-Year Study from Early Adolescence to Young Adulthood." *Journal of Applied Social Psychology* 19, no. 3 (1989): 251–281.

Novotny, T. E., and Siegel, M. B. "California's Tobacco Control Saga." *Health Affairs* 15, no. 1 (1996): 317–326.

O'Connell, D. L., Alexander, H. M., Dobson, A. J., Lloyd, D. M., Hardes, G. R., Springthorpe, H. J., and Leeder, S. J. "Cigarette Smoking and Drug Use in Schoolchildren: Factors Associated with Smoking." *International Journal of Epidemiology* 10, no. 3 (1981): 223–231.

Ogawa, H., Tominaga, S., Gellert, G., Aoki, K. "Smoking among Junior High School Students in Nagoya, Japan." *International Journal of Epidemiology* 17, no. 4 (1988): 814–820.

Orey, M. *Assuming the Risk: The Mavericks, the Lawyers, and the Whistle-Blowers Who Beat Big Tobacco*. Boston: Little, Brown, and Co., 1999.

Perry, C. L., Kelder, S. H., and Komro, K. A. "The Social World of Adolescents: Family, Peers, Schools, and the Community," in *Promoting the Health of Adolescents: New Directions for the Twenty-First Century*, edited by S. G. Millstein, A. C. Petersen, E. O. Nightingale, 73–96. New York: Oxford University Press, 1993.

Perry, C. L., Kelder, S. H., Murray, D. M., and Klepp, K. I. "Community-Wide Smoking Prevention: Long-Term Outcomes of the Minnesota Heart Health Program and the Class of 1989 Study." *American Journal of Public Health* 82, no. 9 (1992): 1210–1260.

Perry, C. L., Murray, D. M., and Klepp, K. I. "Predictors of Adolescent Smoking and Implications for Prevention." *Morbidity and Mortality Weekly Report* 3, no. 4 (1987): 41.

Philip Morris. *Young Smokers: Prevalence, Trends, Implications, and Related Demographic Trends.* The Legacy Foundation Library, University of California, San Francisco, http://legacy.library.ucsf.edu (accessed September 12, 2003).

Pierce, J. P., Fiore, M. C., Novotny, T. E., Hatziandreu, E. J., and Davis, R. M. "Trends in Cigarette Smoking in the United States: Projections to the Year 2000." *Journal of the American Medical Association* 26, no. 1 (1989): 61–65.

Pierce, J. P., and Gilpin, E. A. "A Historical Analysis of Tobacco Marketing and the Uptake of Smoking by Youth in the United States: 1890–1977." *Health Psychology* 14, no. 6 (1995): 500–508.

Pierce, J. P., Gilpin, E. A., Emery, S. L., Farkas, A. J., Zhu, S. H., Choi, W. S., Berry, C. C., Distefan, J. M., White, M. M., Soroko, S., et al. *Tobacco Control in California: Who's Winning the Way? An Evaluation of the Tobacco Control Program, 1989–1996.* La Jolla, CA: University of California, San Diego, 1998.

Pierce, J. P., Lee, L., and Gilpin, E. A. "Smoking Initiation by Adolescent Girls, 1944 through 1988: An Association with Targeted Advertising." *Journal of the American Medical Association* 271, no. 8 (1994): 608–611.

Pollay, R. W., Lee, J. S., and Carter-Whitney, D. "Separate, but Not Equal: Racial Segmentation in Cigarette Advertising." *Journal of Advertising* 21, no. 1 (1992): 45–57.

Public Health Service. *Smoking and Health: Report of the Advisory Committee to the Surgeon General of the Public Health Service.* Washington, DC: U.S. Department of Health, Education, and Welfare, Public Health Service, PHS Publication no. 1103, 1964.

Rabin, R. L., and Sugarman, S. D. *Smoking Policy: Law, Politics, and Culture.* New York: Oxford University Press, 1993.

Richie, J. P., Carmella, S. G., Muscat, J. E., Scott, D. G., Akerkar, S. A., and Hecht, S. S. "Differences in the Urinary Metabolites of the Tobacco-Specific Lung Carcinogen 4-(Methylnitrosamino)-1-(3-Pyridyl)-1-Butanone in Black and White Smokers." *Cancer Epidemiology, Biomarkers and Prevention* 6, no. 10 (1997): 783–790.

Rigotti, N. A., DiFranza, J. R., Chang, Y., Tisdale, T., Kemp, B., and Singer, D. E. "The Effect of Enforcing Tobacco-Sales Laws on Adolescents' Access to Tobacco and Smoking Behavior." *New England Journal of Medicine* 337 (1997): 1044–1051.

RJR Nabisco, Inc. *A Growing Presence in the Mainstream.* Winston-Salem, NC: RJR Nabisco, Programs for Minorities and Women, 1986.

Robinson, R. G., Pertschuk, M., and Sutton, C. "Smoking and African Americans: Spotlighting the Effects of Smoking and Tobacco Promotion in the African American Community," in *Improving the Health of the Poor: Strategies for Prevention*, edited by S. E. Samuels and M. D. Smith, 123–181. Menlo Park, CA: The Henry J. Kaiser Family Foundation, 1992.

Schooler, C., Feigher, E., and Fora, J. "Seventh Graders' Self-Reported Exposure to Cigarette Marketing and Its Relationship to their Smoking Behavior." *American Journal of Public Health* 86 (1996): 1216–1221.

Schwartz, A. G., and Swanson, G. M. "Lung Carcinoma in African Americans and Whites: A Population-Based Study in Metropolitan Detroit, Michigan." *Cancer* 79, no. 1 (1997): 45–52.

Schwartz, G. T. "Tobacco Liability in the Courts," in *Smoking Policy: Law, Politics, and Culture*, edited by R. L. Rabin and S. D. Sugarman. New York: Oxford University Press, 1993.

Semmer, N. K., Cleary, P. D., Dwyer, J. H., Fuchs, R., and Lippert, P. "Psychosocial Predictors of Adolescent Smoking in Two German Cities: The Berlin-Bremen Study." *Morbidity and Mortality Weekly Report* 36, no. 4 (1987): 35–105.

Semmer, N. K., Lippert, P., Fuchs, R., Cleary, P. D., and Schindler, A. "Adolescent Smoking from a Functional Perspective: The Berlin-Bremen Study." *European Journal of Psychology of Education* 2, no. 4 (1987): 387–401.

Skolnick, A. A. "Interview with Victor Crawford." *Journal of the American Medical Association* 273, no. 3 (1995): 199–202.

Smee, C. "Effect of Tobacco Advertising on Tobacco Consumption: A Discussion Document Reviewing the Evidence." London Department of Health, Economics, and Operational Research Division, 1992.

Snell, C. *Enforcement of Texas Tobacco Laws*. Report to the Texas Department of Health, Office of Tobacco Prevention and Control, 2002.

Snell, C., Bailey, C., and Bailey, L. *Law Enforcement Attitudes Toward Texas Tobacco Laws*. Report to the Texas Department of Health, Office of Tobacco Prevention and Control, 2001.

————. *Operation Storefront Texas*. Report to the Texas Department of Health, Office of Tobacco Prevention and Control, 2001.

"Study Finds C-Store Promotions Lacking." *U.S. Distribution Journal* 226, no. 3 (1999): 12.

Sussman, S. "Curriculum Development in School-Based Prevention Research." *Health Education Research* 6, no. 3 (1991): 339–351.

Sussman, S., Dent, C. W., Flay, B. R., Hansen, W. B., and Johnson, C. A. "Psychosocial Predictors of Cigarette Smoking Onset by White, Black, Hispanic, and Asian Adolescents in Southern California." *Morbidity and Mortality Weekly Report* 36, no. 4 (1987): 11S–16S.

Sussman, S., Dent, C. W., Stacy, A. W., Hodgson, C. S., Burton, D., and Flay, B. R. "Project Towards No Tobacco Use: Implementation, Process, and Post-Test Knowledge Evaluation." *Health Education Research* 8, no. 1 (1993): 109–123.

Sussman, S., Dent, C. W., Stacy, A. W., Sun, P., Craig, S., Simon, T. R., Burton, D., and Flay, B. R. "Project Towards No Tobacco Use: 1-Year Behavior Outcomes." *American Journal of Public Health* 83, no. 9 (1993): 1245–1250.

Swan, A. V., Cresser, R., and Murray, M. "When and Why Children First Start to Smoke." *International Journal of Epidemiology* 19, no. 2 (1990): 323–330.

Texas Department of Health. *State of Texas Tobacco Laws*. Austin, TX: Texas Department of Health, Bureau of Chronic Disease and Tobacco Prevention, 2002.

Texas Statewide Tobacco Education and Prevention. *Community Law Enforcement Contractor Training*. San Marcos, TX: Texas State University, Center for Safe Communities and Schools, 2002.

Tobacco Education Oversight Committee. *Toward a Tobacco-Free California: A Master Plan to Reduce Californians' Use of Tobacco*. Sacramento, CA: Tobacco Education Oversight Committee, 1991.

Tollison, R. D., and Wagner, R. E. *The Economics of Smoking*. Boston, MA: Kluwer Academic Publishers, 1992.

Traynor, M. P., Begay, M. E., and Glantz, S. A. "New Tobacco Industry Strategy to Prevent Local Tobacco Control." *Journal of the American Medical Association* 270, no. 4 (1993): 479–486.

Tucker, C. A. Memo from Vice President of Marketing for R. J. Reynolds Tobacco, Legacy Foundation Library, University of California, San Francisco, http://legacy.library.ucsf.edu (accessed September 12, 2003).

Turner-Bowker, D., and Hamilton, W. L. *Cigarette Advertising Expenditures Before and After the Master Settlement Agreement: Preliminary Findings*. Boston: Massachusetts Department of Public Health and Abt Associates Inc., 2000.

U.S. Department of Health and Human Services. *Best Practices for Comprehensive Tobacco Control Programs*. Atlanta, GA: U.S. Department of Health and Human Services, Centers for Disease Control and Prevention, National Center for Chronic Disease Prevention and Health Promotion, Office on Smoking and Health, 1999.

————. *Guidelines for School Health Programs to Prevent Tobacco Use and Addiction*. Atlanta, GA: U.S. Department of Health and Human Services, Centers for Disease Control and Prevention, National Center for Chronic Disease Prevention and Health Promotion, Office on Smoking and Health, 1994.

————. *The Health Benefits of Cessation: A Report of the Surgeon General*. Atlanta, GA: U.S. Department of Health and Human Services, Public Health Service, Centers for Disease Control, National Center for Chronic Disease Prevention and Health Promotion, Office on Smoking and Health, 1990.

————. *Investment in Tobacco Control: State Highlights 2001*. Atlanta, GA: U.S. Department of Health and Human Services, Centers for Disease Control and Prevention, National Center for Chronic Disease Prevention and Health Promotion, Office on Smoking and Health, 2001.

————. *Preventing Tobacco Use Among Young People: A Report of the Surgeon General*. Atlanta, GA: U.S. Department of Health and Human Services, Centers for Disease Control and Prevention, National Center for Chronic Disease Prevention and Health Promotion, Office on Smoking and Health, 1994.

————. *Reducing the Health Consequences of Smoking: 25 Years of Progress. A Report of the Surgeon General*. Atlanta, GA: U.S. Department of Health and Human Services, Public Health Service, Centers for Disease Control, Center for Health Promotion and Education, Office on Smoking and Health, 1989.

————. *Reducing Tobacco Use: A Report of the Surgeon General*. Atlanta, GA: U.S. Department of Health and Human Services, Centers for Disease Control and Prevention, National Center for Chronic Disease Prevention and Health Promotion, Office on Smoking and Health, 2000.

————. *Synar Regulation Implementation: Report to the Secretary on FFY 1998 State Compliance*. Rockville, MD: Substance Abuse and Mental Health Services Administration, Center for Substance Abuse Prevention, 1999.

————. *Tobacco Use Among U.S. Racial/Ethnic Minority Groups—African Americans, American Indians and Alaska Natives, Asian Americans and Pacific Islanders, and Hispanics: A Report of the Surgeon General*. Atlanta, GA: U.S. Department of Health and Human Services, Centers for Disease Control and Prevention, National Center for Chronic Disease Prevention and Health Promotion, Office on Smoking and Health, 1998.

U.S. Department of the Treasury. *The Economic Costs of Smoking in the U.S. and the Benefits of Comprehensive Tobacco Legislation*. Washington, DC: U.S. Department of the Treasury, 1998.

U.S. General Accounting Office. *Internet Cigarette Sales: Report to Representative John Conyers*. Washington, DC: GAO-02-743, 2002.

————. *Tobacco Settlement: States' Use of Master Settlement Agreement Payments*. Washington, DC: GAO-01-851.

Wakefield, M. A., Terry, Y. M., Chaloupka, F. J., Barker, D. C., Slater, S. J., Clark, P. I., and Giovino, G. A. *Changes at the Point of Purchase for Tobacco Following the 1999 Tobacco Billboard Advertising Ban*. University of Illinois at Chicago, Research Paper Series, no. 4, 2000.

Walter, H. J. "Primary Prevention of Chronic Disease Among Children: The School-Based Know Your Body Intervention Trials." *Health Education Quarterly* 16, no. 2 (1989): 81–85.

Walter, H. J., Hofman, A., Vaughan, R. D., and Wynder, E. L. "Modification of Risk Factors for Coronary Heart Disease: Five-Year Results of a School-Based Intervention Trial." *New England Journal of Medicine* 318, no. 17 (1988): 1093–1100.

Walter, H. J., and Wynder, E. L. "The Development, Implementation, Evaluation, and Future Directions of a Chronic Disease Prevention Program for Children: The Know Your Body Studies." *Preventive Medicine* 18, no. 1 (1989): 59–71.

Warner, K. E., Ernster, V. L., Holbrook, J. H., Lewit, E. M., Pertschuk, M., Steinfeld, J. L., Tye, J. B., and Whelan, E. M. "Promotion of Tobacco Products: Issues and Policy Options." *Journal of Health Politics, Policy and Law* 11, no. 3 (1986): 367–392.

West, R. R., and Evans, D. A. "Lifestyle Changes in Long Term Survivors of Acute Myocardial Infarction." *Journal of Epidemiology and Community Health* 40, no. 2 (1986): 103–109.

Worden, J. K., Flynn, B. S., Solomon, L. J., Secker-Walker, R. H., Badger, G. J., and Carpenter, J. H. "Development of a Smoking Prevention Mass Media Program Using Diagnostic and Formative Research." *Preventive Medicine* 17, no. 5 (1988): 531–558.

Young, M., and Werch, C. E. "Relationship Between Self-Esteem and Substance Use Among Students in Fourth Through Twelfth Grade." *Wellness Perspectives, Research, Theory and Practice* 7, no. 2 (1990): 31–44.

Index

About the Author

CLETE SNELL is Associate Professor of Criminal Justice at the University of Houston-Downtown.